Lessel Long

Twelve Months in Andersonville

Lessel Long

Twelve Months in Andersonville

ISBN/EAN: 9783744754095

Printed in Europe, USA, Canada, Australia, Japan

Cover: Foto ©Andreas Hilbeck / pixelio.de

More available books at **www.hansebooks.com**

IN

ANDERSONVILLE.

*ON THE MARCH—IN THE BATTLE—IN
THE REBEL PRISON PENS, AND
AT LAST IN GOD'S
COUNTRY.*

By LESSEL LONG,

Private Co. F, 13th Indiana Infantry.

HUNTINGTON, IND.:
THAD AND MARK BUTLER, PUBLISHERS.
1886.

Entered according to Act of Congress, in the year 1886,

BY

LESSEL LONG AND THAD BUTLER,

In the Office of the Librarian of Congress at Washington, D. C.

ISSUED FROM THE PRESS OF
Montgomery & Vrooman,
PRINTERS AND BINDERS,
TOLEDO, O.

THE STOCKADE AT ANDERSONVILLE.

PREFACE.

This volume is presented to the public by its author with a thorough appreciation of its imperfections as a literary production. There has been no attempt at ostentatious display of learning or boastful show of knowledge, but the volume is simply the plain story of a private soldier who suffered a year in the rebel prison pens of the Southern Confederacy. Originally the sketches appeared in our village paper, the ANDREWS EXPRESS, under the title of "Army Life." The partial judgment of friends and neighbors has encouraged us to revise and re-publish them in book form.

In this, the story of his personal experience, the author has written only the truth. Horrible as was the condition of Union prisoners—terribly as they suffered—the dreadful reality can be but feebly portrayed on paper. The grizzled veteran who wakens from his sleep, twenty years after, with the moans of starving and dying comrades ringing in his ears, whose eyes yet retain the mental picture of the utter wretchedness, hopelessness and misery of Andersonville—he alone can realize the horror upon horror of a year's confinement in the rebel military prisons of the South. God grant that such suffering as fell to the lot of my brave comrades who died, or living, suffered the tortures of death in rebel prison pens, may never again be known in our common country.

THE AUTHOR.

ANDREWS, Ind., 1886.

CHAPTER I.

CAMPAIGNING IN FLORIDA—THE COUNTERSIGN LOST—CAMP RUMORS—OUT AT SEA—KILLING AN ALLIGATOR WITH A PAPER WAD—JOINING THE ARMY IN VIRGINIA—A DISGUSTED REBEL SYMPATHIZER—THE MARCH TO THE FRONT.

DURING the winters of 1863-4 the regiment to which I belonged, the 13th Indiana Infantry, was stationed on Follies Island, South Carolina. It was generally believed that there would be an early and active campaign. Both the North and the South were making great preparations for the final struggle. Late in February our command was ordered to Florida to reinforce General Seymour, who had met the Johnnies and got the worst of the fight. We arrived at Jacksonville about February 26th, and when we landed there was considerable excitement. General Seymour had been out near Ocean Pond and met General Finigan, who gave him battle at once. By some unknown means the rebels secured our countersign, and during the night passed a large body of their men through our lines, thus gaining the rear of the Union army. At daylight the fight began greatly at Seymour's disadvantage, and in a short time his men were on the retreat. It was a hard fought battle for the number engaged. There were several regiments of colored troops in the fight, and they were comparatively new and suffered badly. So when we arrived at Jacksonville the colored troops who were wounded were seen coming to camp. As Seymour lacked sufficient transportation they were compelled to make their way back to camp as best they could. In a short time after we landed we were marched to the eastern part of the town, where we got our supper and were ordered out on the picket line. It was reported that General Finigan was advancing and we might expect a fight at any time, and to make things worse we had no countersign. The location of our lines being new it was somewhat perplexing. At last our officers agreed upon a sign by which we might know our men from the enemy. The sign was the drawing of the saber about one-fourth out of the scabbard and forcing it back with such force as to be heard at least ten paces. This done three times in quick succession was to be our countersign for the night, and the regiment was deployed on the picket line, two men at a place, and each squad about ten to fifteen paces apart. Thus we spent our first night in Florida. Next day the front of our lines was properly explored, and the country scouted over for several miles. Finding no enemy we established our camp and soon fell into the ordinary routine of camp life.

At first our camp was on the edge of the city of Jacksonville. We soon had the place so fortified that we did not fear any danger, as we had several gun boats lying in the river ever ready to throw a Camp Kettle over to the Johnnies, who were always as ready to keep out of range. So things went on very quietly, and we moved our camp outside the works about one-half mile, where we had a nice location and pretty good water, so much better than the water was in South Carolina that it seemed like a paradise to us who had been cooped up on those islands, so long. Now we could go to town, and everything was moving off nicely until one Sunday morning, about the first of April, we heard a pretty brisk fire at the north of our camp, and in a few minutes we could see the orderlies flying in every direction. Soon we received orders to strike tents and get inside of our breastworks. It was said that Finigan was advancing with a large force. All was bustle and hurry until all our camp equipages were inside the works. We saw a large force going out towards where the firing was heard, and in the course of two or three hours we learned that it was only a scouting party which had come on one of our picket posts and had left us fast as their horses would carry them when their fire was returned. We were ordered back to our camp, the boys feeling disappointed that they had so much trouble for nothing, but as it was all for Uncle Sam and cheap glory we were soon fixed up as nice as ever, and all again was quiet.

About this time those of our regiment who had veteranized returned, and all was excitement for a few days. The boys would relate what good times they had while at home, and the many letters that they brought back were read and re-read time and again, and the situation talked over. It was apparent from the activity going on that there was to be a general move all along the line. We heard all sorts of reports as to where we were to go. Some said we were going back to Follies Island, some that they knew we were to form a party to take Savannah, Ga., others thought we would be sent somewhere on the coast to do garrison duty, as the regiment was very much reduced, while others insisted that we would take the field, as we had always done. At last the order came to strike tents and report at the landing, where we would find transports to convey us away from Jacksonville. This was the last of April. At last we were all on board, and down the river we went, arriving at its mouth late in the evening. The weather was clear and warm, when night closed the day; we lay down to sleep, but when we got up in the morning it was raining. We saw several transports anchored out in the bay, and learned that we were at Hilton Head, South Carolina, and that we were to go further north. We soon lay alongside a nice vessel and were ordered to go aboard. We remained at the wharf for two days and nights to receive the baggage of our own and other regiments. Here we learned that all the troops that could be spared from the coast were to go to Virginia, where they would be re-organized into brigades and corps. All the stores, baggage and equipments having been loaded, we put out to sea.

Just here, I will relate a little joke our Captain, H. A. Johnson, played on one of the 112th N. Y. regiment. That regiment belonged to our brigade, and one day while we were at Jacksonville, our Captain was the officer of the day. The Captain always enjoyed a good joke and could laugh as hearty at one as anybody. So while he was making the rounds of the picket line, he came to a post of the 112th. Their post was located at a bridge that had been built to afford a crossing place over one of many marshes or in-lets that put into the St. John's river. The boys who were stationed at this post had discovered a large alligator which had crawled upon a log just at the side of the bridge, and was lying there in the hot sun with the top of his head thrown back for the purpose of catching flies. The boys asked the Captain if they might shoot the monster. He said it would never do to fire off their guns along the line, as it would raise the alarm. At their invitation, however, the Captain went down on the bridge and saw the gent apparently asleep, when it occurred to him that it would be a good joke to have one of the boys draw the ball out of his gun and shoot the fellow with a paper wad. So the Captain gave permission to draw the ball and run down some paper loosely—just enough to hold the powder—and go out and poke the gun as close to his throat as possible and fire, and the effect would be to blow him up, and at the same time the gun loaded in this manner would make no report that could be heard at any distance. No sooner did the boys obtain permission than they proceeded to execute it. The fellow with the gun walked out on the bridge until he was over the alligator, then he poked his gun down as close as he could to its mouth, and fired. At the report of the gun, the alligator popped up like a bladder, but the greatest surprise was when the sentinel looked at his gun. The muzzle was as flat as if it had been placed on an anvil and struck with a sledge hammer. In the agonies of death the alligator clasped his jaws together, flattening the gun barrel as described! The Captain had a hearty laugh at the result. It was just as he anticipated, and he said it was worth a month's wages to see that soldier when he looked at his gun. The jolly Captain is dead. May his ashes rest in peace until the great roll call on the other side.

At the end of five days on the sea, we arrived at Chesapeake Bay. We simply touched at Fort Monroe, where we received orders to go up the York River. While attempting to make the mouth of the York River, our pilot lost his way, and as the wind was blowing a gale, we came near being wrecked on old Point Comfort. After signaling for a long time we got a pilot, who took charge of our vessel and made the river all right, landing at Gloucester Point, opposite Yorktown. Here we remained close to the river for the night, and the next day moved back from the landing about one-half mile, where we established our camp. The troops continued to arrive from day to day, until there was a large body of men, out of which the Tenth and Eighteenth Corps were organized. The Tenth was commanded by Smith, and the Eighteenth by General Gilmore. All was bustle and hurry. Organization of different branches of the service was made from day to day, there were reviews and general reviews without number. We encamped in the old works which McClellan built two years before, when he made his advance "On to Richmond," by the way of the Peninsula. Many were the brave boys who took part in that campaign, who went on the march never to return. Yes, they gave up their lives that the Republic might live and that the glorious old stars and stripes might wave over a land of the brave and a home of the free. Did they give up their lives in vain? It looks that way sometimes when we see the same men that were then doing all they could to destroy our free institutions, now, after twenty years, elevated to the law-making power.

After due time we were assigned a place in the Tenth Corps, and on May 1st, we broke camp and were ordered to go aboard of the transports. What does this mean? We thought we were going to advance on Richmond by the way of the White House, and to confirm our opinion of this fact, several days previous to this there had been a small brigade of infantry and the 11th Penn. Cavalry sent up to White House, and it was reported that the Cavalry were scouting over the country while the infantry were fortifying the landing so as to protect our supplies when they should arrive. As the transports took on their loads, each boat would steam up the river for two or three miles and anchor. This proceeding was going on all day, our regiment embarking late in the evening. When we started after the rest of the fleet darkness had set in. After discussing the probabilities of the campaign we rolled ourselves up in our blankets for the night and slept as only soldiers can sleep under such circumstances.

Imagine our surprise the next morning to find our fleet out on the Chesapeake Bay. The question was now where can we be going? Speculation as to our destination was at last ended by the fleet passing into James River. It was apparent that we were going to land somewhere up the James and opposite from the south side, while Grant was on the North.

It was a grand sight to see all the transports loaded with troops, their bands playing, flags flying, and men cheering. I do not know the number of boats. There were a great many. Some steamers had in tow floating wharfs, while iron clad gunboats were promiscuously scattered amongst the fleet. Near sunset we passed City Point. This had been the place for the exchange of prisoners ever since the war commenced. Here lay a huge iron clad at anchor, seeming anxious for something to do. We passed on up the river to a place called Bermuda Hundred. Here we landed and marched out in a field and encamped. All night we could hear the troops on the move. Next morning when we got up, and the mist cleared away, as far as we could see were troops on the move or in camp. There were several hundred acres of wheat and corn all doing nicely until the troops went into it. After we got our breakfast an old gentleman came over to us and commenced to talk about the war. He said: "This plantation belongs to me. I gave uncle Jeff $50,000 in gold to help carry on the war, and I sent fifty of my best field hands up to Richmond to work on the fortifications. I sowed this wheat with the intention of giving it to him when it was threshed, but here you damned Yankee devils have come and destroyed it as you do everything else." While we were talking, some one said, see those fellows over there in the barn lot! Looking over that way, we saw forty or fifty soldiers after the pigs and chickens or anything else that could be of any use to a soldier. The old man looked at them for a few seconds and exclaimed: "This beats hell," and started off for the house. The boys gave three cheers as he went. We soon got the order to prepare to march with two days' rations in our harversacks. Soon the bugle sounded "fall in" and the regiment formed its ranks. Colonel Dobbs galloped to the head of column and gave the order "right face, forward march!" We know not whether we will ever return. Many never did return, but we hope they were permitted to extend their march to better fields beyond the river.

CHAPTER II.

SCOUTING FOR THE ENEMY—A "NON-COMBATANT" DOCTOR—CAPTURE OF A TORPEDO BATTERY—A SKIRMISH—FRIGHTENED DARKEY—BATTLE OF CHESTER STATION—CHARGE UPON THE ENEMY—TAKING A JOHNNIE PRISONER—THE TABLES TURNED—"THROW DOWN THAT GUN, YOU YANK"—TAKEN INSIDE THE ENEMY'S WORKS—LIBBY PRISON.

AFTER leaving the landing our course ran southwest. We did not go more than one-half or three-quarters of a mile until the boys began to throw away their blankets and extra clothing, it being the 6th of May and the weather very hot. At a distance of about one mile we left the main road and began to scout through the woods and farms. We were told by the officers that we were to thoroughly explore the country between the landing and the turnpike to see if there were any Johnnies in the woods. This operation caused the brigade to break into regiments, each regiment taking a different road, but to keep within supporting distances of each other. As we advanced we observed at every cross-road officers with their maps trying to gain all the knowledge of the country they could. We came to many farms during the day where the men were plowing corn, having no idea of our presence until we were right on them. Some would start to run, others seemed perfectly amazed, having never seen a wild "Yank" before.

All of the white men were put under arrest. This precaution was taken to prevent them from giving any information to the enemy. We spent the entire day in this manner, without finding any armed enemy. Late in the afternoon we captured a young darkey, who said he belonged to a prominent doctor who lived in Richmond, and who owned the farm that we were then on. He said his master had gone to Petersburg and would be back soon. So part of the company went down the road, and taking a good position, soon had the satisfaction of capturing the doctor. He was very wrathy. He said we had no right to detain him, as he was a peaceable citizen. One of our officers stepping up to his horse and taking hold of his holsters, said: "Is it customary for peaceable citizens to carry such things as these?" The old doctor said: "That is my private property, and you have no right to interfere with private property." Nevertheless, the revolvers were confiscated and the horse also. Oh, how he did charge when the horse was taken from him! The boys took the doctor to General Foster's headquarters. From there he was sent to Butler's headquarters. I never heard of him after. About the same time Company D found a negro who said that right "over there is the river, and our folks have a signal station there." So off the boys go, across the fields and through a strip of woods. We were so close to the station before we were discovered that the signal officer left for the fort, leaving his uniform, signal flags, books and everything, which our boys captured and brought to camp. At this station we found a battery for the purpose of blowing up our boats should they attempt to go up the river. The river at this point was sunk full of torpedoes and wires running from them to this battery. By the use of this instrument the signal station officer could touch off any of the torpedoes he desired at any time, but our boys came upon him so suddenly that he left everything. It being now sunset we fell back with the rest of the command, and went into camp for the night.

Early next morning we were ordered up and told to get ready for a march, and probably a fight. Soon we saw the advance cavalry start out, and soon after we followed. The cavalry did not go more than half a mile until we heard a brisk fire, which lasted a minute or two, when all was still. In a short time we saw some cavalrymen coming back guarding a lot of prisoners whom they had taken. We were ordered forward at once, and knew now that we had work before us. As we passed out to the main road we saw the doctors fixing up their tables, getting ready to attend the wounded. We learned that the prisoners just taken were some of General Beauregard's men, and that his army was concentrating at Petersburg. We soon came to the woods and formed in line of battle and advanced in this manner. We were under a pretty brisk fire, but as yet the enemy were not strong enough, and every time we moved up they would fall back and take a new position. In this manner we followed them all day, until late in the evening, when our bugles sounded the order to fall back. So back we went to camp. In this day's fight we had a good many men wounded and some killed. As yet we had not put up any tents but lay down on the ground with our blankets for cover. About midnight we were ordered up and told to commence the erection of breastworks. We were supplied with axes, shovels and picks, and soon had a pretty good line of works. By the time our works were finished it was daylight. This being Sunday, May 8th, no move was made to-day. We arranged our camp, put up our shelter tents, and fixed up for house-keeping. In the evening the right wing of my regiment was ordered out on the picket line. Also the right wing of every regiment in the brigade. We did not go far, and were stationed along a fence, two men at a place, and not more than ten paces between each squad. Thus we passed Sunday night, Monday, and Monday night. Sometime on Monday morning the Eighteenth Corps marched out on the same road (towards Petersburg) that we had fought over on Saturday. They came on the rebels about a quarter of a mile from our pickets, and from thereon, as far as they were able to drive them, they had heavy fighting, continuing all Monday night, and it was the heaviest musket firing I ever heard. Sometime Monday night the left wing of all the other regiments of the brigade was ordered out to guard the rear of the Eighteenth Corps, while they were fighting at Petersburg. Having learned from scouts that there was a considerable force collecting at Fort Darling, who were advancing out on the pike leading from Richmond to Petersburg, Tuesday, May 10th, about 10 o'clock, we were relieved off of the picket line and ordered to join the left wing, which we proceeded to do as quick as possible. After going about three miles we came to the turnpike, followed it for a short distance, the woods being very thick with underbrush on both sides of the road. Here we learned that the left wing of our regiment was on the west side of the pike, so we tried to find them. After going through the woods for some time, we got orders to go back to the pike, where we were ordered to support Battery D, Fifth U. S. Artillery, which had taken position on top of a rise in the pike, with orders to hold. We filed across the pike on the east side and lay down. The fight had opened on the west side of the pike. The musket fire was pretty heavy, and several rebel batteries were firing constantly. As yet our batteries had not opened. As we lay here I heard the orders given to hurry up the rest of the Corps. All the while we lay here the rebels were throwing solid shot and shell in all directions. This was done to get our batteries to reply, so they would know where to concentrate their fire. While laying here we learned that the Major of the 62d Ohio was in command of our brigade, and he, with other officers, was continually riding up the pike to see if they could see anything of the rebels. All at once they came dashing back like a flock of scared sheep. Then some of the officers said to the Major: "Did you see the game, Major?" "You bet I did, and we will smell hell here in a few minutes." Just then the Johnnies fired a volley over us. Our Major's darkey, who had been holding his horse, came leading him up to the Major, and said, "Take the hoss, Majah, I'se gwine back!" The Major looked at the darkey and yelled out: "You d——d black rascal, are you any better to be shot at than I? Hold the horse until I call for him." "All right," said the darkey. Just then there was another heavy volley fired, which cut the twigs over our heads. The darkey again bustled up to the Major and said: "Majah, take the hoss now, I'se gwine back sure." The Major said, as he took the reins, "go, you black devil," and away he went down the pike as fast as he could run, with all the rest of the darkeys belonging to the regiment.

The rebels had by this time crept up through the thick brush so close that they were shooting the artillery horses, when we were ordered to charge, which we did, and a bad old charge it was for many of us. We soon had the Johnnies on the run, and forced them out of the thick brush. We killed, wounded, or took prisoners, all we could see. Many of our men in the front, were killed or wounded in the thick brush, and the noise of the artillery and muskets, the cheering of the men, was terrific as we advanced. After firing had ceased somewhat, we could not see any more Johnnies in our front, but I discovered, about 100 yards in advance of me, a Johnny laying behind a log. Having just fired off my gun, I rammed down a cartridge as quick as I could and started for him. He threw up his hat and cried out "don't shoot me, I am a conscript and don't want to fight." I said, "throw down that gun and accouterments and come up to me." He did so. Just then the firing had ceased on our side of the pike. I thought we had made a clean victory of it. I talked with the fellow for a few seconds and learned that he belonged to the 4th Alabama regiment. So I went back and picked up his gun and accouterments and then we started back. I could not see any of the boys but thought they had got back in the the thick brush. As I went along I picked up one of the nicest little rifles I ever saw. So I was going along leisurely, thinking I could make a good report when I got to my regiment with one prisoner and two extra guns. Just then I saw Quarter Master Gordon. He was coming towards me. I soon discovered that he was bearing off too far to the left to come to me, when I yelled out to him, "what shall I do with this fellow?" The Quarter Master turned in his saddle and seeing who it was, said, "throw down all of those accouterments but yours and hurry back. They are flanking us," at the same time motioning to me to bear off to the left and still yelling at me to hurry. Then all the artillery opened up, and such a yelling and firing I never heard. I bore away from the pike as directed by the Quarter Master. The woods had taken fire and it was a fearful hot day. I ran as fast as I could until I came to the edge of a field when I had to stop and rest. While we stood on the edge of the field I said to my prisoner, "if we can gain the woods, the other side of this field, I think we are all right." We had to run about thirty or forty rods in the open field to gain the woods. The bullets were falling as thick as hail. We could see the dust rise where they struck the ground, creating about as much dust as a drove of sheep would make running over the ground. But take our chance we must, and dashing across the field we were successful in gaining the woods. On the opposite of the field from where we entered the brush, the balls were coming through the brush, which sounded to me like heavy rain drops falling on dry leaves. We had not gone more than three or four rods in the brush until I heard a noise on my right. Looking in that direction I saw two of my company. One was dead and the other badly wounded. The wounded comrade was making a noise, and I was just in the act of stepping to him when I heard some one on my left hello, and looking in that direction, I saw a rebel sergeant and two privates, with their guns at a ready. The sergeant yelled out, "throw down that gun, you Yankee s— of a b—, or I will blow you through!" Now, you see there was no time for parley. I threw my gun in the brush, when they came up to me and the sergeant said, "I never will shoot a man until I give him fair warning. I could have shot you, but I knew you did not see us, and I would not do that." Imagine my thoughts. Here I am, a prisoner, and not one of my comrades in sight. My prisoner had been ordered back to take a gun. How quick I had changed places with him! We did not stand here long until several of our boys were brought up—eight of my company and fifty-two of the regiment. Seventy of the brigade all told. One of my company Charles Weibel, was badly wounded in the head. While we were standing here we heard great cheering on our left. Looking in that direction we saw several men running, who proved to be part of Company I, Captain Beebe, of my regiment, and thirteen men. They had tried to cross a swamp, could not do it, and on coming back saw the rebel regiment drawn up behind. Taking them for our own regiment they set up a cheering to think they had got back to their own command. They did not discover their mistake until they were within three rods of the rebels. The rebels were clothed in blue Kentucky jeans, which looked like our uniform when off at a distance. They were ordered to surrender, which they did, and we were started back to the rear, while the woods were full of shell falling in amongst us. A good many were wounded. After surrendering we followed an old road for about one mile, when we came out to the turnpike. Here was a rebel general's headquarters, and here we were halted and questioned as to who they were fighting. When told Butler's men it seemed to make them mad. They said they would soon have the "beast" in the same condition that we were in. The rebel general, Ransom, was in command of the Johnnies, and while they were talking with us our batteries moved upon the pike and commenced to shell them. All of their ambulances and transportation wagons were corralled on a large farm on the west side of the pike. Our shells fell thick and fast in that mass of frightened beings. Ambulances overturned, white men and negroes were running in all directions. We were ordered to form between two lines of guards, and down the pike we went at a run, myself and another of my company taking charge of our comrade, who was wounded, one on either side of him, with his arms over our shoulders. In this manner we were compelled to run for about a mile. All this distance we could see soldiers running back, and it seemed to be a regular panic. We came to a creek, where we were permitted to get water and wash the blood off of the wounded. Then we went down the pike about one-half mile, when we took a road leading to Fort Darling. We were soon inside of their works, from which we were taken to the James River and went on board of an old boat. We were told that we would go up to Richmond. Here we remained for about two hours, when an officer came down and told the guard to take us up on the hill to the old government graveyard, where there was plenty of shade. Here we remained until late in the evening, when we went on board of a steamer and started up the river for Richmond. On our way up we saw the Confederate fleet, which was lying in the river between Fort Darling and the

BATTLE OF CHESTER STATION, VA.

city. There were several substantial looking vessels. Just at dark we landed at Richmond, and were ordered out between two lines of guards, who conducted us to the famous, or rather infamous, "Libby Prison." The following members of my Company were with me: Charles Weibel, Greenbery Cruse, Nathan Lowder, Martin Harden, Luther Robbins, Samuel Weeter and William Cromer—all still living except Weibel, who died in Andersonville.

CHAPTER III.

LIFE IN LIBBY—SEARCHING THE PRISONERS—A CONTEMPTIBLE OFFICER—THE PEMBERTON BUILDING—NEGLECT OF THE WOUNDED—A BRUTAL GUARD SHOOTS A HELPLESS PRISONER—HOW THE PRISONERS GOT THE NEWS—SENDING WORD TO MY PARENTS - OFF FOR THE "SUNNY SOUTH."

WHEN we marched up to the Libby building, the doors were opened, and we went in. Our Alabama guards left us at the boat. Now we were under a different set of fellows. A fellow that they called sergeant ordered us in line, single file, that he could count us. We were in a large room, and there were half a dozen or more clerks at work on the prison rolls. After he got through counting us, he then said to us that we should give our names, rank, company and regiment as we were called, commencing on the right. The clerks would enter the names as given on the rolls, and as fast as each prisoner gave his name, etc., he was ordered into another room. Here was the Provost Marshal's office, and another clerk who took your name, rank, company, regiment, State, and the branch of the service that you belonged to. When it came my time to go into the room the Provost Marshal looked up at me and said: "Have you got any money?" I answered: "I have a little." He then said, "I want it. If you give it up here it will be given back to you when you are exchanged." So I took out my money, which consisted of two ten dollar greenbacks and one two dollar bill, with seventy-five cents in postal currency, and handed it to him, when he threw the postal currency back to me, and said: "Take those rags, I do not want them." I thought, good-bye greenbacks, I will never see you any more, but such was not the case, as we shall see after awhile. He then said, "Have you any more? If so, you had better give it up here, for if any is found on your person when you are searched in the next room it will be confiscated." I said, "that is all I have." He then said, "Guard, take him to the next room." I observed that the clerk registered my name, etc., and the amount of money given up, in a large ledger.

As the guard led the way to the next room and opened the door, I saw some half dozen or more of my comrades, some taking off their clothing and others putting their's on. In this room were several rebel officers to see that we were properly searched and robbed of all of our valuables, such as money, which had not been given up to the Provost Marshal. There were a number of soldiers searching the boys for what they could find. I was ordered to take off my clothing, and as I did so the fellow searched the seams of my blouse, pants, shirt, drawers and cap, running his fingers through my hair and beard to see what he could find. After he was satisfied, he said, "you can put on your clothes." I did so, when he took up my canteen and rubber blanket and threw it on a pile of such articles in one corner of the room. Emptying out my haversack, he threw that on the pile, at the same time scattering its contents on the floor and taking such articles as he wanted. Then he said, "If there is anything there that you want, take it." I picked up a few crackers, a cup and spoon, they being about all there was left. This search was continued with all the boys. When completed we were formed in line, counted, and a little fellow they called Adjutant came strutting up to us and said that we would now go over to the Pemberton building. So the command was given, and off we went across the street to the Pemberton building, where we were conducted to the third floor and told to remain for the present.

There were about three hundred men already in this room. It was about ten o'clock and no supper was given us. The prisoners gathered around us and besought us as to the prospect of exchange, and wanted to know how our army was making it. If we did not think that this spring's campaign would end the war. etc. We told them all we knew of the prospects, which we thought looked encouraging, and we thought we would soon be back to our regiment. Imagine our surprise when some of them told us they had been in this building for ten months! As we were very tired we lay down for the night on that part of the floor that had been assigned to us. We had no blankets, nor did they furnish us with any, so we lay on the bare floor.

Early in the morning I got up and took a good survey of the room and the surroundings. We were on the third floor of what had once been a large tobacco factory and warehouse. There were no sash or glass in the windows, they having been broken out or taken out before we arrived. Right across the street was the Libby building. Down the street we could see Castle Thunder, where men and women were confined for their loyal sentiments, and many of our boys who were held as spies. If this building could talk, it could tell a terrible tale of horror. Many were the poor fellows who went inside of those barred doors that never saw the light of another day. This building was a large brick; the windows were all barred with iron rods. We could see some of the inmates through the grating of the windows. Still further on was the Rebel Capitol, with the Southern flag floating over it at that time. On the South, and directly in front of our building, were the James River and

Canal; on the opposite side of the river was a large tract of land, now entirely destitute of fence or trees. This I was told belonged to General Scott, and was once a very fine farm, but was now used by the rebels to try their guns which the large factory was turning out. The Tridegar Gun Works, of Richmond, was the largest of any in the Confederacy, and at this time was run to its full capacity, day and night. We could see the smoke from its tall stacks, and could also see away down the river to Fort Darling, where Butler was contending against the rebels.

After viewing our situation I made some inquiries in regard to the rules of the prison, and was told if I put my head out of the window I might get shot, as all prisoners are forbidden to sit in the window or put their heads out. There was a line of guards around the building, placed about fifty feet apart, with instructions to shoot any prisoner who should violate any of the prison rules. The guards were old men, too old to go in the field, or too young for active service. They had no more judgment than a mule, and seemed to try and see how mean they could act. After having learned all I could from the old prisoners, I took a seat on the floor to await developments. About half-past eight o'clock up came a little fellow whom they called Adjutant. He was followed by a sergeant and a big burly Irishman, who carried an old musket barrel for a cane, and always marched close to the sergeant. The Adjutant ordered us in line and proceeded to tell us how mean we looked and how ignorant we were. Said he could compare us to nothing but East Tennesseeans, as they were the most ignorant people in the Confederate States. The sergeant called the roll and then counted. Then the Adjutant gave us another lecture and went below. I made inquiry who this fellow was, and was told it was Adjutant Ross. I will tell you what became of him after awhile. He was the most contemptible little devil I ever saw, and I think he is receiving his just reward before this time.

All was quiet until about ten o'clock when the same burly Irishman came up to the head of the stairs and sang out, "fourteen men and bread boxes." At this every old prisoner jumped up and wanted to be one of the fourteen to handle the bread boxes. The sergeant of the floor gave orders who could go, and in a short time they returned with one day's rations, which consisted of corn bread, bean soup, and bacon. Each man got a piece of corn bread about one-half as big as a brick, and one pint of bean soup, with a few beans in it, and three ounces of bacon. This we learned was for our day's rations. We could eat it all at once or save a part until evening and have it for supper. I thought I would make two meals of mine. I would eat the soup and a part of the bread and save the balance for supper. I tried this for several days until I got so hungry that I ate all at one meal, and I never tried to make two meals off one day's rations after that, in all of my confinement, which was twelve months. After we had finished our meal every one seemed more cheerful. We marched up and down the room for exercise and sung patriotic songs, such as "Rally Round The Flag," and "Old John Brown's Body," everybody joining in the chorus. After we had got tired of this, orders were received from our own sergeant to wash the floor. This done, then the boys would gather in groups while some one would relate his experience as a soldier. I was looking after the welfare of our wounded comrade whom I spoke of in my last chapter. I had an old knife which we sharpened on a brick and I proceeded to shave the hair from the wound and wash it in cold water. This I did every day for three weeks, when the wound healed up, and did not give him much trouble. The rebels never offered to do anything for him, although it was a bad wound. When night came, we lay down to sleep. This was my first day in Richmond. Little did I think I would have more than 300 days within the Confederacy. Almost every day we could see squads of prisoners marched up to the Libby and go through the same ordeal that we had gone through. After three or four days, a large lot of prisoners from Butler's army came in, and a few of them were from our brigade. I sought them out and learned all I could about my own regiment. All I could learn was that the regiment had lost heavily in the fight on the 10th.

One night there were some cavalrymen put in our room. Next morning one of them sat down in the window with his face resting on his hands, when one of the guards fired at him without giving any warning. Three buckshot took effect in his shoulder blade and ranged up. The man fell forward almost over me. He never spoke. The rebel sergeant of this floor came up and ordered him taken to the hospital. The man that did the shooting was quite an old man, from fifty to sixty years of age. He was wearing glasses. There was nothing but pure cussedness that caused him to shoot, for the soldier was at least thirty feet from the ground and not aware that he was violating any rule. Our first day's experience was a fair sample of all the rest of our stay in Richmond.

About the 15th of May we discovered a terrible excitement in the streets. Soon saw the rebels moving freight cars from the Petersburg to the Danville road. We inferred from this that Butler had taken Petersburg, and to confirm our opinion, we saw in a Richmond paper that there had been very hard fighting going on at Ft. Darling and Petersburg. The paper called on all citizens to open their houses to receive the wounded and for every able-bodied man to arm himself and form companies for the defense of the Capital. As General Custer, with a large cavalry force was threatening Richmond, while Grant was holding Lee, and Butler was holding Beauregard, the excitement was intense. About this time there was a large lot of prisoners came in. A portion of them were crowded in our room. Amongst them were some of the Eighth Connecticut regiment, with whom I was acquainted, and from them I learned that a few days before that Butler had made an assault on Fort Darling and had been repulsed with heavy loss, being compelled to fall back to his works, the rebels following them. The Connecticut boys said, "we were put in your old works which you built, the second night after we landed. You know how thick the little pine trees were in front of your works. Well, they were all cut down and fell in such a manner as to form a great impediment to a charge on our works. The Johnnies came up in the thick timber and massed their men, and charged through this tangled mass of logs. We lay behind our works, and you know we were armed with repeating rifles. We just gave them h—l. They fell back, but in a few minutes they came again. They made five different charges before they drove us out of the works, and they would not then have succeeded but the 62nd Ohio, on our right, ran out of ammunition, and before we knew it, they were driven out. So we had to run to keep from being flanked. You see we were too busily engaged in our front, and did not hear the order to fall back until it was too late. When we started to run they had cut us off from the rest of the troops, so we had to give up. I tell you that was the worst fight I ever saw. It looked like foul murder to shoot those poor fellows that were trying to get through that abatis in front of our breast works." I said, "how do you think Butler is making it." "I hardly know. It seems as though they had kinder bottled him up." We now noticed that our Alabama guards were doing duty as prison guards. I afterwards had a talk with one of them. He said: "We thought it was a pretty hard fight the day we captured you, but I tell you it was not like the fighting on the 13th. Our regiment was so reduced then that we have been sent here to do guard duty until it can be filled up with new recruits or consolidated." I said to him, "when do you think the war will end?" "I don't know," he said, "it looks like they will never quit until all the men are killed or wounded." He said, "I am very tired of the war and wish it was over. Do you not think there will be a compromise?" I said I did not, I thought all the compromise that could be expected was for the rebels to lay down their arms and return to their allegiance to the government of the United States. He said, "I don't care how they settle it so they stop the war."

The weather was getting warmer all the time, and our room was so crowded we thought we could hardly endure it. We said, surely they will exchange us; we can't live this way very long. There were no seats in the room. When we sat down it was on the floor, and the room had become so crowded at this time that it was almost impossible to sit down, and when we lay down for the night we were so crowded that you could not turn over unless the whole squad turned. When you got so tired laying on one side that you could not stand it any longer in that position, you would call out: "Sergeant, give the order to right or left turn," (as the case might be), when he would give the order: "Squad No. 8, right turn," when the whole squad would flop over on their right sides, but not without some one giving vent to his wrath for being disturbed so often.

About this time Adjutant Ross came up to our room and said: "If any of you fellows want to write to your friends North you can do so, provided you say nothing about the condition of the army, or anything that will give any information as regards military operations, the same to be inspected before being sealed." So I thought I would write a few lines home, although I did not have the least idea that it would reach its destination. I will give the letter verbatim, as I recollect it at this time:

RICHMOND, VA., May 17, 1864.

Dear Father—I am a prisoner of war here in Richmond. Eight of my company are with me. All well.

LESSEL LONG,
Co. F, 13th Ind. Inf.

When I handed it to Ross he looked at it, and looking up to me, said: "That is all right—it will go." Then the old prisoners laughed and said, "yes, it will go—to the flames." But for once Ross told the truth. In about a month or six weeks my father received the note.

Every day some one would start the report that there had been a general exchange agreed upon and we would soon be exchanged. This would revive the drooping comrades for awhile. Our rations grew smaller in quantity almost every day, and before it was received we would be so hungry that it would almost drive us mad. Everybody would be ill, and you could get up a quarrel or fight at any time. So things went on from day to day. At last one day Ross came up and ordered us in line, counted us, and then took our names, rank, regiment, etc., and said we should be ready to leave at any time when called on. Every one thought this meant exchange. The old prisoners said that is the way they always do when they send a lot to be exchanged. Now our hopes were high, and we felt sure we would soon be with our friends.

On the following evening, a little before sunset, Ross came up and said: " Fall in and go down stairs, and you will spend the night in the east room with those that are to go with you." So down we went, and up to the east room, where we met a lot of fellows like ourselves, buoyed up with false hopes of being exchanged. The room was badly crowded. Ross told us to be ready to leave early the next morning. There was not much sleeping done that night. In that room some one would lead out in singing some patriotic song, when all would join in the chorus. When they had sung until they were exhausted, then they would talk of what good times they would have when they got back to " God's country." The majority that were in the room were old prisoners taken at Chickamauga. At last morning came, and a little after sunrise the order was given to fall in and go down stairs single file, where we would receive our rations for the day. We moved down the steps, and when we came out on the street we saw two lines of guards drawn up, extending down the street toward Castle Thunder. The line of guards extended from the foot of the stairs to the center of the street, where it turned to the right. At the foot of the stairs were large boxes filled with corn bread and bacon—bread on one side and bacon on the other. As we passed we were handed a piece of bread and a piece of meat. The piece of bread would weigh about three-quarters of a pound and the meat about six ounces. This was for one day. We were not allowed to stop, but as soon as we filed to the right, were ordered to form two abreast, and move down the street towards the rebel capital. As we passed Castle Thunder, we could see men and women crowding up to the grated windows trying to see what was going on below. We moved through the city for a good ways, when we filed to the left and crossed the long bridge that spans the James River. At this place we did not go far until we came to the cars which had been provided for us. We were now guarded by the Fourth Alabama, and I asked quite an old man why they did not take us down the river on the boats. "Where do you think you are going," he asked. "To City Point, for exchange," I said. He shook his head. The thought flashed through my mind that we had been deceived, and were not going to be exchanged but moved to some other prison. I said, "where do you think they are going to take us?" "I do not know," was his answer, "we are ordered to go to Danville with you," but, said he, "I think you are are going to Andersonville, Ga." I had never heard of that place before so I plyed him with questions about its location until I learned that it was a place that had been built expressly for the safe keeping of prisoners, and he said it was a large piece of ground which had been enclosed for the purposes of a prison, with plenty of shade and a nice stream of water running throught it. He said, "that is what I have heard." We got aboard of the cars while Grant's artillery was thundering away at Frazier's Farm, north of the city, and were soon en route to the "sunny South." It was the 31st of May, 1864.

CHAPTER IV.

THE JOURNEY TO ANDERSONVILLE—TRADING A PEN HOLDER FOR A BLANKET—COMPARATIVE VALUE OF UNITED STATES AND CONFEDERATE MONEY—A CONVINCING ARGUMENT—REMOVING DEAD MEN FROM THE CARS—TWENTY DOLLARS FOR A TWENTY-FIVE CENT RING—ASSIGNED TO DIVISIONS AND HUNDREDS AND MARCHED INTO THE STOCKADE.

WHEN at last, we got aboard of the cars, there were found seventy-five to eighty men in a car. The cars were freight cars, no seats, no straw to sit upon, but crowded in like so many hogs or cattle. Many of the cars were just as they had been left when used in hauling cattle and hogs, and as filthy as they well could be. The signal being given, our train began to move. We were guarded by the Fourth Alabama, and I soon became acquainted with one of the guards who was stationed at the door. He was very talkative, and from him I learned that we were on the Danville Road, and their orders were to go as far as that city, when we would be handed over to some other parties. We did not go far before we could see what war does for a country. Kilpatrick's cavalry had a short time before made a raid on this road and destroyed bridges, depots, water-tanks and many miles of track. My Alabama friend said this was the reason that we had been detained at Richmond so long. They had to repair the road before they could move us. He said all of the prisoners would leave Richmond as fast as transportation could be had. All along the road for twenty miles or more, were large bodies of men building breastworks and forts to guard this road. They seemed very much excited, as Butler was on the South, and Grant's army was only nine miles on the North, and his guns were thundering away as we left the city and could be distinctly heard for many miles. This road runs through a pretty fair part of the country. It looked more like our Northern farms than any part of the South I had yet seen. Our train made very slow time. We had to side track for all incoming trains, and when we had the track I do not think we made over eighteen or twenty miles an hour. The day was very hot, and owing to the crowded condition of the cars, it was very unpleasant and tiresome. Many of the men were sick with the diarrhea. We suffered badly for water, having nothing to carry any in. All the way we could get a drink was when the train stopped by some branch or pond and we were allowed to get off the cars to get water. Then we would go many miles without getting any more.

Along in the afternoon, my friend said to me, "you have no blanket." I said I did not. He said, "have you anything to trade me for mine?" I said, I did not think I had, for they took everything when they searched us. He said, "if you have, I will trade it to you, for you will need it." I felt in my pockets, and finally found a silver extension pen-holder which had been broken some but could be used. I said, "how will this do?" "All right, just what I want, and I have another blanket back at Richmond." "Then we will call it a trade," I remarked. "Yes," was his answer. I handed him the holder. He said, "keep it until we leave the car, then I will hand the blanket to you and you can hand the pen to me." I thought that is another rebel lie, he will never give me the blanket.

It was a very long day to us but nothing to compare with the night. As soon as darkness set in they shut one door and fastened it, closing the other all but about a space of two feet, and two guards stood in that. The heat was terrible. We could not sit down or lay down, but simply had to stand or "squat." Many of the men were too weak to stand, and to add misery to misery men had to be helped to the door continually, so they could attend to the calls of nature. Now just imagine yourself in this position for twenty hours. It is impossible for any one who never experienced these horrors to realize the misery. At last just as the sun began to show itself in the East, the whistle sounded, and the guards said we were at Danville. Our train stopped at the foot of a street where two lines of guards were drawn up to receive us, the same as at Richmond. I remained in the car until nearly all were out when I stepped to the door. My friend hung the blanket on my shoulder. As he did so I passed him the pen-holder. As I struck the ground he said, in an under tone, "good-bye, I am sorry to see you go." We were formed between the guards that were drawn up in line, single file, and ordered to move. Soon we came to some large boxes filled with corn bread and bacon, and as we passed, a man on our right handed us a piece of bread and another on our left a piece of bacon, about the same quality and quantity that was given us as we left Richmond. We were kept moving until we came to the Charlotte & Danville Road, where a train of freight cars, with engine attached, was waiting for us. We were hurried aboard, while a large crowd of citizens gathered along the train all anxious to see us. While we were waiting I fell into conversation with quite a nice looking man. He said he lived in North Carolina. While we were talking a fellow came along peddling corn cakes, which he was selling for one dollar in Confederate money. I said to him, "I have no Confederate money, but I have a piece of silver I will give you for one of those cakes." He said, "how much is it?" I said, "a sixpence." He said, "let me see it." I handed it to him, when his eyes glistened, and he said, "all right—here is your cake," handing it to me at the same time. I took it and remarked to the gentlemen from North Carolina, "it looks as though you did not have much confidence in your money." "Well, you see that fellow don't know what hurts him." I said, "I think there are a good many more in the same fix, for I have heard the old prisoners say that for the last ten months you could get from five to ten dollars for one at Richmond, and while we were there we could get $20 for one." Adjutant Ross made a regular business of buying all he could get hold of at from five to twenty for one.

The whistle again sounded and we moved South. The road over which we now passed was very rough, having just been finished and ballasted. It seemed as though the cars would leave the track at every turn of the wheels. We now had a new set of guards—the Virginia Home Guards—composed of young men from twelve to twenty years of age. They were right in for argument, and when one of our boys talked to them and got the best of the argument, they would straighten up and say, "shut your d—d Yankee mouth, or I will run this bayonet through you." Of course, the boys would have to shut up or the whelp would have put his threat into execution. They were the most contemptible set of curses I ever saw. Take them as you would, you could find nothing good about them. They were ignorant, overbearing, self conceited, and very cruel to the men under them. Would push and knock the sick men as though they were brutes, and much worse than any drover does his hogs or cattle. This day we arrived at Greensboro, North Carolina. Here we got off the cars about sun set, and were allowed to go to a small grove about ten rods from the road. There were several dead men taken from the cars who had died since we left Danville in the morning, and a good many who were so sick that they could not walk. They were laid under the shade trees on the grass with those who had died on the cars. I wish to call the attention of the young men to this one point. No doubt but some one will read this narrative whose father or brother was left there. It is a fact that they were "some one's" brother or father—some mother's darling—who had given up his young life, away from home, with no one to pity or console them, or even give them one drink of water. Left to die alone and in a strange land. May the Supreme Ruler be merciful to their ashes.

We left Greensboro about ten o'clock at night, and were ordered on the cars and did not stop until about ten or eleven o'clock the next day when we arrived at Charlotte, N. C. Here we again changed cars. We were marched to a little grove south of the town, and a guard line established around us. We were told that we would draw rations here, as we had had nothing since we left Danville the morning before. We received our rations, and being very hungry, soon dispatched them, when we felt in a better humor. I was setting by a tree when one of our boys came up to me and said that there was a rebel officer out there that wanted to buy a finger ring. I had a cheap one, worth about twenty-five cents. It was very large and had a glass set in it. So we went over to see him. When I approached him he said, "are you the Yank that's got the ring?" I said, "I have a ring." He said, "I want to buy one." I said, "I will sell this one." He looked at it and said, "what do you want for it?" I said, "one dollar in greenbacks, or twenty in Confederate money." He said, "I have no greenbacks, but will give you twenty in Confederate money." He took out his money and counted it over, saying, "I have only sixteen dollars and sixty cents here, I will go and get the rest." I said, "hand that to me, or the ring, until you come back with the rest." He handed me the Confederate money and started off, saying he would get the other three dollars and forty cents which he owed me. As yet, I never got the three dollars and forty cents, and should the fellow see these lines, and write to me, I will forgive the debt and send him a receipt in full of account.

About the middle of the afternoon we started again. Reached Columbia, South Carolina, that night. Traveled all night and all the next day, reaching Augusta about one hour before sunset. Here we crossed the Savannah River and got off the cars. It was Saturday, and we were put in to some cotton warehouses to remain over night, and also over Sunday and Sunday night. Here we received the best treatment accorded us on our trip. Our Virginia guards left us, and the guards here were old soldiers and treated us pretty fairly. A son of ex-Governor Hicks, of Maryland, was Provost Marshal of Augusta, and showed us considerable attention. It was my fortune to get hold of a paper here, and I learned that Sherman was pressing Johnson very hard, up at Marietta, and Governor Brown was talking of surrendering the state to Sherman, in order to save their property. It would have been the wisest thing he ever did, had he done so, but Davis was too much for him. Hence the destruction of life and property which followed. Monday morning we took the cars for Andersonville, there remaining no longer any doubt of our destination.

We arrived at Macon a little after daylight Tuesday morning. Here all the commissioned officers were taken from the train and left at a prison established for officers only. Captain Bebee, of my regiment, was left here, and about fifty other officers, among them a Brigadier General, whose name I have forgotten. The guards had been telling us what a nice place Andersonville was. They said it was a large tract of ground, surrounded by a board fence, having plenty of shade and tents, with a nice stream of water running through it. We began to think after all this is not so bad. About eleven o'clock we arrived at the station, were ordered off the cars, and formed in line in order to march to the stockade. When we arrived at the outer gate we were met by a Dutch Captain, who began to curse and swear at us, and said he would soon tame us. It was June 7th and very hot. We remained in line until we could be assigned to Hundreds and Divisions. While we were waiting, I was within a few feet of a tall pine tree. I thought I would step around it and get in the shade. When I got on the north side of the tree I could stand with my back against the tree, and set my foot in the sunshine. The tree did not cast a shadow at noon more than two feet, the sun being almost directly over us. You could stand with your face to the North and look up and see the sun at noon almost as well as you could with your face to the South.

After we had been assigned to divisions and hundreds, we were taken inside of the stockade, it being about 1 o'clock. The stockade was crowded to its utmost capacity, there being over 20,000 men confined in a space of less than seventeen acres. We were perfectly amazed at the horrible sight that met our eyes. At every step we saw men prostrated by disease, men dying from neglect, men almost naked, men blackened by smoke, men begrimed by dirt. All the horrible sights of suffering humanity could here be seen in a few minutes time. After much crowding to make our way through this crowd, we finally found the hundred that we had been assigned to. After the rebel sergeant informed the sergeant of the hundred that we had been assigned to his hundred, he gave him our names, and proceeded to say to us that we could go anywhere in the stockade, but must be at this place at roll call, and at the time of issuing rations. There were no rations given us this day, having arrived too late, so we were doomed to go very hungry the rest of the day. There being eight of my company, we were divided and four of us put in the 28th hundred and the other four in the 30th hundred.

It was now necessary that we should look out a location where we could lay down when night came. We traveled until almost dark before we could find a place that we could pre-empt. At last, when almost ready to give up, a young man from Maine said to us, "you had better stop here by my place. This ground is used only when they haul in rations, and then you can put your traps up against my tent until they get through." We accepted the offer and pitched our tent. There was where my blanket came in good play. Four men and one blanket, one tin cup, one-half canteen, two spoons, one fork and one old jack-knife was our entire outfit. This piece of ground we held until the last of June, when the addition to the stockade was finished and we removed to new quarters.

CHAPTER V.

THE HORRORS OF ANDERSONVILLE AS SHOWN BY THE OFFICIAL RECORDS OF THE WAR DEPARTMENT—HEROISM AND LOYALTY OF THE PRISONERS—ORGANIZATION OF THE REGULATORS—FIGHT WITH THE RAIDERS—AN EXECUTION IN PRISON.

THAT my readers may form an idea of the deliberate cruelty of the Confederate Government in selecting this particular location for the stockade, I here add the testimony which I have copied from the official records on file at the War Department at Washington. This information was gained from a native of Georgia, a citizen of the vicinity at the time, and was brought out in the trial of Captain Wirz, after the war:

"Andersonville is situated on a railroad running North and South between Macon and Americus, Ga. Four or five straggling rough board structures, resting drowsily on the yellow sand west of the road, twenty or thirty people as vapid and rickety as the buildings. Such was Andersonville before the Confederacy made it synonymous with all that is cruel and brutal. West of the railroad and but a few dozen yards removed from it, are two marshes in which spewings of toads and reptiles and swamp ooze, decaying wood, weeds and rank grass are distilled into poison. The marshes are fifteen hundred feet apart—one above and one below the town. From the marshes the poison runs off in two leafy brown, sluggish currents, across the railroad track, and unite fourteen hundred feet east of it. From this confluence of poison the stream in lethargic floes, runs nearly due east between hills rising with gradual swell on either side until it is lost in the Little Sweetwater, less than a mile below. Five hundred yards from the confluence of the two little streams that ooze out of the marshes there is another marsh. Around this the Andersonville prison pen was constructed. As finally completed, the pen is an oblong, 780x1620 feet. The stream creeps through its narrowest part about one hundred feet south of the center.

"General Winder superintended the building of "the pen." When he began, in December, 1863, the marsh and the hills that rise on either side of it were clothed with heavy timber. The people of the surrounding country came to look on. The whole population of Americus, a little town a few miles below, were on tiptoe of excitement. "Got so many Yank's, don't know what to do with they'uns all. Gwin ter build a prison at Anderson," so the people said. Among those who went to see was Ambrose Spencer, a resident of Americus. When he arrived negroes were digging a long trench, other negroes were felling trees, others again were hewing their sides. "What are these for?" said Spencer. Winder looked at him and said: "What, the trees hewed on two sides?" "Yes," said Spencer. Winder said, "we put one end in the ground in that trench, the hewed sides close together, then pack dirt about them. The result will be a close pen with walls twenty feet high." Spencer said, "Are you going to erect barracks or shelter of any kind?" "No, the dratted Yank's who will be put here will have no need for them." "Why, then, are you cutting down the trees. They will prove a shelter to the prisoners from the heat of the sun at least." "That is just why I am cutting them down. I am going to build a pen here that will kill more Yank's than can be destroyed in the front. That marsh in the center of the pen will help kill them mighty fast." "But why," said Spencer, "don't you put the pen below or above the marsh?" "I don't want to," said Winder. "There is the Little Sweetwater five feet deep and twenty feet wide, not five hundred feet from where you are putting the pen, and not a marsh on it. Why don't you put the prison there?" "This is better." "You could go below the marsh and take in both creeks, Little Sweetwater and this Double Branch run." "Yes, we could." "Then they would have an abundance of water for cooking, bathing, every purpose, and good healthy ground." "Yes." "Why in the world don't you put the pen there?" "This suits us better." "It looks like you wanted to kill them." "Yes, kill the miserable Yank's. Better that than have them in the front shooting our boys." Spencer went away, the construction progressed, the pen was completed, the marsh lay a festering sore in its center. Then came the captives, 800 first from New Hampshire, Connecticut and Michigan, weary, worn and hungry, from prolonged travel cooped up like beasts in freight cars. Down from the depot they marched wearily on through the shifting sands amid the jeers and taunts of a gaping crowd. The gate opened. The stockade swallowed them. Then they saw walls of pine, a slimy brown creek six feet wide and five inches deep, struggling through the soft mud, and a waste of yellow sand dotted with huge stumps. And there were no buildings, no sheds, no tents, no shelter, no concealment from pelting storms; no screen from the blazing sun. That was the 15th day of February, 1864. "A desert," cried one. Wait—a desert is mercy to this. The volume of captives swelled; the heroic plucked from the front of battle; the daring tricked by guerrillas; the devoted who sacrificed liberty to save a brigade or a division of an army. They rolled into the pen, a continuous stream of captive humanity. The deadly dews drenched them. The lightnings flashed in their unscreened faces. Hungry, emaciated and torn with pain, shelterless, tattered and naked, the pitiless storms beat down upon them and they froze. The fierce rays of the tropical sun followed the storm, and they consumed. Human ingenuity exhausted itself; they made storm covers of blankets and of coats. They burrowed in the ground. The storm pursued them, searched them out, penetrated them. The eight hundred became more than thirty thousand. The Confederate guards camped on the stream that flowed through the stockade. The water flowed from their camp to that of the prisoners. It was morbific at first. The Confederates camped on it and it became virulently sceptic. The soil was saturated with their garbage, their offal, and their filth. The storm is a scavenger and a creek is a sewer. The scavenger swept the excrement, the washings of rottenness of carrion, of compost, down through the stockade. It was bilge water nastified. Hideous spume. The creek was a serpent, breathing death, its mouth full of corrosive poison. The earth and the air—boundless creation—was full of life giving water, and thirty thousand Union prisoners were condemned to drink of Double Branch. Double Branch was a Confederate executioner. Then came the morass. A morass is an infinity of craters, ejecting pestilent vapors. Slime and green scum were already upon the morass in the stockade. The scavenger—the storm—carried down upon it the sewage of the pen. It permeated it, became a mass of putrifaction. Out of putridity came a loathsome life—maggots. And the hot sun was upon it all. The earth abhors nastiness. It flings it off in effluvium. The subtile, noisome exhalation loaded the air. Then came scurvy, that is born out of storm and exposure and want of proper food. Faces puffed. Syncope from slight exertion followed, with weak vision, blindness and inability to sleep; then dysentery. Old sores opened. Broken bones that had united came apart and grated together within the body. Horrible music! Mouths and throats and bodies ulcerated. Teeth loosened and fell out. Gums, nostrils, bronchial tubes, and intestines poured out streams of offensive blood. Limbs rotted off. Worms devoured living bodies. The fetid breath of disease aggravated the noisome exhalation from the creek and the morass. Poisoned by the earth, poisoned by the air, poisoned by the water, tormented with vermin, irritated by gnats, mosquitoes and winged ants, devoured by maggots, blackened with smoke, befouled by mud, with matted hair, shelterless in the midst of mills and lumber piles, thirsting for water, with limpid streams but a few yards away, perishing for fuel, while boundless forests nodded to them from the surrounding hills, rotting for vegetables, while potatoes blossomed and corn tasseled before their eyes, goaded to madness by brutality, writhing in helpless impotence under taunts and jeers and murderings, perishing by hundreds, by thousands, with death marching by their side—a putrid horror living and dying—these martyrs stood firm and to the end. The shattered fragment of the wreck never faltered in their devotion to the American Union."

We had been in the stockade but a few days until the Regulators were organized. From our location on the north side of the branch we had a pretty good view of the prison on the south side, the banks on the north being steeper and higher, which gave us a good opportunity to see what was going on. We could see the south gate where the prisoners were brought in and where the dead were taken out, and we could also see the teams hauling the dead away from the dead house, from this place. The Regulators were organized to keep order inside of the stockade, to enforce certain rules, and to prevent murder and robbery. There were a lot of men from the large cities who had made a profession of bounty jumping, and had either deserted or were taken prisoners. These fellows had formed themselves into a kind of organization and made a regular business of robbing other prisoners of their blankets, or anything they had. They became so bold that they were a regular terror to the other prisoners, and no one seemed secure who had a blanket or anything of value. They were always trying to gain favor with the rebel officers, and would report any plot that was made to escape. Would report all tunnels that the boys were digging. By so doing they could secure some favors from the rebels. The better class of prisoners saw that something must be done to stop this, hence the Regulators. The Regulators were organized in companies and officers appointed over them. Every man mustered into these companies promised to obey the officers selected. The officers were mostly western men, and the Regulators were armed with a club about 14 inches long, with one end larger than the other. To this club was attached a string at the small end, and this string was fastened around the man's wrist. When all was ready, the chief, whose name was Leroy L. Key, of the 16th Illinois cavalry, sought an interview with Captain Wirz, and obtained permission to arrest the Raiders, (that was the name they went by), and Wirz said he would furnish a guard to guard the men that were arrested. All being ready, the order was given to commence operations. The Regulators went for the big tent where the headquarters of the Raiders were. About one hundred of the Raiders were in line and ready for the boys. The Regulators moved up in good order, and when they were close up to them the Raiders wanted to know what they wanted. They said, "Sergeant Key wants you to go outside." Then the Raiders said, "do you think we will go?" The answer came from a hundred throats, "yes." "Well we are not going, and you can't take us." "Well," said a little

Irishman, " we will be after trying about as hard as any set of fellows in these parts." By this time the two lines were within a few feet of each other, when a big fellow made a dive for one of the Regulators. This was the signal to commence and as nice a little battle as one could wish to see resulted. The Regulators beat the Raiders with their clubs for a few minutes, and it was hard to tell who would come out best. Thousands of men were watching the fight. At last the Raiders gave way, and tried to escape, but would be set upon by a lot of Regulators, and would have to give up. There were many broken heads in this melee. As fast as one of the Raiders was arrested he was taken outside of the stockade, where Wirz had a guard ready, and put in an old house and strictly guarded. There was a great deal of fighting for the next three or four days until all the leaders of the Raiders were captured and taken out. Then Sergeant Key organized a court and tried them. They had a fair trial and six of them were condemned to death. The proceedings and findings of the court were sent to General Winder who approved of the findings and sentence, which were carried out on the 11th of July. The lawyer who acted as prosecuting attorney was sergeant Higgins, of my hundred. He was from Illinois, and a very fine young man, and for the manner in which he conducted the trial he was sent to our lines. Well do I remember when he came in and bade us a last farewell. I saw the tears roll down his cheeks as he said, " I hate to leave you here, but I can do you no good by staying." He had been a prisoner over twelve months and his health was poor. Said he, "I can not live much longer in here and I will go and do all I can to get an exchange."

It was several days after the trial before it was known what the sentences of the Raiders were, and it was rumored one day that they would be put back in the stockade. This caused a great deal of uneasiness, as it was expected things would be worse than before. About 2 o'clock, one day, the word was received that all the Raiders would be turned back into the stockade, but six of the leaders, who had been condemned to be hung. The Regulators were called out and formed in two parallel lines from the gate up the street and about eight feet apart. This was done to punish the Raiders who had not been condemned to be hung. They were let into the stockade one at a time and told that they had to run the gauntlet. So they would start to run, and as they did the Regulators rained blows on their heads, backs, arms, and many of them were badly hurt and some killed. By this time it was apparent that the Regulators were much the strongest and were well organized, and it was getting unhealthy to be caught stealing, and things began to be more quiet in the prison. On July 11th the gate opened and some timber was brought in on the south side of the stockade and some carpenters went to work to erect a gallows to hang the six raiders. This was soon noised over the prison and created much excitement. The friends of the Raiders said they never should be hung. It was generally expected that there would be a general row when they were brought in. A company of the Regulators were ordered on duty and were placed around the carpenters. By noon they had the gallows finished. Everybody was anxious to know what the result would be. At last the gates opened and in they came. Wirz rode a white horse; behind him walked the faithful old priest reading the Service for the condemned. The six doomed men followed, walking between double ranks of rebel guards. All came inside of the hollow square and halted. Wirz then said, "Briziners, I return to you dese men, so goot as I got dem. You haf tried dem yourselves and found dem guilty. I haf had notting to do wit it. I vash my hands of eferyting connected wit dem. Do wit dem as you like and may Gott haf mercy on you and on dem. Garts, about face. Vorwarts, march." After Wirz left the stockade, Key and his assistants went about the preparation as fast as they could. One of the condemned said, "You do not intend to hang us do you." "That is about the size of it," said Key. They were soon ordered to mount the scaffold, which they did, when the ropes were adjusted about their necks, when Key said, "Two minutes to talk." This time was improved by them in giving instructions to their friends as to what disposition to make of certain property which they had stolen. Key said, "time up." At this there were meal sacks drawn over their faces and the men jumped to the ground. Then Key raised his hand and said, "all right." At this signal, the props were pulled out from under the scaffold, and five of them were left swinging. The rope broke with the sixth man and he fell. Some of the Regulators went to him and discovered that he was not dead. The sack was pulled from his head and water thrown in his face, which soon restored him to consciousness. "Limber Jim" went about fixing up the platform. When all was ready, and a stouter rope had been secured, Limber Jim picked him up and placed him on the scaffold. He begged to be saved. Limber Jim was in no mood for that, for this same fellow had killed Limber Jim's brother some time before. He was soon swung off, and they were left hanging until life was extinct, when they were cut down and the sacks removed from their faces. The Regulators formed in two lines, and all the prisoners who wanted to, marched past and viewed their remains. The names they gave were as follows: John Sarsfield, 144th N. Y.; William Collins, *alias* Mosby, Co. D., 88th Pennsylvania; Charles Curtis, Co. A., 5th Rhode Island Artillery; Patrick Delaney, Co. E., 83rd Pennsylvania; A. Muir, United States Navy; Terrence Sullivan, 72nd N. Y. It was generally believed, however, that these names were fictitious, as they were understood to be "bounty-jumpers," enlisting for large sums of money, and remaining with no regiment after a chance was given them to desert.

CHAPTER VI.

ORGANIZATION OF A PRISON POLICE—SHOOTING DOWN PRISONERS—SHORT RATIONS AND SCARCITY OF WATER—CONDITION OF PRISONERS WHEN TURNED INTO THE STOCKADE—OUR NATIONAL HOLIDAY IN PRISON—MODES OF PUNISHMENT—THE MIRACULOUS SPRING.

AFTER the hanging of the six men, it was apparent to all that it was necessary to have a regular police to preserve order, so a regular system was organized. Key was made Chief of Police, but owing to the active part he had taken in the hanging of the six raiders, it was thought best that he should take a parole and go out on detail duty, as the Raiders were determined to avenge the death of their leader. Key sought and obtained a parole outside. Sergeant A. R. Hill, of the 100th Ohio, was made Chief in his place. Hill first came to notice on Belle Island, where he had an altercation with one Jack Oliver, of the 19th Indiana. Jack was a powerful man and thought it was his duty to thrash everybody on the Island. He got into a fuss with one of Hill's mess, and, as usual, proceeded to give him a thrashing, when Hill interfered and knocked Jack down, giving him a tremendous thrashing. Ever after this Hill was considered one of the best men in the prison. He was not quarrelsome but was very firm in his judgment, and was considered very fair in all his decisions.

Jack Oliver died a few months after he went to Andersonville. As I said, we were on the north side of the branch and close to the north gate. The path that led from the north side to the south side was close to the dead line, and where it crossed the branch was where we got the water we drank. At this place many of the boys were killed. This was about the way it was brought about. The stream was so small that it was very easy riled up, and in order to get a little pure water the next fellow would reach up the stream a little farther, and so on, until they would reach beyond the dead line, when the guard would fire at them without any notice, and it as often happened that some one else was hit as the one that was getting water, owing to the crowded condition of the pen. Just on the north side of this little stream was a "guard's perch," and it was said, and was never denied by the rebels, that every guard that shot a prisoner was allowed a furlough for thirty days. Hence they were very watchful, and this being a favorable post, owing to the men coming here for water, many were shot down at this point. I have stood on the bank and watched the guard at this post for hours, to see how eager he would be to get a shot at some poor, unfortunate prisoner. They would cock their guns, raise them to their faces ready to fire at the very slightest pretence of the prisoners getting over the dead line. The little board had got broken off the stakes at this place so you could not tell exactly where the line was. Many new prisoners coming in were killed here, not knowing that they were violating any rule whatever. It was terribly interesting to see how the eyes of the guard would flash when he thought he would get a good shot. There was no excuse for this. It was nothing but cold-blooded murder, premeditated from day to day, by these curses who were too low down in the scale to be classed with the human family.

Our rations consisted at first of mush, made of corn meal

ground, not bolted, no salt, and of this we got for one day's rations about one quart, and a small piece of meat. Often this mush had soured before it was given to us. Occasionally we would get about one-half pint of peas. Every pea had from one to one-half dozen bugs in it. This was our rations for several days after we went in the pen. Then they gave us corn bread, which was much better than the mush, and occasionally we would get a little molasses. The weather was desperately hot. Many of the men fell sick in a few days and could not eat such food. To make matters worse, they had made the cook house over the stream just outside of the stockade and when they had cooked the meat they would let the water out in the branch and it would be covered with grease. This was all the chance we had for water for several weeks. The mortality was fearful, as high as one hundred and twenty-five would die in twenty-four hours. Go where you would, you could see men dying. Hundreds and thousands were turned in this pen without blankets, tent, cup or anything in the line of cooking utensils. Many came in here bareheaded, barefooted and almost naked, having been robbed of their clothing by their captors. The rebels never seemed to think that we needed anything of the kind. The boys of my regiment were put in different hundreds, yet we managed to see each other every day, or nearly so. Of my company, four of us remained together until September. We got four little sticks upon which we would spread our blanket during the day. This offered us a little shade, and at night we would take it down and spread it over us, having nothing to lay upon but the bare ground. During the month of June and up to the 10th of July, it rained almost every day. Then the sun would come out and the heat would be fearful. The skin on the men's bare backs would raise up in great blisters and make running sores. These sores would be covered with great big green flies. Soon you could see those sores full of maggots, then the gangrene would set in, and death soon followed. In this manner hundreds died. Many soon got the scurvy, and then it soon run to the dropsy. I have seen hundreds of men with their ankles swelled to three or four times their natural size. Their legs would puff up until they seemed transparent. To make things worse there was no arrangement made for the men to attend the calls of nature. They would crowd up to the little stream as near as they could, but it soon became so filthy that you could not sit within three or four rods of the stream. Reader, let your imagination take in the situation. Thirty thousand men, all of them having the diarrhoea, and all must go to attend the calls of nature, and that on as limited a space as one acre of ground. What condition do you think it would be in in the course of two or three months? Do you think you would like to be compelled to breathe this kind of an atmosphere? This is not all. Hundreds who were too sick to go to this place would dig out little holes in the ground and use them until almost full when they would fill them with dirt. Thousands of such holes were inside the pen; then there would come a rain. The hot sun, the thermometer ranging up to as high as one hundred and twenty and even forty. Now how would you like to lay down in this place and take a sleep? How would you like to take your breakfast in this pleasant parlor where you could look in any direction from you and see dead men and men dying? Don't you think this would be a pleasant place to have a picnic or the Fourth of July celebration? Well, I celebrated the Fourth of July in this pen in 1864, and the surroundings were much worse than I have described them, as language fails me, and no man will ever be able to write it as it should be written. Many stout men would come in here and, after looking at the horrible condition of things, would sicken and die inside of ten or twelve days.

As for myself, I was very stout, and I determined if it was possible that I would live through it. I did not want to give the curses the satisfaction of seeing me carried out dead. I took all the exercise and precaution I could that I might beat them in the end, and thanks to the Supreme Ruler, I got out of this living hell. But when I think of the many brave boys who perished there, I feel very sad, as there was no just cause for this inhuman treatment.

No, our misery was not due to the inability of the rebels to provide for us comfortably. It was deliberately planned by that arch traitor, Jeff. Davis, and his subordinates. May God have more mercy on their souls than they showed to the poor, helpless and starved Union prisoners who surrendered their lives—the victims of their damnable cruelty—in this horrible place of confinement.

In this chapter I will tell the rebel mode of punishing the prisoners. I have often been asked why more of the prisoners did not try to make their escape. Every 400 men made a division. Over this division there was a sergeant appointed to take charge of the men, and he was held responsible for his division. Over every hundred was a sergeant appointed, whose business it was to see that all his men answered to roll call, draw rations, make details to look after the sick, carry out the dead, bring in wood, etc. He was held personally responsible for his hundred. For instance. A man was detailed to go after wood, and while outside of the stockade made his escape. The sergeant of his hundred would be punished for his offence. This way of dealing kept many a prisoner from trying to get away. Sometimes the rebels would punish the entire hundred by cutting off their rations for a day. No prisoner wanted a man put in the stocks, or one hundred men to go without anything to eat for twenty-four hours, on account of his offence. You can see at once that the rebels hit upon a pretty good plan to keep the men from trying to escape.

During this month, I think it was in January, while I belonged to the tenth hundred, the sergeant was one of those good-natured fellows, and I think, strictly honest. While a detail of his hundred was out after wood, one cold, raw, damp day, a prisoner tried to make his escape. As soon as it was found out, the rebels sent in for the sergeant, who was taken out and put in the stocks. He was kept in the stocks four days, until the fellow who had tried to escape was returned. I saw him while he was in the stocks. He said to me, "this is getting worse than death, but I will try and stand it." He was lying flat on his back, or rather on his shoulders, his feet about two feet high, with his ankles securely fastened in the stocks, on the cold, damp ground. He was compelled to lie in this position for four days. At night they would release him and bring him into the stockade as soon as roll-call was over. In the morning he would be taken out and fastened as described. Remember he was not the only one that was put in the stocks. There were hundreds who were punished in this way. The sergeant of my hundred did not live long after he was released. Having taken a severe cold, he soon sickened and died. You see there are not many men who would try to escape, knowing that the innocent would have to suffer on their account. Some one might say, "how could the rebels tell when one tried to escape." Usually ten men went out of a hundred. After they got through the stockade on the outside they formed in line, the number of the hundred given, and the men counted by a rebel officer stationed at the gate for that purpose. After all were counted, about six or eight guards would accompany the squad after the wood. When they returned, all were halted at the gate and re-counted. If a man was missing, the officers were notified at once. There was no chance of getting away while out on detail duty without some one getting punished.

Towards the last of June the prison was crowded terribly. The rebels seeing the stockade was not large enough to hold the prisoners, had been at work on an addition, which was finished about the first of July. This addition gave us plenty of room for a time. As soon as it was open and the order given to go inside of it, my squad did not lose any time in getting there. We made our way to nearly the center of the new addition, where the most of my regiment took up quarters. We got a pretty good place and secured some brush and wood enough to last us for several days. We now suffered the most for water. While we were near the branch, we used to scoop out little holes near the edge of the marsh and by watching close we could get a little water, although every night the holes would fill with from one dozen to five times that many maggots in them, as the earth near the branch was covered with maggots. But we soon got used to them, and would scoop them out, and in an hour or two there would be enough water to give us a drink. Being removed from those places we could not watch them, so we were compelled to use the water from the branch. Close to where we lay in the new stockade were some marines who had been captured and were allowed to bring in some of their traps. They had a small rope which they thought they would use to assist them to haul the dirt out of a well which they proposed to dig. They commenced to dig their well and continued it over forty feet deep with no signs of water. There were several wells dug at different places without any better success. The marines, about this time, camped near the brow of the hill on the north side of the branch. Suddenly the ground began to get damp and soon became so damp that the men staying there had to remove their quarters. In a few days, water began to trickle down the side of the hill. There was a young fellow who had been outside and had picked up a piece of bark, which he rolled up and formed into a trough or spout. This he placed where the water seemed to come out the strongest, raising the lower end until you could set a cup or hold a canteen under it. A small stream of water began running all the time. This stream grew stronger from day to day, until it got to be a large spring and afforded plenty of water for the entire prison. Many prisoners will remember how we used to form a line and take our turn to get water, and how they would cry out, "look out for flankers." This was while the stream was small and required several minutes to fill a canteen. The rule was, if any one fell out of line and ran ahead to get a chance, he was compelled to go to the rear of the line. This gave all an equal opportunity to get water. I often stood in the line for one hour to get a chance at the spring. After the spring was an assured fact, the rebels caused boxes to be made about fourteen inches wide and about the same depth, and fourteen feet long, which they placed at the spring, commencing at the branch, placing the first one with just sufficient fall to carry off the water. The end of the second one was placed on the end of the first, the other end extending up the hill, and so on until six or eight of these boxes were so placed and afforded plenty of water for the entire stockade, and of a good quality. This spring is still running to this day. After this we had no more trouble for water. You can call this a miracle, or what you please. We were satisfied with the water without asking any questions. There were more than one dozen wells on that side of the branch, dug out from 40 to 60 feet deep, without getting any water.

Poor Charley Weibel, my partner, had fallen sick with the diarrhea and rheumatism. He could not walk a step.

This was very annoying to him and he fretted over his misfortune very much. Soon another of the mess, Luther Robbins, now of Huntington, fell sick, but after a time he got able to walk around, and finally got back to God's country. Weibel never got any better but gradually grew worse from day to day, until death ended his sufferings.

CHAPTER VII.

Efforts to Escape—Tunneling—Tattooing a Traitor—Plan to Force the Stockade—Wirz Informed of the Plot—Carrying Out the Dead—Thoughts of Home—How We Learned of the Capture of Atlanta—A Night of Great Excitement.

As it was useless to try to escape while out on detail it became necessary to try other means. So tunneling was resorted to. In order to tunnel we were compelled to dig downward at least five feet to get under the stockade. Tunnels were usually started as though you were going to dig a well. Then you would start at right angles and keep on a level as near as possible. The tunnels were from fifty to seventy-five feet long, and men would work in them day and night. During the day the dirt would be hauled back into the well, and at night it would be carried out and scattered around or put in any little depression and covered up with top-soil so as not to attract the notice of the guards in the day time. It would take several days to complete these tunnels. Now the great trouble was that some of the raider crowd would inform on you, and the leaders of the tunnel would be taken out and punished, and the tunnel broken in without any one making his escape. Whenever any certain set of persons had made up their minds to dig a tunnel, they would try to keep it a secret, yet these fellows would find out many of them and report the same to the rebels. It began to be discouraging to try to get out that way, although there were parties at work all the time digging. Another trouble was that the rebels sent in some of their own men, disguised as prisoners, to watch for tunnel diggers. One day quite a commotion was noticed in the prison. It was soon learned that a large tunnel had been almost completed and some one had reported the boys and they were taken out for punishment. Some one suggested that the fellows who were suspected of giving the information be punished. So several of them were caught and had one side of their heads shaved as close as it could be done, when they were let up and had to run the gauntlet. This was pretty severe punishment. One fellow was caught close to where I was stopping, and there seemed to be no doubt of his guilt. Among the fellows that he had reported was an old sailor, who was very mad at not having an opportunity of going through the tunnel and at least making the attempt to get to God's country. He proposed that they put a mark on the fellow that all might know who he was. The old sailor understood the art of tattooing with India ink, and having a supply with him, said to the boys, "Lay him on the ground a while till I mark him." He was laid on the ground, while some held his feet, others his hands, and the old sailor took his head between his knees and began operations by picking a large letter "T" on his forehead, the stem, or large part of the "T" running down his nose. The sailor, like all other sailors, used tobacco pretty freely, and as his work proceeded he would stop and deliver a well directed shot of spittal on the fellow's forehead, which he would rub over the part he was at work on. After he had finished his work the fellow was let up, and there was a large letter "T," that could be seen for several rods away. He was then compelled to run the gauntlet. He made for the gate

Twelve Months in Andersonville.

and was taken out. It was soon understood that he was a rebel who had been sent in to watch the prisoners and report tunnel digging. Soon a guard came in and took the old sailor out with some of the other boys and put them in the stocks, but did not keep them there long, and when the old sailor came in he remarked that that fellow had a mark he would not lose this side of the grave, and said some more fellows would get the same kind of treatment if they did not stop their meddling with other people's business. From the trouble experienced in trying to get out by tunneling, the case seemed hopeless. Enemies without and enemies within. What should next be done? By this time there were thousands of good able-bodied men, captured in the spring campaign, who had not become reduced much and who were anxious to be outside. There was a plan proposed to force the stockade, and this seemed to meet with the approval of all the prisoners that were let into the secret. They then commenced to form companies. Fifty men were to form a company, and every man had to take a solemn oath to obey the officers appointed over them. The work of organization progressed nicely, and everything seemed to be working well. Men were detailed to dig tunnels to the stockade and then to follow along the stockade for twelve or fifteen feet, hollowing out the ground, so that when the time came to make the break by running against the stockade it could easily be pushed down. There were several of the tunnels prepared, or nearly so. When the time came the men were all to rush against those places and push the stockade down, and through these gaps the men were to rush out and try and capture the star fort, which had twelve guns. It was thought this could be done before they could fire more than one round. There were companies of artillerymen organized to take charge of the guns who were to turn them on the rebel camp. The other companies were to overpower the guards and take their guns from them. It was supposed that the guards would throw down their guns, as most of them were young men and conscripts. After once getting outside and capturing the guards we were to form and make our way to Florida. It was certain then we would have at least twenty-five thousand good effective men. With this army we could drive everything before us. We meant to take all the teams that we could find on the march. The prisoners would reason that Sherman was holding Johnson so that he could not spare any of his troops, neither could Lee, nor could they spare troops enough from any point to cope with such a force. It was reasonable enough to suppose that our plans would have been successful could we have made the attempt. A few days before the break was to be made, Capt. Wirz sent in and arrested our leader and we never heard of him afterwards. I think his name was Wilson, and he was from New York. He was a cool and brave man. As soon as Wilson was taken out Wirz sent in for all the Sergeants of hundreds to report to the gate, which they did. He took them outside and informed them that he had been apprised of the plot for some time and had taken extra precautions to guard against it. Said he: "Should you have made the attempt, you could not have forced the stockade, as I have caused it to be so braced that you could not have forced it, and you would have caused thousands of deaths, as I should have opened on the stockade with every gun I could have brought to bear on it." And we had good reasons to believe that he would have done so. Thus this plan all came to naught.

As soon as the Sergeants were returned to the stockade, Wirz sent in some men who hoisted a line of poles across the stockade with a strip of cloth on them and issued orders that if there should collect fifty or more men in one mass between the poles and dead line, he would conclude that they had a design on the stockade and should open on them with grape shot. As this plan had fallen through, we turned our attention to other matters for a few days.

I was detailed one morning to help carry out a dead man. We got to the gate where we found several others waiting for it to open. We laid the dead man down and had to stand around him. The sand was very loose and dry. I was in my bare feet, and while standing here in the sand, the gray-backs would crawl over our feet as if you had put your foot in an ant hill. There was a large space around the gate that was used for the examination of the sick, and they would be brought here by their friends and laid on the ground until they could be examined. The dead also would be laid here for some time, and the lice would crawl over the ground. It was literally alive with gray-backs.

All the news we could get from outside was from the new arrivals, or "fresh fish," as we called them. Whenever a new lot of prisoners were seen coming, they would be asked by the old prisoners for the news. Everybody wanted to know what the prospect was for exchange. As a general thing they learned but little about an exchange. Occasionally some one would come in and make the statement that a few days before his capture he saw in the New York *Herald* or Baltimore *American* the statement that there had been an agreement made whereby all prisoners were to be exchanged, and he had no doubt but what, in a few weeks at farthest, we would all be out of the pen. If he had no doubt at the time he made the statement, it is fair to suppose he had many doubts before we were released. The Branch was a good place to go for news. As all could go there, you were free to visit it almost any time and engage with the boys in conversation, either relating the part they had played or how they came to be gobbled up. Every soldier thought he belonged to the best branch of the service, and had the best and bravest officers.

One of the most trying and aggravating things that a prisoner had to endure was to hear boys and men tell what good victuals they used to have at home, and what good times they would have when they got back. They would begin this way: First boy would say, "I know my ma can beat the world to make good light biscuits. I tell you they would almost melt in your mouth." Second boy: "I tell you my ma was lightning on buckwheat cakes; oh, how I wish I had some of them instead of this everlasting corn meal." No one knows what effect this kind of talk would have on a fellow until he is starved as we were. Go where you would you could hear this kind of talk, and they would keep it up until some one would bawl out, "Stop that racket. You know it is not allowed in this glorious Sunny South."

The fate of Sherman's Army, then on its triumphant march to the sea, was a matter of which we were extremely solicitous. Few prisoners were received after the month of July, and although our hopes were high, our apprehensions were of the gravest character. The defeat of Stoneman's Cavalry, with the loss of its commander, and a considerable number of his men, followed by the defeat of our infantry at Etowah Creek, had a very depressing effect. Such news as we received came at long intervals, generally through rebel sources, and always colored to suit themselves. To show the officers that they were attending to duty, the guards in the stockade perches called the number of their posts and the time every half-hour. The formula was as follows: "Post number——, half-past ten o'clock, and all is well." This was repeated until it had made the rounds, when silence would again prevail. One night our ears were startled by the call from one of the perches, "Post number four, half-past eight o'clock, and Atlanta's gone to h—l!" Every prisoner in the stockade, apparently, heard the call. Our astonishment at this announcement may be imagined. Every heart took courage, and in an instant the prison was a scene of great rejoicing. Cheers followed cheers. The sick were made almost well by the glad news, the strong leaped for joy, and the handshaking and hurrahing was indescribable. Atlanta was won, Sherman's army was safe, and we almost felt that we were once again with the loved ones of our Northern homes. Sleep was banished from our eyes. You could hear patriotic songs all over the prison. I believe Boston Corbet and some others organized a praise meeting. The "Star Spangled Banner" was sung, "Rally Round the Flag, Boys," and "Tramp, Tramp, we are Marching." The most of the night was spent in this manner until the men actually became hoarse from cheering and singing. So great was the excitement that the rebels became alarmed lest we should make a dash on the stockade and a grand rush for freedom. The guards were placed under arms, and not until exhausted nature forced us to rest, were they withdrawn. It was a night never to be forgotten by any comrade in Andersonville.

CHAPTER VIII.

A Promised Exchange—Death of My Partner—Transferred to Savannah—Deceiving the Prisoners—Improved Prison Fare—Futile Attempts at Tunnel Digging—The Story of the Arrest of the Commander at Savannah as a Rebel Spy—His Death at Fort Delaware.

A FEW days later, early in the month of September, the rebel sergeants who called the roll visited the stockade, and each addressing his squad, stated that a general exchange had been agreed upon. They said that United States vessels were then at Savannah waiting for the prisoners, and that twenty thousand men would at once be sent to that place, ten detachments to leave the following morning. As stated, the first detachment left in the morning, but as my hundred was not included, I had to wait a few days. I took my station the next morning near the gate, and soon the column that was ordered out began to move. I never saw men so rejoiced as they were. Some could hardly walk, others had to hobble along with the assistance of a stick, but all seemed cheerful, and you could hear from all sides, "We will soon be in God's country." The long column soon passed out of the gate. I walked to the top of the hill, where I could see them move off towards the station where the cars were waiting for them. As soon as they were gone, I approached the guard and had a little conversation with him. He said every man would be taken out of the pen as fast as they could furnish transportation. The well ones would go first, then the sick. I went back to my quarters and told Charlie Weibel what I had seen and what the guard had told me. It so elated him that he sat up for awhile, but as soon as the excitement began to wear off he seemed worse. I talked to him, and said to him I did not have any doubt but that we would all be removed in a few days. He said, "I am not strong enough to stand the trip." We told him it was not so far to Savannah, and the rebels said they were going to make different arrangements for the sick, and as soon as we got to our boats we would be taken care of. He said, "I will try and keep up." In a day or two the guards came back and said, "You ought to have heard your fellows holler when they first saw your old flag." This kind of news put us all on tiptoe of excitement again, and another squad was ordered out. By this time it began to thin out the prisoners so that one could move around with a little ease. In a few days the guards were back again. This time the hundred to which I belonged was included. We were ordered on the south side of the branch and a guard was put between us and the branch. This was done to keep out "flankers." We went over there in the evening. I was now compelled to leave Weibel for the first time since our imprisonment. Before I left him I took my blanket and fixed him as good a tent as I could, supplied him with water, and there was a young man from Ohio who stayed close to us. We had become acquainted. He said he would draw his rations for him and keep him supplied with water as long as his hundred remained in the stockade. We remained on the south side all night. The next morning we did not go out. Ten o'clock came and no orders to leave, so I obtained permission to go back and see my comrade. I found him very much depressed. He said he felt that he could never make the trip. By talking with him for awhile he revived up. I had to go back to the squad, and about 3 o'clock in the afternoon the young man from Ohio came over and said Weibel wanted to see me. I went as quick as I could. I found him much worse. He said to me, "Long, I can't stand this any longer. I am sure I cannot live through another night. I have here some letters, memoranda book, and gold rings. Take them, and if you ever get home take them to my sisters at Indianapolis and tell them where I died. The letters are written in German. They will forward them to their destination." I said, "Charlie, I think you will soon be better; cheer up; I heard an officer say that the next to go would be the sick, and I am sure you will be able to go." By talking to him for a short time he cheered up, and I handed him his goods back. I remained with him until near dark, when I reported back to my hundred. The next morning I went back to see him and found him very bad. I remained awhile and got him some breakfast. He ate a little. I brought him some fresh water, when I was again ordered to my hundred, but for some reason we did not go out. About two o'clock the young man from Ohio came over and said that Charlie wanted to see me. I hurried over there as quick as I could. When I approached him, he handed me his traps and said: "Do with them as I told you yesterday." I said, "Do you not feel any better?" "No," said he, "I want to die and be out of this misery. Do not talk to me to cheer me up, for I cannot live any longer in this misery." I made several attempts to talk to him, when he would say, "Don't, I will soon be out of this misery." Four or five of the boys that I was acquainted with came up, and we sat on the ground close by him. All at once he turned over, and I went to him and found that he did not breathe. He was dead. We straightened him out, removed the blanket, tied his hands across his breast, tied his big toes together, and I wrote his name, Company, Regiment and State, date of death, on a little slip of paper and pinned it on his breast, after which we carried him out. I was now alone as far as any of my Regiment were concerned. We had been so scattered that now we were all gone. While I felt the deepest sorrow for poor Weibel, I was truly glad that he was out of his misery, as his imprisonment had been terrible. Wounded at the start, then the diarrhea, and then rheumatism, he had not been able to walk for weeks, but was compelled to lay on the bare ground day after day, and night after night.

About sunset we were ordered out, and off we go, as we suppose, to God's country. After we had embarked, the train moved slowly along at a rate of speed not exceeding eight miles an hour, and when we recollected that the reported distance to Savannah was 240 miles, it seemed as if we should never reach our destination. Macon was the only town of commercial importance along the line. Its population at that time was about five thousand. At regular distances along the line of the road would be seen an open shed which served as a station. The country through which we passed consisted principally of pine barrens, and for miles and miles there was no sign of habitation. The inhabitants—such as we saw— were of the class known as "low-downers." They were lazy, ignorant and stupid, dull-eyed and open-mouthed, lank and lean, and had evidently never made the acquaintance of a barber or hair-dresser. We looked upon them and their poverty-stricken land with undisguised contempt, remembering the culture, intelligence and comforts of the sturdy yeomanry of our Northern homes.

The morning of the second day after our departure from Andersonville we reached the city of Savannah. Contrary to our expectation, we found it almost a deserted village. The unbroken stillness, so different from what we expected on entering the metropolis of Georgia, and a city that was an important point in Revolutionary days, became absolutely oppressive. We could not understand it, but our thoughts were more intent upon the coming transfer to our flag than upon any speculation as to the cause of the remarkable stillness of Savannah. Finally some boys came close to us, and we opened up a conversation. "Say, boys, are our ships down in the bay yet?" "I don't know." "Ain't they going to exchange us here?" "Don't know." "Well, what are they going to do with us, any way?" "They have got some of uns around by the old jail." "What, are there any prisoners here now?" "Yes, around by the old jail there is a place fixed for uns all." How our hearts sank within us. The truth flashed across our minds that we had been deceived, and for a purpose. We soon learned that there had not been any prisoners exchanged, and that there had been no exchange agreed upon. They had lied to us for the purpose of allaying our fears and preventing our trying to make our escape while being transferred from Andersonville to Savannah. By this means they could do with many guards less than it would have required if we had known we were going to another prison. So you can see how well they succeeded in deceiving us. Soon the guard formed into lines, one on either side of the street. We were ordered off the cars, formed between the guards, and after a short march through the city we came out to an old jail, where we saw a high board fence erected enclosing a large tract of ground adjoining the old jail. We soon came to the gate, where we were counted off into hundreds, names taken, and then turned into the pen, where we met our old comrades who had left Andersonville some twenty days before. Among them were some of the 5th Indiana Cavalry. I soon found the 5th boys, and among them my old friend, Bob Fisher, who at this time is a doctor, and lives somewhere in Kansas. Bob was not long in telling me how they had been deceived. He was in the first squad that left Andersonville. I said, "Bob, what do you think about exchange now?" "Oh," said he, "it is all right. We will soon be exchanged. There was a little difficulty arose between the rebels and our folks," said he, "in regard to our boats coming up the Savannah river, and that has delayed the exchange for a few days. We will soon be out of here. You see this is not near so strong a place as Andersonville, and if they did not intend to exchange us why did they go to the trouble to send us here?" I said, "I hope you are right, but I don't believe a word the cusses say in regard to exchange, for I know they have lied to us this time. They said that they saw you go on our boats, and said, 'you ought to have heard your fellows holler when they saw your old flag.' Now you see that is a lie, and if they will lie one time they will another when it suits their purpose and they can accomplish anything by so doing." Bob said, "What do you think?" "Well," I said, "I think they have got a little scared and have moved us to keep us from falling into Sherman's hands. You see Atlanta is ours, and how long it will be before Sherman gets down here no one knows. I think they were more afraid of that than anything else." "Why, don't you think we are going to be exchanged?" "Not a bit of it; at least, not now."

As I was entirely alone now, as far as any of my Regiment were concerned, and there was no room with Fisher for an extra man, I began to look around for some place to stop, which I could call my own. At last I met two men from Ohio. They had not been prisoners long. They lived in Cincinnati, and had been captured in the Shenandoah Valley. They had each a blanket and I had one, and so we went together and fixed up a place to stay. I soon found them to be gentlemen in every particular, and very kind. Their names were Khalor and Ellis. Khalor was well educated and well posted in regard to the war. He would set for hours and tell us his views as to the final outcome of the war. He had no faith in an exchange. He had kept himself posted before his capture, and said that there was not the least prospect for exchange, nor never would be, unless the rebels would exchange colored troops the same as other soldiers. This, he said, our government was lawfully bound to do, and could make no other arrangement that would be honorable or just. The weather was fine, it being the 1st of October. There was not so many men here as at Andersonville. After we got fixed up we thought, after all, this is a much better place than Andersonville. The guards treated us much better; in fact they were gentlemen by the side of those brats we had left. The guards here were marines enlisted for the Southern navy. As Uncle Sam had blockaded all the ports, the South had but little use for marines, and they refused to take the field. Many of them had belonged to the U. S. Army before the breaking out of the rebellion, and didn't seem to care whether the South gained her independence or not. We felt relief to know that we were not to be ruled over by that villain, Wirz. There was a young man in command of the camp. He had been at Andersonville a short time. His name was Davis—a lieutenant in the rebel army. His home was in Baltimore. He had taken an active part in the mob which assailed the old Sixth Massachusetts Regiment when they were on their way to Washington. As usual such men as would engage in a mob did not like the idea of meeting the enemy face to face on equal terms, and being wealthy, he got the position of commanding the camp at Savannah. He was a very foul-mouthed fellow. Would make terrible threats of what he would do if his "ordahs" were not obeyed. He was one of those fellows that could swear by note and never miss a bar or skip a quarter note.

Our rations were much better here than they had been at Andersonville. The meal was ground finer and was sifted, which was much more palatable, and we got a little salt every few days. Our ration of meat was larger and of a better grade. We soon began to be glad that we had been transferred to this place. Our ration of wood was limited and required a good deal of economy to make it do our cooking. There were no new prisoners coming in and we soon began to be anxious to know what was going on outside. When the first prisoners arrived at Savannah they were put inside of the enclosure. The boards did not go down into the ground, but rested on the sod. The prison was located on a piece of commons, which was sodded over, and the soil being sandy it was but a few minutes work to dig under the fence and get outside. As there was no dead-line established, the men were allowed to crowd up to the fence. Many of them took advantage of this opportunity and dug out. There were several hundred got out the first night. When morning came, look anywhere along the fence and you could see holes where the Yank's had dug out. The alarm was given and men and dogs started out after the fugitives. By night, all or nearly all, were back in the pen, as all the bridges were guarded and all boats broken up. It was simply impossible to escape. The boats had been broken up to keep their men from going out to our fleet. When the last squad was brought in Davis said he would stop that "d—n business," so he established a guard line about twelve feet from the fence and issued orders to the guards to shoot any prisoner who came inside of the dead-line. This did but little good, as the sod was very stiff, and underneath the sand was very loose, it only required a little more time to tunnel out, three or four hours being sufficient to complete a tunnel. The next morning several tunnels were discovered and some fifty or a hundred men had passed out during the night. This made Davis very mad. He said, "I will stop this business." There was a great revolution going on in his dull brain. At last Davis hit upon the plan to find out if any tunnels had been commenced during the night. Every morning he would come in with a lot of guards and a cart with a mule attached to it, the cart loaded with stone. They would go on the inside of the deadline and when the wheels of the cart crossed a tunnel they would break the sod and the tunnel would be exposed. Davis was wonderfully elated over his plan. He said, "I guess I am a match for the d—n Yank's." He supposed that it would take two or three nights to dig a tunnel with the implements at hand, while three or four hours was all a brisk Yankee wanted. So the next morning there were a lot of men out. Davis came in and said, "You fellows beat the devil." "Oh yes," said one of the boys, "I guess that is about the size of it, for we have been beating the rebels of late badly and we think they are worse than the devil." Davis seemed terribly excited and said, "I can fix you. I will let you know that I can keep you in this prison and I will keep you there." He went out and in a short time we saw a large gang of negroes at work digging a ditch around the outside of the fence. This ditch was dug about twelve feet wide and five feet deep. Davis had this filled with water from the city water works and kept it full all the time. This ended the tunneling. There was no use to try that any more.

When we first arrived at Savannah great numbers of her citizens came out to the prison or stockade, to see us, and would crowd up close to us, as the stockade was not entirely finished. When we first arrived there was only a guard line to keep the citizens and prisoners apart, and as they seemed anxious to talk and the prisoners equally as anxious, they would be continually crowding up to them. One day one of the guards saw a young man standing in the crowd of prisoners whom he thought was a citizen from his dress, and ordered him out. The young man walked out and sauntered away and endeavored to make his escape, and got within twenty miles of Sherman's lines when he was recaptured and returned to Savannah. When he was brought back to the stockade Davis was standing near the gate. He looked sternly at him and at his rebel garments, and muttering, " By God, I'll stop this," he caught the coat by the tail, tore it to the collar, and took it and his hat away from him. The name of the young man was Frank Beverstock. In a few weeks Beverstock was included in an exchange, and was sent to his home at Newark, Ohio, on a furlough. While on the cars, on his road home, I think, Beverstock met and recognized Davis, who had been sent out of the Confederacy to Canada with dispatches for Southern emissaries then harassing the Northern borders from the Dominion. Davis had made an effort to disguise himself, but could not conceal his identity from the young man, who, with the assistance of some comrades, placed him under arrest, and delivered him to the authorities at Camp Chase, near Columbus, Ohio. A court martial afterwards tried Davis as a spy, and he was found guilty and sentenced to be hanged. When the trial was over, Beverstock stepped up to Davis, and reminding him of the incident at the prison gate, remarked, " I believe, Davis. we are even on that coat now." Davis was to have been executed at Johnson Island, but through family connection with border State Unionists, his sentence was commuted to imprisonment during the war. He was taken to Fort Delaware for confinement and died soon after. So ended the life of a foul-mouthed tyrant and traitor whose name, with that of Wirz, ought only to be remembered with infamy.

CHAPTER IX.

EFFORTS OF CONFEDERATES TO SECURE MECHANICS FROM AMONG THE PRISONERS—FLANKING INTO A SICK MAN'S PLACE—DECEIVED AGAIN—TRANSFERRED TO MILLEN—TUNNELING AGAIN ON AN EXTENSIVE SCALE ONLY TO MEET WITH ANOTHER DISASTROUS FAILURE.

THE weather continued fine, with but little news to break the monotony of prison life. No new prisoners came in, and we had little opportunity of hearing from our armies. We had about made up our minds that we would have to stay here through the winter, when one day a rebel colonel came in and posted up notices that the Confederate Government wanted all the blacksmiths they could get, and if any of the Yankee prisoners would go out and work for them they would give them a parole of honor, take them out and would pay them in Confederate money or greenbacks. They wanted blacksmiths, machinists, shoemakers and a few carpenters. The notice stated that the colonel would visit the prison from day to day and take out such as chose to go. As winter was just here and my clothing was very thin, I could not see how I was to pull through the winter. So Kahlor went down and saw the colonel, as Ellis and myself were blacksmiths. We agreed that if they would take all three of us out, we would go out on parole, and by so doing we might meet an opportu-

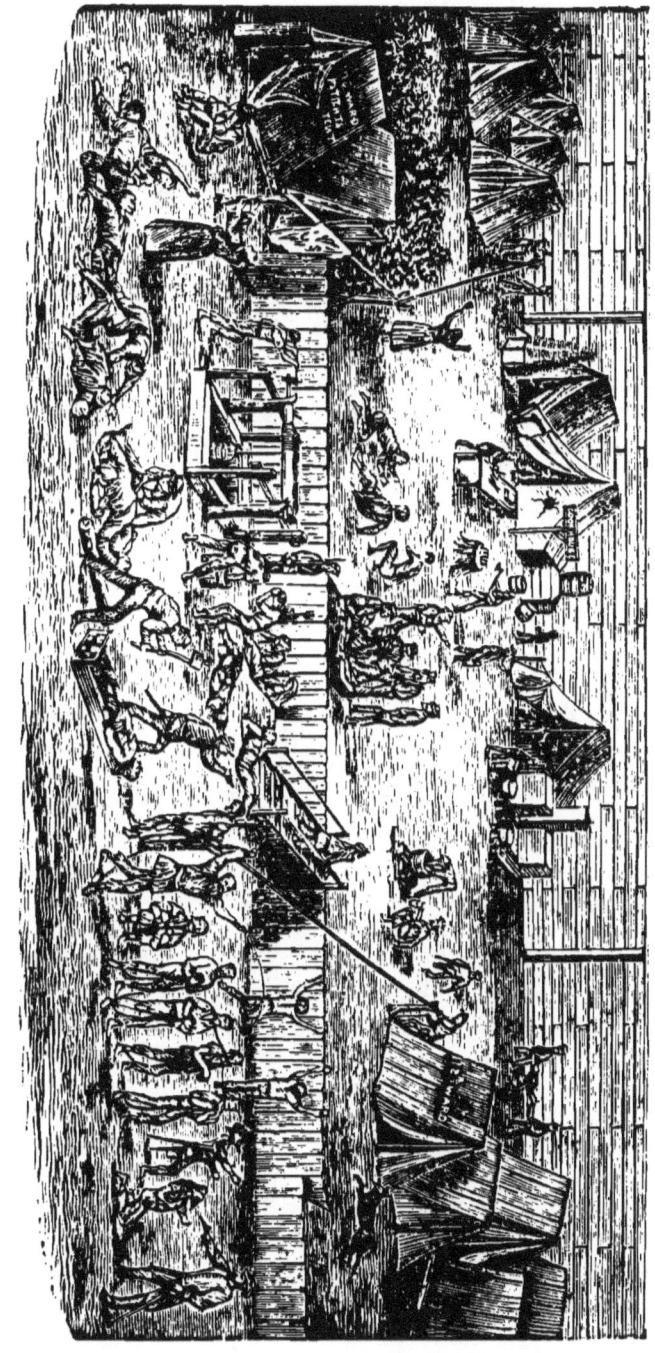

HOSPITAL AT ANDERSONVILLE.

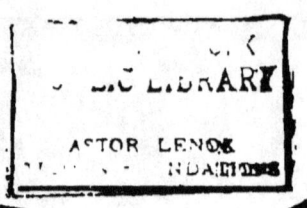

nity to make our escape. At any rate it could make matters no worse than they were. When Kahlor returned he said he had made the arrangements and we were to go out the next day. Several of our friends found out that we were going out and came over to our tent. Some wanted us to do all we could to get them places, while others said, "It is all wrong," and whenever we got exchanged we would be punished for working for the enemy. I almost backed out, as I did not like to work for my enemies. Kahlor reasoned with us, and said he did not believe that our government would punish us at all, and said he: "If we have to remain here all winter without shelter or clothing the most of us will be dead by spring," and he thought the best thing to do was to go out, as he had made arrangements. So we decided to go. About 3 o'clock in the afternoon my old friend, Bob Fisher, came up to our tent much excited. Said he: " I told you we would soon be exchanged. Do you see that squad of rebel officers down there? Well, they just came in and ordered from one to ten detachments to get ready to leave at 6 o'clock this evening and I want you to take the place of a sick man in my hundred and go out with me. I know we will soon be at home." By this time the entire camp was in a blaze of excitement. I said, "All right, I will go." Turning to Kahlor and Ellis I said: "It will not be long till you will follow." " We hope so," said they, "yet we have our doubts." "Oh, I guess we are all right this time." I took up my blanket and cup, which was all of my outfit at this time, and bidding my friends good bye, saying to Kahlor: "Tell that Irish Colonel to mend his own dilapidated machinery, as we propose to work for Uncle Sam in preference." I went with Fisher to the sergeant of his hundred and assumed the name of the sick man. The sergeant said to me, " I will do the best for you I can, but if you get in trouble do not blame me." " All right," said I. Six o'clock soon arrived, and the word was given to fall in, and I took my place in line. We were marched outside of the gate amidst the cheers of the entire camp. We could hear patriotic songs all over the camp as we marched to the gate. When outside of the gate we were formed in line, and Davis marched up and down the line, swearing that if there was a man who had flanked out he would shoot him. As soon as it was known, I began to wish I was back inside of the stockade, but all I could do was to stand still and await the result of the roll call, which was commenced in a short time by a rebel sergeant, who, like all the sergeants who had been over us, were very poor hands to call names. As they approached near me I almost sank down, but was close to the sergeant, who said, "Be quiet." When the sergeant called out the man's name, I answered in an undertone. Imagine my relief when he and Davis passed on. I felt that I had passed a terrible ordeal, for I believe Davis would have put his threat into execution at that time. We were told to remain here for awhile, and about eight o'clock the order was given to move. So here we go with high hopes of soon being in God's country.

We soon arrived at the cars and were literally packed into them. There was no room to lay down or hardly sit down. After considerable confusion with the guard, the old, squeaky cars began to move. We could not tell in what direction we were going, but supposed we were going to Charleston and the rebels encouraged us in this belief. They said there had been some difficulty in allowing our fleet to pass the fortifications of Savannah and hence it was the cause of our having to go to Charleston for exchange. After pounding along all night, morning came, and we were not long in discovering that the country through which we were traveling was the same we had covered in coming to Savannah. It soon became painfully evident that we were returning to Andersonville. When we reached the junction at Millen, we haulted at the "Y" and waited the orders of the officers with intense anxiety. The left hand road was the route to Andersonville, the right hand road led to Charleston or Richmond. The left hand road meant a return to our wretchedness. The right hand road hinted a hope of speedy exchange. Our engine took the right hand track, but after running about five miles, stopped in the middle of a heavy pine forest. We were ordered out of the cars, and marching a few rods, came in sight of another of those hateful stockades, similar to that at Andersonville, with this exception, the logs in the stockade at Andersonville were hewed, at Camp Lawton they were in their rough state. We were marched up to the gate of the prison. Oh! how our hearts sank within us at the idea of again being confined inside of those gloomy walls.

There were a lot of rebel sergeants at the gate who proceeded to take our names, Regiment, Company and State. This was a tedious operation, as no rebel was ever an expert at writing names, and especially Yankee names. We were formed into hundreds. Over each hundred a sergeant was appointed, and ten hundreds formed a division over which a sergeant was appointed. It took until dark to get the prisoners arranged, when the gates opened, and we were marched inside. For the first and only time in my prison life, we had plenty of fuel. There was an abundance here, the refuse of the stockade. The night was very chilly and we soon had regular log-heaps on fire. After we had been inside for about one hour we received about one-half pint of corn meal. This was our rations for the night. We soon found some water, and making our meal into mush, talked over the situation and how we had been fooled, or how the rebels had lied to us. After we had finished our supper I said to Fisher, "what do you think of exchange now?" "Oh," said he, "these rebels are the worst liars I ever saw." He said, "what do you think?" I said, "I think that whenever a man gets mean enough to be a rebel he is mean enough to do anything that is dishonorable." "Well," said he, "I guess that is about the size of it. I do not believe I can ever put any confidence in them any more, for this is twice they have fooled me." The ground was covered over with a thick coat of wire-grass which had formed a regular sod. We selected a place, built a large fire and lay down for the night to dream of home and the good things in God's country. When morning came we got up and took a general survey of the inside of the stockade. It was, in every respect, similar to that of Andersonville. The guards were mounted in little perches at the top of the stockade, just the same, and they called out the time of night the same. It only differed in this respect. Whereas, Andersonville was built around a swamp and was surrounded by swamps, Millen was built on good dry ground, with a large clear stream running through it, the banks of which were firm and solid and the stream afforded plenty of good, clear water for all purposes. The guards were of a different class from those brats at Andersonville. Here they were mostly old men from fifty to sixty years of age, natives of Georgia. They did not show a disposition to shoot one at a pretended violation of the prison rules, but would give notice that you were trespassing and warn you away. After making the rounds of the prison, we came to the gate, where we learned that one Capt. Bows, was in command of the "camp" as the rebels call it. (They never say stockade or prison, but always say camp.) Capt. Bows had the appearance of being a man of about 45 years of age, rather good looking, and seemed rather pleasant. He was so much different from Wirz or Davis that we soon began to be glad that we were under him in preference to either of the others. After we received our rations for the day we were ordered on the south side of the stream where places were assigned for each hundred. We began to fix up for housekeeping. We lost no time as it was necessary to use the material while it lasted. Fisher and two others of the 5th cavalry and myself composed our mess. We commenced at once to fix up so as to make ourselves as comfortable as possible. We dug out a place about eight feet square and one and a half feet deep. By this means we could keep warmer than if we built our tent on top of the ground. We gathered up a good quantity of pine leaves, placing them in the bottom of our tent. This formed our bed and was much better than any we had had before. We then took some sticks, sticking one end in the ground near the side of the pit, coming together over the center, same as a rafter on a building, tying the ends together. Then we took other sticks and laying them on these they answered as lath or sheeting. Now we were ready to put on the roof. We gathered up the long leafed pine and thatched it over and closed up the ends in the same way. When completed it made a warm place to stay in. Our roof turned the rain very well. In this place we spent most of our time while at Millen. Our rations were pretty near the same as at other prisons, with this exception, the meal was ground much finer and was bolted, which made it much more palatable. In a few days we were all fixed up and fell into the regular routine of prison life. Every few days there would be a train load of prisoners arrive from Savannah. In about ten or twelve days after our arrival at Millen, I was going to the branch, when I saw Kahlor, who had just come in. He said after we had left they concluded not to go out, thinking that perhaps there was an exchange. He said the Irish Colonel was very much out of humor when he could not get any one to go out. Kahlor said, "I now wish we had went out. We would have had much better chances to escape than we can have here." Said he, "if we had gone out, we could have got the papers and learned where our armies were and kept posted all the time, but here we can get no news unless it is from some new prisoners, and there are not many coming in now." Said he, "I intend to try and make my escape the first opportunity." I said to him, "I know of a tunnel that is in process of construction, and I am interested in it. I will let you know when it is done, so you can go out with us." He said, "I will work in it and help to complete it." I said, "I can not take you there now, as the number that can be used is full and we are on our honors not to let any one know where it is until it is completed, when those who dug it will go out first, but before going, we have the privilege of telling our friends how to find it. It will not be many days before it is completed, as there are one hundred men interested in it, and they work day and night. It is the largest tunnel that has yet been dug, and we feel confident that some one will make their escape and get to our lines. The arrangements are that but two men are to go together and no two are to go in the same direction. Some are to go south, others east, others west, while the majority are to go north or northeast. By dividing up, the guards would be thrown off the trail." He seemed much elated over the prospect of getting outside of the stockade. I said, "I will keep you posted from day to day, so you can be ready." About one week after this the word was given out that the next night the tunnel would be completed, and we notified our friends. We had saved up all the meal we could and had baked it for the purpose of having some rations to take with us. It had been raining all day and was raining very hard at dark. The order was to cut the hole out. There were some fifty men in the tunnel, with twice that many ready to go in as soon as the way was cleared. Imagine our surprise when we went to cut the hole out, we had only got to the stockade, coming up by the logs on the inside. When this was learned it was several minutes before we could get the men out of the tunnel. Some almost smothered owing to its crowded condition. When the tunnel was cleared they commenced work again. It would take several days to complete it, as it would have to be dug at least twenty feet further, but at it we went with a will, hoping to complete it before it was found out. The leader gave orders that we should all return to our quarters and remain there until called for. This we did and when the time came we responded to a man.

As soon as it was learned what the trouble was there was a detail formed to prosecute the tunnel with all possible speed. By commencing back a little from the stockade and running the tunnel on an incline we could get under it. There were as many men placed in the tunnel as could be used. Each one would remove the dirt as far back as he could, when another one would receive it and conduct it in the same way until it reached the place of beginning. Here the dirt was left until night, when it was carried out in pieces of old blankets or anything that would answer the purpose. The dirt was put in any little depressions that could be found and covered over with top soil, so as not to attract the attention of the guard. The rain continued to fall at times in regular torrents, but the work went on, as it was thought if we could get out while it was raining we would have a better chance to escape as the dogs could not follow us so easily. The second night it was thought that we were far enough outside to cut out. About eleven o'clock the word was given to cut the hole out. The man detailed to do it found out that the tunnel had been run to much on an incline and was too deep for him to reach the top of the ground. The tunnel was cleared and it was found that there was not a man in the squad who could reach the surface. So one of the boys brought up a corporal from some

Michigan regiment who was over six feet high. He was taken into the secret and asked if he would try and cut out. He said he would, and all parties were now notified that the tunnel was completed and ready. So in goes the corporal and soon had a hole cut through. By working the hole a little slanting he was able to get his head outside, while he took a good look at the surroundings. After he had rested a bit he made the attempt to raise himself on top of the ground. As he did this the entire ground gave way and fell in, fastening him as though he was in a vise. As the dirt fell in it made considerable noise, so that the guard heard it, but could not see any one. It was just time to relieve the guard and as they came up the sentinel said to the sergeant that he believed the Yankees were digging out. The sergeant laughed at him and said, "I guess you are a little scared." As soon as the sentinel was relieved he went to the place where he heard the noise and there he found the corporal, who could not get out of the tunnel or back into camp. The rebels raised the alarm and they soon released the Yankee, building up a big fire at the place and putting a stop at any further attempts to escape. It was some time before the tunnel could be cleared, and you can imagine our disappointment, after having worked so long and hard, and not one man had made his escape. The next morning a rebel officer came inside with a lot of negroes, and broke in the tunnel its whole length, filling up the ditch with stone. I walked down there the next morning and heard the rebel officer say to some rebel sergeants who had been calling the roll, that he was "getting pretty d—m tired of this kind of business."

CHAPTER X.

Preparing for a Winter's Residence—An Exciting Election in the "Precinct of Millen"—Disgust of Rebel Officers—Tricking the Rebels as to Our Nativity—A Base Proposition Bravely Spurned—Wanton Plunder of the Camp and Robbery of Prisoners—A Fiery Speech—A Scene of Awful Excitement—Almost a Massacre.

AS the weather was getting pretty cool and our clothes were very thin, a great many fell sick from the effects of the continued cold rain. After the great disappointment narrated in the last chapter, my squad about concluded that there was no use in trying to escape, and we began to fix up our shanty the best we could, as it looked as though we would have to remain the guests of Captain Bows all winter. There was nothing to create any excitement for several days, until just before the Presidential election of 1864. Both the rebels and the prisoners were greatly interested in that event. The re-election of Lincoln meant a continuation of the war to a successful conclusion on the part of the United States. The election of McClellan meant a possible compromise, and a probable cessation of hostilities. It was represented to the rebel officials by a few of the raiders who had accompanied us from Andersonville, and who lost no opportunity to ingratiate themselves into their favor, that the prisoners were so hostile to the administration of Lincoln for not acceding to any terms offered by the rebels for an exchange, that if a vote could be taken an overwhelming majority would be cast for McClellan. The idea seemed to please the rebels, who probably thought such a result might be used in the North for the purpose of political capital, and be a benefit to the rebel cause. Accordingly, an order was issued for an election in the prison the same day of the Presidential election. The prisoners selected their own judges of election, and the votes were deposited in ballot boxes supplied for that purpose by Captain Bows. The contest was hot, although one-sided. A large number of rebel officers, including the commandant, came in during the day to see how the voting was going on. If they had any confidence in the raider crowd up to that time it must have been dispelled when they watched the voting. Instead of all of us voting for McClellan, the polls were surrounded with ticket peddlers, shouting, "Vote the Lincoln ticket," "Come right this way and get your Union, unconditional surrender, Abraham Lincoln tickets," "Don't gratify a d—d rebel anywhere, but vote to whip them and make peace with them after they have laid down their arms," "Don't vote for McClellan, the candidate of the Northern copperheads," etc. The rebel officers remained in the stockade but a short time, and their disappointment could plainly be seen. When they strutted out it was amid the jeers of the prisoners, and the boys were as happy as if they had won a battle. The result of the vote was over seven thousand for Lincoln and but three or four hundred for McClellan. I was told an election was held the same day at Florence, with a similar result. If the rebels ever sent any report North of the "Precinct of Millen," I am not advised of it.

When the excitement of the election had died down, and

after several days of weary monotony, orders came in to make out rolls of all those who were born outside of the United States and whose terms of service had expired. No reason was given for the order, but by common consent it was agreed that it meant a partial exchange of prisoners and the rebels were going to still further punish the men born in the North by discriminating against them, and sending home a class of men who would be of least service to the Government. Acting on this suggestion, a great majority of the prisoners proceeded to have themselves enrolled as foreigners. I was classed as a German, but from my appearance and dress might equally as well have claimed nativity near the sources of the river Nile. When the rolls were finished and sent out, I am told that they did not show the names of five hundred native Americans in the prison. If the rebels didn't make up their minds that the battles for the Union were being fought by foreign mercenaries, it was no fault of ours, for the rolls mentioned England, Ireland, France, Germany, and the names of almost every habitable country on the globe, as the place of our "bornin."

The day following the completion of the rolls, an order came for all those whose names appeared thereon to "fall in." We did so almost as one man. We were on hands by hundreds and by thousands, and the few " native Americans " left were hardly large enough in number to have organized a lodge of "know-nothings." We were marched outside the stockade and massed around a stump on which a rebel officer was standing for the purpose of making a speech to us. When all had marched out and silence had been restored, the officer began. He said the Federal Government had abandoned us, refusing all offers of exchange upon the part of the Confederacy; that Stanton and Halleck had both declared they had no use for the prisoners. Continuing, the officer congratulated the men on their loyalty to the cause they had espoused, and arraigned the

Government for its inhumanity in throwing them to one side, leaving them to starve and die. "The Confederacy," said the speaker, "is certain to secure its independence. It is only a question of a few short months. You have already endured all your Government has a right to demand of you. If you will now join with us, become our allies until the close of the war, you will receive the same rewards as other Confederate soldiers. You will be taken from the prison, clothed and fed, and when peace crowns our efforts, given a warrant for a good farm, a large bounty,——"

At this point the sergeant of one of the Divisions, a man with stentorian lungs, sprang out of the ranks and shouted, "Attention, First Division!" The command was repeated down the line by the sergeants of the other Divisions. "First Division, about face," commanded the stout-voiced sergeant. The same order followed to the other Divisions. "First Division, forward, march," came next, and in an instant each man in all the thousands of prisoners turned on his heel and away the boys marched to the stockade, leaving the crest-fallen officer by himself on the stump.

The rebels were wild in their fury at the way their base proposition had been received, and we were hardly in the enclosure before several companies of the guards came in with loaded guns and fixed bayonets. We were driven from one point to another of the stockade, and the guard, under pretext of searching our quarters for contraband articles, such as spades, axes, etc., tore down our huts, stole our blankets, and proceeded to destroy and plunder us indiscriminately. It was a sight to provoke us to the last extremity. Robbed of the little we had, in pure wantonness, because we refused to surrender our principles, our indignation made us almost desperate. Among the prisoners was a young man named Lloyd, a member of the 61st Ohio. He was illiterate, but full of patriotism and common sense. Mounting a stump he began a fiery address. He denounced the statement that the Government had deserted us as an infamous rebel lie, and predicted that before the spring came the "hell-born Confederacy and all the lousy moss-backs who support it, will be so deep in hell that nothing but a search warrant from the throne of the great God of the Universe can discover it. The stars and stripes will wave in triumph over this whole Nation as sure as God reigns and judges in Israel." The burning words from the lips of the speaker aroused us to the highest pitch, and we began cheering tremendously. A rebel officer came running up and demanded of one of the guards that he should " shoot the Yankee son — - ——." Before the order could be put into effect Lloyd was jerked from his position and his life saved.

Then ensued a scene that beggars description. Shouts were made to charge on the guards ; take their guns and make an assault on the gates of the stockade. We quickly formed in line of battle, and the rebel officers hurried behind the line of guards. The guards were badly frightened, but held their ground, their muskets leveled to receive our assault. Captain Bows, from an elevation outside the prison, had discovered the condition of affairs, loaded and shotted his cannon and stood ready to give the command to sweep the stockade with canister and grape. The long roll was sounded, and for a moment it looked as if the massacre was to begin. Cooler heads among the prisoners realized the desperate danger and lent themselves to an effort to dissolve the line from its menacing attitude. Slowly the boys deserted their line of battle and spread over the prison grounds. The guards by an indirect march, that they might keep their faces toward the prisoners, cautiously withdrew. The agony was over, and all drew a breath of relief. Had a collision occurred the carnage must have been dreadful. By evening all were engaged in an effort to fix up their tents and huts, that we might again make ourselves as comfortable as possible.

CHAPTER XI.

TRADING A COMPOSITION PEN FOR TOBACCO—A MCCLELLAN BADGE WORTH ITS WEIGHT IN GOLD—HOW THE SICK WERE NEGLECTED—CARTING THE DEAD AWAY—WAITING FOR THE CLOTHES OF DEAD MEN—ANOTHER DREARY RAILROAD RIDE—AN ESCAPE FROM A MOVING TRAIN—THROUGH SAVANNAH TO BLACKSHEAR, GA.

AS the days and nights were very damp and chilly we had made use of all the refuse that would answer for fuel and now had to make details to go outside after wood. Every time we went out after wood we would bring in some of the long leaves of the pine to repair our hut with, which the rebels had destroyed to a great extent. One of my squad tried to go out on as many details as possible, in order to get material to fix up our hut.

One cold, damp day I got out. As soon as I passed the gate a man about 45 or 50 years of age stepped up to me and said, "I will go with you." As we walked along towards where we got wood he said to me, "Have you anything to trade me for tobacco?" I said, "I do not know as I have, as I have traded all my buttons off and have nothing left but these old rags, and they will soon be gone." He said, "I would like to get something from the Yankees to send home to my daughter. I promised her I would send her something when

I left home." I said, "How far do you live from here?" He said, "I reckon it ain't more than 40 miles. I never was here before. I never traveled around much before I was conscripted. I always liked to stay at home, and it would please my daughter to get a present." I examined my old rags to see if I could find anything. At last I felt something in my vest pocket. I got it out of its hiding place, and to my surprise it was a composition pen, one of those that looked like gold. It had worked through the pocket and was secreted between the outside and the lining of the vest. I looked at it and found the point badly bent, so much so that it was entirely worthless. But it was bright and nice looking. I layed it in my hand and said to him, "How would this suit you?" "What is is it?" he asked. I remarked that it was a gold pen. How his eyes flashed. Said he, "It is just what I want; my daughter has always wanted one of them." I said "that I hated to part with it, but as it seemed as though I never would have any more use for it, at least while I was in the South, I would trade it off if I could get a good trade." By this time we had got near several pine tops that had fallen together and formed a large body of brush. Said he, "let us go under the brush and I will show you my tobacco." We entered the tangled mass of brush and were soon concealed from the gaze of any other guard. I said to him, "This pen is very valuable, since gold brings such a high premium." "Well, I will give you a good trade for it." He wore a long-tailed coat with pockets in the tails which would hold something less than a peck each. He commenced to disgorge, piling his tobacco on the ground, I still insisting it was not enough, when he would lay on another twist. At last his supply was exhausted. I said, "Is that all you have?" He answered, "It is all but a little which I want to keep so that if any one asks me for a chew I can give him one." I said, "there is not enough." "Well," said he, "take this and let me have the pen, and I will be on duty again day after to-morrow, and you come out and I will give you some more." I said to him, "all right." We broke off some pine leaves, laying them on my arm, then the tobacco, then some more leaves and a little wood. We moved back to the gate; I went inside, and when I arrived at the hut I was about played out. I threw down my load, when the boys said, "Why did you not bring more wood?" I said, "Open that bunch of leaves and you will see." When the tobacco was displayed they asked, "How did you get that?" I told them, but I never called for the balance of the tobacco, nor do I know how the pen suited the young lady.

This transaction opened up a new field for my mess for a few days. We could trade the tobacco for meal, beans and meat, and adding this extra to our rations did us a world of good. At this time one of the mess had come into possession of a medal which was composed of a yellowish substance which resembled gold. Upon examination we thought we could erase the letters that were on it and pass it for a $20.00 gold piece. So going to the creek we found a piece of sandstone which we took to our hut and began to rub the medal with it. By this operation we erased the letters and by means of pieces of old cloth we gave it a good polish. Taking it in your fingers and holding it up it looked very much like a $20.00 gold piece. Myself and one of the other boys started out to trade it off. We followed around the line of guards, but could find no one that had enough stock in trade to strike a bargain with, but we kept trying from day to day. The usual question would be asked, "how much do you want for it?" We would say, "five hundred dollars in Confederate money." They would say, "we would like to have it, but we have not so much money." We began to think we could not get a trade. We knew that if we offered it much lower they would suspicion us of some Yankee trick, so we held to our first price. Going down the line one afternoon we accosted a young guard with, "do you want to buy some gold?" He said, "yes, how much have you?" We said $20.00, holding the piece up in the sunshine. He said, "how much do you want for it?" We said, "five hundred dollars in Confederate money." He answered, "I have not got that much money, but my lieutenant has and I know he will buy it. I will soon be relieved and will see him. I will be here again in two hours, and if you will come then I know you can sell it to him." We said, "all right, we will be back at that time." We watched when the relief came on and went back to the perch. Sure enough, there was the rebel officer. As we came along we heard the sentinel say to the officer, "there they are." When we came opposite the post we halted, when the officer said to us, "are you the Yanks that wanted to sell the $20.00 gold piece?" We answered we were, holding the piece up. He said, "I have not got $500; can't I trade you something else for part?" We said, "we will take some meal, peas and sweet potatoes." He answered, "I will give you a good big haversack full of each and $300 in Confederate money." We told him we could not do that. He said, "that is all I can get now, but if you want to trade I will give you that now and the balance in a few days." We said, "you must give us the meal, peas and potatoes as interest for waiting on you." He said, "all right. I will be back here in about one hour." At the appointed time he was back. "Now," he said, "I don't want to cheat you, and I don't want you to cheat us. You tie that piece of money in a cloth while we look at you, and tie the cloth to this club (throwing us a small club at the same time), then you must hold it up all the time until I tell you to throw it over the stockade. Here are the meal, peas and potatoes, (holding them up so we could see,) and here is the money. I will put it in this sack of meal. Now I will go down, and when I am ready you throw the piece of gold over and this guard will throw these sacks to you." "All right," we said. So down he goes, and when the word was given my comrade threw the piece over. We heard him say to the guard, "all right, Johnnie, I have got the gold, throw the sacks over." Here they come. We gathered them up and hurried to our hut as fast as we could. Upon opening the sacks we found the fellow had done as he said he would. That is now more than twenty years ago, and I have never heard how he came out with his gold.

The Prison at Millen differed from all the other prisons that I was at in this respect, that others had a hospital outside of the regular stockade. This can be accounted for by there not being so many at the prison as there were at other points. There was some vacant ground inside of the stockade, and no prisoners were allowed on the south side of the branch except the sick. They were corralled in the southeast corner. We could go over and see the sick at any time we chose, but could not build our huts there. There were no tents or shelter of any kind provided for their accommodation. They simply lay on the bare, cold, damp ground. At night some of the well men would go over and piling up the logs in heaps, fire them so they would have fire all night. This was kept up as long as there were any logs to pile up. After the cold, rainy spell that I spoke of in my last, the sick died very fast. They had become greatly reduced and the cold nights were too much for them. The thermometer would almost register at freezing point.

I do not know how many died here, as there was no record kept of the dead. I cannot say in what condition they were buried, as I was never at the burying ground. All I know now about the dead is what I saw. I often went to the gate and saw them hauling off the dead by wagon loads, without giving any attention whatever to where they belonged or who they were. As the weather was very chilly and our clothing very thin, we did not know what to do, for winter was just here. One day I was talking with some Kentucky prisoners who were almost naked. They said that some of their squad had been watching the sick and as soon as a man died, if he had any clothes on they took them off. "In this way," they said, "we have got much better clothes and we do not think there is any wrong done any one, as the clothes can do the dead no good, but can do us a sight of good." We talked the matter over in my squad. My clothes were the nearest gone of any of the squad. I needed a coat badly, as I only had on, when captured, a blouse, and it was nearly gone. They said they thought I had better go over and see if I couldn't get a coat. As I had not been over to see the sick for several days, I went over and took a look through their part of the camp. I shall here relate what I saw, and no doubt many will say that I have misrepresented the condition of the sick and dead, but, God being my helper, it is the truth and nothing but the truth, and every word can be substantiated by living witnesses.

As soon as I crossed the branch and came to the part occupied by the sick, I could see what the cold rains had done for the poor fellows. There were several hundred scattered over a small space. Many were already dead, many more were dying, others could not walk or stand, some were lying in the mud unable to get out of it. This was amongst the hardest sights I saw while I was a prisoner. Those who were dead were entirely naked, laying where they died, scattered over the ground in every direction. I walked over the ground and took a good look. When I went back to the hut the boys said to me "What luck had you?" I told them what I had seen. "Oh, well, we can't help it. If I were you I would go over there every day until I got a coat or any other garment." The sight that I had witnessed seemed impossible for me to shake off. When I lay down that night I could see the poor fellows clawing up great handfulls of dirt and leaves as they were in the agonies of death, others begging for water, and still others making complaint of how cold they were. I could see in my imagination, those poor boys who were dead and had been stripped of their clothing. They had become so reduced before death that they were only skeletons. Their sunken eyes, extended check bones, and regular claw fingers, they seemed to haunt me for days, and to this day I can see them in my imagination as plain as I could on that cold November day in 1864. I got up early the next morning and went over again. I saw several men who were dying and there would be from one to four men standing or sitting near by to strip him of his clothing as soon as the breath left his body, and I have no doubt but what many were stripped before they were dead. At last I came to a man that I saw was dying. He had on pretty good clothes. I thought now is my chance, so I sat down on a stump near him as I saw he would be dead in a few minutes. I was not there long until up came two more men when one of them said, "Are you waiting for this man's clothes?" I said, "That is what I am here for." "Well, that is our business, so we will divide them as soon as he is dead. As you seem to have the oldest right which garment do you want?" I said I wanted the coat. "All right," he said, "We will take the rest." I sat there a few minutes, and as it became lighter and I could see the horrible sights I felt sick. Getting up I walked away and returned to the hut. When the boys said, "Didn't you have any luck this time," I said no. I related what I had seen, and said to them, "If I freeze, all right, I will never take the clothes from a dead man's body." "Well, what will you do? You can't live through the winter without clothes." I said "I will do the best I can, and when I turn up my toes you can carry me out like the rest of the poor fellows."

There was no excuse for the rebels treating the sick in this way, for we were in the midst of a pine forest, and any number of the prisoners would have gladly prepared shelter for the sick if they could have had the privilege to do so. But such privilege was denied them. It was not down on the plan of Jeff. Davis, John H. Winder and the rest of the rebels. Their plan was to kill off as many as they could, and as fast as they could. It is a well known fact and a matter of history, that John H. Winder boastingly said that he was killing and disabling more men than Lee was at the front. The prison at Millen was located on land owned by General A. R. Lawton. Lawton was educated by the U. S. and held the rank of Major I think. He deserted the flag that he had sworn to protect against all of its enemies and joined the so-called Confederacy. The prison at this place was named in honor of this man and he arose to the rank of Commissary General in the Confederate army.

Time began to wear very heavily on our hands. No new prisoners came in and we could hear nothing from the outer world. The weather had cleared up and was most delightful, only a little cool for those whose clothes were so thin that they afforded scarcely any protection. There was nothing of any exciting nature occurred until late in the month, when one night about ten o'clock, the Rebel sergeants who called the roll of the prisoners, came in and ordered the first and second divisions to prepare to march at once, and the rest of the camp to be ready to leave at a minutes notice. It was one of the most cheerless nights I ever saw. The rain was pouring down in perfect torrents. There was a perfect confusion in the camp. All sorts of rumors were rife. The rebels said that the difficulty that had existed about our vessels coming up the Savannah River to the city had at last been adjusted, and we were going back there to be exchanged and there were boats enough to take us all at once, and they were in a great hurry to get us there. They said all would go. There would be a special train for the sick as they intended to abandon this stockade. After an enormous amount of swearing by the Rebel officers and guards, we got outside of the gate and marched to the railroad, but there were no cars there. The officers seemed very impatient. It was near noon before we got aboard of the cars. The rain continued to fall, at times very hard. Many of the cars were flats. I was lucky in getting in a box car. Again our hopes were revived with the thought that we should once more see the Stars and Stripes.

After we got aboard the cars we soon moved off. When we came to the "Y" our train took the road to Savannah. The car that I was in was filled with men from Ohio, Indiana, Illinois and Michigan. I fell in conversation with a man from Ohio who had been captured late in the summer campaign. I asked him what he thought of our prospects of getting exchanged at Savannah. He said, "I do not believe it. It is only another rebel lie told to deceive us, and you will find it out." I said, "What in the world do they mean by moving us from Millen so soon after going to such expense as they have to build such a stockade?" "Well," said he, "I think their plans have been badly frustrated, and they are a little puzzled to know what to do with us." I said, "What do you think is the cause of our removal?" "I think," said he, "they are afraid of Sherman. You see as far South as Sherman is, he can conduct a campaign better in the winter than in the hot summer, and I believe he has cut loose from Atlanta and is coming this way, and they have to get us out of his line of march." I said, "Do you have any idea that Sherman is able to force his way through the heart of the Confederacy?" "I certainly do. You see Grant is holding Lee at Petersburg so he cannot reinforce Johnson or Hood. I understand that Hood has superceded Johnson, and is in command of the Rebel army near Atlanta, and I heard just before my capture that Hood was trying to flank Sherman and had gone to Tennessee. So you see that Sherman has nothing in his front but Joe Brown's Reserve Brats, who will be no hindrance to him whatever, and I think Sherman will strike for the coast, either at Savannah or Mobile. Should he go to Savannah, we are right on his line of march. Should he strike for Mobile, Andersonville would be too close to his .lines to be safe." I said, " if we are not to be exchanged where do you think they intend to take us?" "I do not know, nor do I believe they know themselves, but we shall soon see." The rain continued to fall in showers all day and part of the night. Our train thumped and pounded along over the road as usual, the axles fairly squeaking in the worn out boxes. I do not think they had received any oil for weeks from the noise they made. The Confederacy was getting hard up for materials to operate a railroad. Toward evening the man from Ohio said to me, "There are a lot of my regiment who have made up our minds to try and make our escape to-night, and if you wish would like to have you go with us." We talked the matter over. He said, " If we can get off the train we are going back North, and we think we will soon meet Sherman's army." I said, " My shoes are so hard I cannot wear them, and could not travel more than one night barefooted, and I fear it would only make my case worse." " Well, if you do not want to try it, I want you to help us off the cars at the proper time." I said I would do all in my power to help them. About 10 o'clock at night he came to me and said, "I will now tell you our plan. There are twelve or fifteen of us, and we have discovered that we can open the door on that side of the car (pointing to the door). We want you and this man here to take your blanket and hold it up in front of the door, while, one at a time, we go behind it and drop to the ground. Your blanket will make a perfect screen between us and the guard in the other door, so that he will not be able to discover us as we drop to the ground. We will lay perfectly still until the train passes, then we will get together and start back." The train was moving along very slow and the rain came down in a brisk shower. At last all the arrangements were completed. The leader was to go first. I took hold of one corner of the blanket and the other man took the other, holding it up before the door. It made a perfect screen. The leader passed behind it and pushed the door open. Then he took another man behind the screen, when he took hold of the leader's hands and lowered him to the ground. As there was no alarm given the next man was dropped; in this way we let fifteen off, and the most of them got to Sherman's army. In a very few days, by some cause they became separated and a few were recaptured and returned in a week or so. I learned the full details from them when they returned.

At last morning came, and at the dawn we approached Savannah, pulling in on the same street as when we were first taken there. The train halted. We were ordered off the cars. There were dead men in almost every car. The poor fellows had received an exchange over which Jeff Davis, John H. Winder and the rest of the rebel curses had no control. Details were soon ordered to carry the dead from the cars to a place designated for them. They were laid in a row, when soon some negroes came with carts and took them off and sunk them in a sand bank. No record of their names, regiment or the State to which they belonged, was made. They were simply blotted out of existence as it were, and for what! For doing their duty as U. S. soldiers. They had given their lives that the Government might be maintained and the American flag not dishonored. Were their lives given in vain? I think not. They have not been forgotten, though no record of their deeds can be found. Their light will shine when traitors will be banished to everlasting perdition.

We were given a few substitutes for hard tack, something similar to what we received when we first went to Savannah, and were marched to the other side of the city and put on cars on the Gulf railroad, and soon started down the road. We were told this was only temporary, and that we would return in a few days as soon as our vessels came in. They said the city authorities objected to having us quartered in the city, and we would be run down the road. Of all the roads we had traveled over this was the worst. All the rolling stock and machinery that was good for service had been removed to other roads of more importance, as this road was of very little use to the Confederacy. Every few miles something would break down, either the cars or engine, and the train would come to a standstill when the rebel officers would coax the prisoners to get out and help push the train over the grade or help patch up the old wheezy engine. There was no wood prepared along the road and no facilities for taking water. There were some negroes who rode on the tender who would gather up pine knots and fill the tender. When the water gave out they would stop by some swamp and fill it up with buckets. They insisted on the prisoners helping do the work but we informed them that as we were on an excursion for pleasure, having been ordered down here by Jeff Davis, we thought it hardly good manners to do any work. Whenever the train stopped we were allowed to get off and build up fires while they were getting ready to move. We would often remain for hours at the same place. This did us lots of good. We could see through the woods, see the birds flying about, see something free once more. We also instituted a raid on the graybacks which had become very numerous. Here was the first cremating that I had seen done. Our clothes had become so badly infected with the graybacks that it was too much of a job to pick them off. Some Yankee found that by building a fire out of pine knots, taking off your pants, putting two sticks crosswise in the waist, and taking the pants by the ends of the legs and holding them up over the fire, the legs would serve as stove-pipe to draw the heat. Then hold the pants high enough above the blaze so they would not burn, and the heat would draw up the legs, which would puff up every grayback to his fullest capacity when you would give the pants a shake and the lice would fall off in the fire. This was the most effectual way of getting rid of the pest I ever tried. Any ex-prisoner who was on that trip will tell you that this was a God-send to us.

The country over which we were traveling was very poor. In all of our trip on the Gulf road of eighty-five miles, from Savannah to Blackshear, there was not a single town or collection of over one-half dozen houses. It was almost one unbroken forest, the soil very sandy and poor, and nothing seemed to thrive but the long-leaf pines. We were so long on the road that our rations gave out, and the guards were almost as bad off as we were. Our makeshift of an engine would give out oftener as the trip lengthened and take longer to fix it up. There were some good mechanics among the prisoners, so at last they consented to go and repair the old wheezy concern on the promise that as soon as we got to Blackshear we would get rations, and not until we reached that point could we get any. When the boys came back to the car from repairing the engine one of them declared that he believed this was the road that he had heard of where nothing remained but two streaks of rust and the right of way. The scurvy still lingered in our systems and we were in need of something green. When we made the stops we would get off and pull up what the natives call bull grass. It has a small white root, which was almost tasteless, yet it seemed to supply a long-felt want, and it was eagerly sought after. After thumping along in this manner for five or six days we reached Blackshear, the county seat of Pearce county, Georgia, the largest county in the State, and having 500 square miles of territory to every inhabitant.

CHAPTER XII.

A Camp Without a Stockade—Signing a Bogus Parole—Kilpatrick's Cavalry—The Story of the Escape of Three of my Companions to the Coast, where they were Picked up by a Government Vessel.

WHEN we arrived at Blackshear, the train halted and we were told to get off. I looked about to see the town, but could not see as much as a respectable dwelling. Was told that this was the county seat of Pearce county, Georgia. Here the same scene took place as at Savannah. There were dead men on most of the cars. They were taken off by order of the rebel officers and collected in one place near the railroad track, where a detail was made to bury them. They dug a long trench and laid the poor fellows in it. When this was finished we were ordered to fall in and marched out through the woods near a stream and were told that we would establish our camp here for the present. We were in a heavy forest and the boys commenced to build shanties the same as we did at Millen. We thought we would make use of the material while it lasted. There was no stockade here. They placed a heavy guard around us, and several sections of artillery, in commanding places. After receiving rations, all hands began to erect their huts, as though we were to remain here for the entire winter. We were so far south that the

PRISONERS IN CAMP AT BLACKSHEAR, GA.

weather was very warm although it was the 1st of December. After we had been here for several days, a rebel officer came out and ordered the first division to fall in, and marched them outside of the guard line. Massing them close together he presented a paper, which he said was a parole, which he had been instructed to have us sign in order to save time when we returned to Savannah for exchange. We did not understand this and thought it was a rebel trick they desired to play on us. When some one said, "read it," the officer read it over, yet we were not satisfied, and said, "let some of our boys read it." "All right," he said, when a young fellow stepped out and taking the paper in his hand, the officer said, "get up on this stump and read this to these d—n fools that they may know for themselves that it is all right." The young man read off the parole carefully, and when he had finished it said, "this is all right, boys." Then the men said, "we will sign that," and such a cheer as they set up we had not heard since we heard of the downfall of Atlanta, while at Andersonville, three months before. The cheering was taken up by those inside of the guard line, and when the boys got through cheering the officer said, "you will arrange yourself alphabetically, and sign the rolls as fast as you can." When the rolls were finished there were two day's rations of corn meal issued to the men and they marched to the railroad, went aboard the cars and started back for Savannah. This process of paroling continued from day to day. Each day a train load was taken away until a number of trains had left. At last no more were taken out. The rebels said we would go in a few days.

About a week after the last train load had left, one day we heard a big noise up towards the railroad. Looking up the road we saw a large crowd of men coming down. Soon they came near enough that we could see they were prisoners and had a strong guard on each side of the road. We almost held our breath. At last some one said, what does this mean?" "It means," said a prisoner from Ohio who was standing near me, "that the d—d rebels have been lying to us again." Soon the boys came inside of the guard line. The guards were doubled, the artillery manned, the pieces were shotted and we were ordered to make no demonstration. Said the officer, "If you do we will open on you with these guns." The prisoners that came in were the last train load that had left us. Before they could reach the Charleston & Savannah railroad, Kilpatrick's cavalry had made a raid on it, destroying the road and capturing many rebels. There was nothing left for them but to return to us. Hence the strong guard and the secret of the paroling was out. It was apparent they had fears of our cavalry, and that was why they paroled us. They had no idea of exchange. They wanted to get us to Charleston, or Florence, South Carolina.

Ever since we had left Millen, up to this time, the guard and officers had been very mild, and did not seem to care whether we left or not. They would say, "If any of you are d—n fools enough to run away and lose your chance of exchange what do we care? It will be the worse for you." This kind of talk kept many a fellow from trying to escape, but now the secret was out and they changed their tune. They gave strict orders and established a dead line at once. After the first squad had left, we traded off our blankets and almost everything we had, thinking we would soon be in God's country, where we could get much better blankets, etc. I had kept my woolen blanket that I got of the guard on my way from Richmond to Andersonville, but I was so very hungry that I traded it off for an old quilt, getting a few sweet potatoes as "boot." The rebel that I traded it to seemed so honest that I could not help but put confidence in what he said, and I yet think he was deceived. He said, "I know you will go home, for I heard the Captain say so, and this old quilt will do you until you get back to Savannah, and the blanket will do me so much better this winter."

After the return of the boys we knew there was no prospect of exchange at this time, so we commenced to make arrangements to try to escape. We made all the inquiries about the country and the distance to the coast. A number made their escape here, amongst them three of my acquaintances. I will here narrate what they told me after we got in God's country. All of my squad had gone out in the first lot that left, so I was alone as far as acquaintance was concerned, but I soon fell in with three fellows from Ohio who had been captured late in the campaign. The next day after the squad returned the boys said to me that they were going to move that night, and if I thought I could stand the trip they would do all for me they could. They said, "We have made up our minds not to go to any house unless we are on the eve of actual starvation, and then only to the negro huts." I do not remember any of their names except one. His name was Cochrane, and he was the oldest of the three. He was to do all the talking for the squad. It was impossible for me to travel, as I had no shoes that I could wear, and one night in the brush would take off all my rags. I said, "It is useless for me to try it, and perhaps I would be a hindrance to the rest of you. I will not try it." They said, "We have here several things that we can not take with us. You can have them if we succeed in getting away; if we are captured and returned before you leave here we will all stay together." Cochrane said, "I have bribed one of the guards to let us pass, to-night. I am to give him this blanket. After we have got beyond the lines several rods, he is to fire his gun into the air, so as to clear him should we be discovered by any other guard. We are to go at ten o'clock to-night. That post right there is where we are to go out. You can see from here whether we got out or whether he actually shoots at us or in the air." All arrangements being ready I gave them the address of my father, and they said, "if we get through we will write your folks, tell them where we saw you, and all about things in general." We built up a good fire. It blazed up nicely. At last the relief for ten o'clock came on duty. The boys taking up their few things and each of them taking me by the hand and bidding me good-bye, marched up to the guard, and I saw Cochrane hand the guard the blanket. As he took it, he turned and marched up his beat. The boys passed out, I saw them start on a run. The guard turned about, stood for a few seconds, and then I heard the click of his musket. As he cocked it I fairly held my breath, for the next instant I saw the flash of his gun, but could not tell whether he shot at them or not, but I could hear no noise outside. At the same time he called out, "Corporal of the guard, post No. 4." In a very short time the corporal and officers of the guard came running up to the fellow. They inquired the cause of alarm. "Well," said the guard, "I thought I saw some Yankees out there and I fired, but I did not hear anything after I fired." The officer went out, looked around a little, but soon returned and reprimanded the guard for giving a false alarm. He said, "You do not want to get scared at the shadow of these d—d Yankees, and before you fire any more you want to be sure it is a real live one, and then give it to him." But the boys had made their escape. I sat by the fire for more than an hour. I was now entirely alone as far as acquaintances. At last I lay down to dream of the boys and home.

I had the pleasure of meeting all three of these boys five months after this time, and under very different circumstances. We met this time in God's country, in a land of plenty, and where traitors were not allowed to dictate to us. The boys said the first night they were out they made good time, traveling fully twenty miles before day-light. They secreted themselves in a thicket, and two would sleep at a time while the other kept a lookout. As soon as it was dark they started again and again made good time. This night they crossed a field and found a sweet potato patch. Taking all they could carry not to load themselves down, they made their way south. The weather was warm and clear so they had no trouble in shaping their course. They made for the coast of Florida where our blockading vessels lay. The second night they made good time and again hid in a thicket. In this manner they traveled for several nights, at last coming to a poor stretch of country where they could find nothing to eat. Being worn out by traveling through the swamps and thickets, they became so hungry that they thought they would have to give up. At last they reached a turpentine orchard, and secreted themselves in a thicket. As the warm sun came up they fell asleep and when they awoke it was late in the afternoon. While the party were deliberating what they should do they saw a black man gathering the turpentine from the trees, and made up their minds to surround him and capture the fellow should he try to make his escape. They worked their way round the fellow unobserved when they closed in on him. He was badly surprised at first but when told who they were, and what they wanted, he said he was the overseer of the orchard and it was several miles to his masters or any other white persons. They asked him if he would give them something to eat. He said he would, and they concluded to go to his cabin, as he assured them that there was no danger. His wife soon had their supper ready, which consisted of corn bread and fat pork. The couple also provided them with some provisions and the man guided them through a swamp, giving them all the information he could. He traveled with the party until in the after part of the night, when they came to another old darkey's cabin, whom he called up and told who the visitors were. And when the fugitives wanted to go, he said he would go with them to a certain darkey's, who would conduct them further. In this manner they were piloted through by the darkies, each one going as far as he could, so as to get back before daylight. After many nights they came to a place where the darkies said they could take them no further, as they could not cross the swamp and get back the same night. As they would have to go many miles around in order to cross, and all the roads leading through the swamp were picketed by the rebels, they did not know what to do, but again thought they would have to give up. Finally a young darkey said if they would take him with them up North he would go. This was readily agreed to. The party had a terrible time getting through the swamp, but finally succeeded, and early next morning they came to the beach. The darkey said, " Right out there the boats lay." The fog was so heavy they could not be seen. The sun came up, the fog disappeared, and they could at first see the outlines of a boat, and soon discovered that it was one of the Union vessels. They hoisted their blouse on a pole and signaled the boat. Along in the afternoon they saw them lower a small boat and start towards the bank. They came more than half way when they turned and went back. Oh, how their hearts sank within them. The next day they kept signaling all the time, but no boat came out. The third day they became almost wild, as they knew they could not stay much longer, as they had nothing to eat. They made a more determined effort than ever, and could see the officers on the boat watching them, and from their actions were certain they were using their glasses. They tried every way they could to make them understand they were friends and not enemies. At last they saw them lower a boat, three men getting into it, and pulling direct for the shore. They came rapidly towards the shore until they were within forty or fifty rods, when they halted.

The refugees could see that there was some trouble. In a minute or so the sailors commenced to row, and the escaped prisoners met them at the beach, when the officer asked who they were. They told their story. He said, "Get into the boat and let us hurry back, for the woods here are full of guerrillas, and we may be fired upon." They stepped into the boat and pushed out for the vessel. When the boat stopped while it was coming to the rescue, it was on account of the sailors refusing to row any further. They said that the party were rebels and that they did not want to be made prisoners. The officer having a glass could see better, and had been thoroughly convinced that they were escaped prisoners. When they stopped and refused to obey the officer, he took out his revolver, cocking it, and holding it in his right hand, he took out his watch with his left hand and said to the sailors: "I give you two minutes to commence to row, and at the expiration of that time, if you persist in your mutiny, I will kill you." The sailors, knowing the officer, felt that it was a case of life or death with them, and thought they had better obey the officer and take the chance of being made prisoners.

Arrived at the vessel, the boys were received kindly and treated with all the care that could be lavished upon them. They were clothed with a new suit of clothes and given plenty to eat, remaining on this boat until the supply boat came, which was several weeks later, when they were sent North, stopping at Hilton Head, South Carolina. They remained there for several days, when they were sent to New York. From there they came here, landing this morning. I said to him, "How long were you getting to the coast?" He said, "Six weeks from the time we left you until we reached the coast, and we never saw a white man or a woman during that time." "What did you do with the negro?" "We left him at New York. A doctor took him for his coachman and said he would take good care of him and write us occasionally how he was doing." Remember, this conversation took place five months after we parted at Blackshear. I went up to the barracks and saw the other two fellows. They seemed very glad to see me, and said they had often talked about me. "But," said they, " we never expected to see you here. We thought you would reinforce some of the sand banks in Georgia before this, but we see you have outgeneraled them this time."

CHAPTER XIII.

ANOTHER MOVE—THE REBELS FIRE THE HUTS—SEVERAL PRISONERS CONCEALED IN THE TRENCHES BADLY BURNED—A SHORT STOP AT THOMASVILLE—SOUTHERN UNIONISTS—A SEVEN DAYS' MARCH—TERRIBLE SUFFERING OF THE PRISONERS—A BEEF BROTH FROM A BONE THROWN AWAY BY THE GUARDS—ESCAPE OF A NAKED BATHER—ONCE MORE IN SIGHT OF ANDERSONVILLE STOCKADE.

A FEW days after the boys left we were ordered to be ready to leave our camp. All being ready we started for the railroad. After we left camp and got out on the road we were halted. It seemed that after we left our huts some of the guards found one of our boys concealed and raised the alarm. Some of the rebel officers went back and upon examination of the camp they found several of our boys concealed. Our boys, upon learning that we were to be moved and go further South, dug ditches in their huts long and deep enough to hold a man, covering them over with fine brush, and when the order was given to leave they crawled in this ditch and were covered over by their friends. They hoped to remain concealed until the rebels had left and then try and get to Sherman. When the officers went back to camp and discovered the situation they ordered all the huts fired. They burned readily and made a very hot fire. There were a number of boys severely burned; being in the trenches they could not get out until they were badly burned. They came up to the rest of us, receiving no attention whatever. Some were so badly injured that they could scarcely see. All the hair was burned off their heads and their arms and faces were dreadfully scorched. It was reported that some were burned up, and the rebels never denied the charge so far as I ever heard. Several years ago I met one of the prisoners who was burned. He was badly disfigured about the face.

We went aboard the cars and started down the road. The same old squeaky cars and wheezy engine. We made very slow time. The rebels were bringing up the Florida coast guards to assist in keeping Sherman out of Savannah. We were run in on a switch at one place while a train load of those fellows halted beside us. They had on board of their train a very fine battery from Tallabassa, Florida. They were on flat cars the same as we were. Our boys would halloo at them. We would say, "Hurry up! Uncle Billy will put on the second relief!" "Yes," they said, "you will see we will have Bill Sherman and all the rest of his cut-throats in the same fix as you are before many days." We would say, "Go ahead. You will never get to load those guns if you get within twenty-five miles of Sherman. Some of his bummers will take charge of them, when you will get a free ride up North." At last they pulled out and left us in high glee at the idea of capturing Sherman. We saw some of these fellows after the war was over at Jacksonville, Florida, when we asked them about their success. Said they: "We went down the road at a rapid rate until we came within about twenty miles of Savannah. All at once our engine gave a fearful blast. The engineer called for brakes, the train came to a halt, some of us jumped off and ran ahead to see what was the matter. Just as we got to the engine we saw that the rails were taken up, and when we looked out in the woods we saw a line of blue coats with a battery ready to fire at the word of command. What could we do?" I said, "I suppose you could surrender." "That was just what we did do, and as quick as we could, as we saw there was no time to parley, and in a few minutes we saw the Yanks take charge of our battery."

Our train thumped and pounded along at a slow rate for a day or two. At last we came to Thomasville, and were told to get off the cars. It was raining pretty hard. It was about ten o'clock at night. We were marched out to the woods about one-half mile from the town, and went into camp. The next morning I got up and took a good look at our camp. No one seemed to be inclined to build shanties. There was plenty of wood, so we kept up big fires all night. This was a much better part of the country than we had left. The soil was pretty good. The town seemed to have some life. We were told that before the war many rich planters made this place their home. There were some very handsome residences in the place. We had not been here long until a large lot of negroes came out and commenced a ditch around the camp throwing the dirt up in a ridge. It formed a pretty good breast-work. The guards walked on top of the ridge. The artillery was planted at suitable places. There was a heavy guard kept around us all the time. While we remained here the weather cleared up, and was very warm, so much so that we were glad to get under shade during the greater part of the day. We did not stop at Thomasville more than ten or twelve days until we were informed that we would go back to Andersonville. They said, "We have sent up there after more guards and as soon as they arrive we will start for that place." So one evening we heard quite a commotion up at the station. It was caused by two regiments who had just arrived from Andersonville. In a short time we received orders to be ready to start on the march. The next day while we were in this camp many citizens came out to see us, and some seemed to be very much affected at the sight they saw, and manifested much sympathy for us. I have reason to believe that there was a strong union feeling in this town. I made some inquiries about the distance we would have to march, and was told that we were about sixty-five miles almost due south of Albany, which place, at that time, was the terminus of the Georgia Central Railroad. We would have to march across the country to that place and from there we would go on the cars to Andersonville. The next morning after the arrival of the guards, we broke camp and started on this march which lasted six or seven days. We did not make more than eight miles the first day. That night there came up a heavy rain storm and the weather turned cold for that country. We camped in the woods, receiving a small quantity of corn meal and a small piece of fresh beef. The next morning we resumed our march. It was terrible. The roads were muddy and we traveled through a low, wet country, most of the day. Many of the boys gave out. What became of them I do not know. Should anyone who reads these lines know what became of the boys who gave out on this march, and let me know, it would be a great favor. At night we again camped in the woods close to a large plantation, receiving the same amount of rations as before. We now crossed a better stretch of country, passing many small farms, and on every farm was a small field of turnips. The guards would help themselves, throwing us the tops. Many lively tussels were had to get those turnip tops. They were very careful never to throw us a turnip. Thus we plodded along from day to day. The weather on the 23d of December got so cold that it froze the mud in the road. We started early in the morning so we could reach the Flint river that day. As no one had any shoes and had marched over fifty miles barefooted through the mud and sand, their feet were worn out. This day you could track the men by the blood. Many of them did not take a step without leaving blood in their track. We reached the river late in the afternoon of December 24th and went into camp at Blue Spring, about two miles below Albany. While on the march this day I was lucky in picking up a beef bone which the guards had thrown down when they had marched over the road some ten or twelve days before. I carried it until we went into camp when I got an old hatchet from a friend, spliting the bone up in small pieces. It being the knuckle joint there was some nourishment in it. I took the pieces and boiled them, drinking the broth. I have been very hungry since that time and before it, but I never tasted anything half as good as that broth did at that time, for I had been so hungry that I had chewed sticks during the day to satisfy the cravings of my stomach. I had no salt. After drinking at least one quart of the broth and chewing the bones I lay down to rest and fell asleep. When I woke up I was very sick. The bones had laid so long in the sun that they were badly tainted, and I had drank too much of the broth. Next morning, Dec. 25th, the sun came up clear and nice. Many people came out from town and the surrounding country to see the Yankees, we being the first that had ever been in that part of the country. During the day the boys were allowed to go to the river and bathe. For my part I did not feel like going into the water. I was sitting on the bank watching the boys. There were two or three hundred in the water. The guards did not seem to think there was any danger of the boys trying to cross the river, being entirely naked. I noticed some fellows that kept working their way out farther and farther. At last one fellow struck out for the opposite side of the river. The guards did not notice him until he was near the middle of the stream when they called to him to come back, but he had no intention of coming back, but made greater efforts to reach the opposite bank. At last they commenced to fire at him, but their aim was bad and he soon reached the opposite shore. Pulling himself up the bank, he was out of range of their guns. He turned and saluted and then started off at a lively pace. What became of him I do not know, but I know that it stopped the bathing mighty quick. About noon it clouded up, and along in the evening it commenced to rain. The wind blew a perfect gale. This was as disagreeable a night as I ever saw. We had used up all the wood that was inside of the guard line, so we had no fire and no shelter. About three o'clock in the night orders came for us to go up to the bridge that spanned the river. It was a covered bridge and would afford us some shelter. When we got there we were met by some officers who ordered us to go over to the railroad and get in the cars; we were more dead than alive. We remained aboard the cars until morning before the train started. As the depot was right in the town, we could see that it was a place of considerable importance. There were hundreds of cotton bales piled up along the track. At last the signal was sounded and our train moved up the track. It did not seem to make much difference to us where we went for our fare was just the same. The country looked about the same and the inhabitants seemed to be near relations to each other. We did not expect much sympathy from them and did not receive much. At last our train reached Americus, where we halted for awhile. There was an old gentleman standing on the platform at the depot who commenced to talk to us. From him we learned more than we had from any one else. He said they were filling up the stockade at Andersonville. He said Bill Sherman and his cutthroats had gone clear through the State and had fetched up at Savannah, and he did not know where the trifling whelp would go next, but said, "I think he will try to prance around in South Carolina same as he has in this State, but I tell you he will have a different set of fellows over there and if he does not get his head in a halter I am fooled." We asked him what Hood was doing. "Oh, he thought he would slip away from Sherman and go over in Tennessee and maybe he would get up in Kentuck." "Well, I guess Hood has found his match up there. Old Pap Thomas is enough for him." "Well," said he, "they have been having some pretty hard fighting up there." We asked him why they did not stop Sherman before he went clear through the State. "Oh! we did not have any troops to set afore him but Joe Brown's Reserves, and they are a powerful ornery set in a fight." "Yes," said some of the boys, "that is what we think. They would find it quite different to face a regiment of blue coats to what they do in guarding us poor starved Yankees." At last the train started, and we passed over a pretty fair part of the country. Along in the afternoon we halted and were told to get off the cars. The first man we saw was Captain Wirz. He was flourishing his big navy revolver and swearing terribly. The weather was cloudy, cold and damp. We were formed in line when the old process of counting began, Wirz walking up and down the line making all kinds of threats. From where we stood we could see over in the stockade. At last we had been arranged in hundreds and divisions and started for the stockade.

CHAPTER XIV.

My Return to Andersonville—Homeless, Shelterless and Friendless—A Five Cent Row—I Open a Tin Shop and Become Known as the Tenth Street Tinker—Supplied with Raw Material Unexpectedly—Fresh Arrivals—How "Old Baldy" Revived our Hopes and Stirred up the Anger of the Rebels.

ARRIVED at the gate of the stockade we were halted for a few minutes when the gates opened and we passed inside. Imagine our despondency when we took a survey of the situation. The weather was cold and very damp, and you cannot conceive a more cheerless situation than we were then placed in. No tents or shelter of any kind were given us, no wood to build fires with. My worldly possessions consisted of one old quilt and a small cup. Many of the boys were alone as far as old comrades or any member of their regiment were concerned, having been separated from them in our several removals. I was one of the number. I walked over the prison to see if I could find anyone that I knew and at the same time looking out for a place to stay; but, after spending considerable time I gave up all hope of finding any one of my former friends. About the time we left the prison in September the rebels had allowed our boys to erect two long sheds on the north side of the prison. They were to be used as a hospital. There was no siding put on them, just simply a rough frame and roof of split boards. I went over there late in the evening and found fifty or more like myself looking for a place to stay. There were about a dozen of us who went together and fixed up a place in one of the sheds which we called our own. There we remained several days and nights. The weather was very cold and having no clothing we suffered terribly. We would all lay down together and crowd up to each other as close as we could to get all the warmth possible, one from the other. In this way we spent our time, only getting out long enough to answer at roll call and draw our rations. After eating our scanty supply we would lay down and remain as quiet as we could. We had been here but a short time until we were bothered terribly with the graybacks. As soon as we would begin to get a little warm they would commence their daily and nightly drill. They would have division, brigade, regiment and company drills, ending up with a general review. When those large fellows began to prance around in front of the lines it would make some one halloo out, "I must turn over, I can't stand this any longer!" So we would all turn to the right or left as the case might be. This would stop the chaps for a short time. The weather remained cold for a number of days with rain every day or two. At last one cold rainy evening, a lot of guards came over to the sheds and ordered us out. Said they were ordered to move us to the south side of the Branch and no one would be allowed on the north side but the sick. This was a dreadful blow to us. While we were very cold we could keep dry under the sheds. Now to be turned out in a cold rain was terrible. But go we must, for it was the order of Captain Wirz and must be obeyed. I wrapped my old quilt around my body to keep me as warm as possible. After we crossed the Branch, we commenced to patrol the camp to see if we could find anyone we could stop with. After spending one or two hours in this manner, just about sunset, I was standing at the foot of what was known as Tenth street. It was raining very hard, and I had about given up all hopes of finding a place to stop. While I was standing here I noticed two young men in a dug-out near and from their actions I thought they were talking about me. Pretty soon one of them spoke up and said, "Are you one of the boys that have just been sent over here from the sheds?" I said I was. He said, "Have you no place to stop?" I said I had found no place yet. He said, "How would you like to stop with us? We have room here for three. One of our boys was taken sick and has gone out to the hospital and you can take his place if you like." I was more than glad to accept the offer. They had dug a hole in the ground about eighteen inches deep and had covered one side with an old blanket. The other side and end was thatched with pine leaves. The place was just large enough for us to lay down in and be comfortable. We could use my old quilt for a cover. I felt very fortunate to get so good a place and they expressed themselves as being more than pleased in getting a partner who was the owner of so much worldly goods!

After we had fixed up for the night the usual inquiry was made as to what command do you belong. I said, "I belong to Company F, 13th Regiment Indiana Volunteer Infantry." "Where were you taken?" "At Chester Station, Virginia." "What regiment do you belong to?" "We belong to Company K, 53rd Illinois regiment; were captured at Guntown, Mississippi. We were taken while on the raid under General Sturgis. We do not think Sturgis is much of a General or he would not have been drawn into such a trap and lost the most of his command." I found my new friends to be nice fellows. I would like very much to hear from them if they are living

Their names were David Scolstock and Herman Hensler. Scolstock lived near Livingstone, Illinois, and Hensler lived near St. Louis. I have Scolstock's photograph which he sent me after he got home. I have written to him but can get no answer. If any one should read these lines and know of his whereabouts and would let me know it would be thankfully received.

I remained with these boys during the rest of my imprisonment. We fixed up our tent as fast as we could, and in the course of ten days or two weeks we had a pretty good house for Andersonville. Upon looking around and making inquiries I found that most of the boys in our immediate vicinity, like myself, had been separated from their regiment. We formed a squad for our own mutual protection out of this class of boys. There were not more than three or four from any one regiment, and our squad numbered about forty. After we had become acquainted we felt secure, felt that we were able to secure our rights with any other squad in the prison, and during the rest of our confinement there was not one of our squad proved untrue to us, but were always ready to help any of the squad in need of help. To illustrate this, I will narrate a little incident that happened a short time after our acquaintance. I commenced to repair tin cups, spoons, etc., and was fortunate enough to get ten cents from a fellow for repairing his bucket. I took the ten cents and went up the street to a squad of New Yorkers who had peas for sale. I bought five cents' worth and handed the fellow ten cents. He took it. I said, "Why don't you give me the change?" He said, "There is nothing coming to you." I said, "I gave you ten cents and have here but five cents' worth of peas." "Five cents is all you gave me," he said. I said, "That is a mistake. I gave you ten cents, and there it is now." He said, "You are a liar." I said, "I am not, but you are if you say I did not give you ten cents." He said, "If you repeat that I will slap your mouth." I said, "Try that, and I think I will give one lying Yankee all he wants." I thought I could handle the fellow and I saw that he was not over anxious for the job, but just back of him lay a big burly fellow, who raised up and said, "Billy, if you don't slap that fellow I will slap you." I knew now that I had stirred up a hornet's nest. The fellow started for me, and I thought the best thing I could do was to "git and git," which I did with the fellow after me. We went down the street at a lively pace, and when near our squad a big fellow by the name of Rood, from Michigan, raised up just as the fellow was reaching for me. Rood was very tall and had long arms. He yelled out, "You s—n of a b——h, what are you after?" At the same time he gave the fellow a good blow, which stopped him. As he started back Rood started after him, applying the toe of his boot to the fellow's lower extremities. In the excitement Rood followed him too far, and a half-dozen or more of the fellow's companions made for him. Rood succeeded in getting away without getting hurt. A few days after this Rood was up to the sutler's, and some of the New Yorkers saw him, when the whole squad made for him. He tried to get back to our squad, but they had cut off his retreat; he took around the sutler house with two or three after him. They had it around and around. Every little while they would get a lick in, and as often he would return it. He found he was getting tired out, made a desperate effort to break through their lines, which he succeeded in doing, but not without receiving many bruises. When he came to the squad he was bleeding freely. After we learned the circumstances our squad was for going up and cleaning out the New Yorkers, and would have done so, but for the timely advice of Mr. Ellis, of Boston, Massachusetts. He said he thought we had better let it go. If we went up there we would all get bruised up more or less and we had better drop the matter. By the way, this Mr. Ellis, I think, ranked much higher than First Sergeant, as his stripes showed. I have always thought that he ranked as high as Colonel or Brigadier, and had concealed his rank from the rebels for purposes best known to himself. I do not think his real name was Ellis; I think that was a fictitious name. He was a perfect gentleman, and remained in our squad until our release. I spent many hours in conversation with him. He told me that his occupation before the war was that of boot and shoe dealer in the city of Boston. From him and two men from Maine I received many favors. The favors consisted in supplying me with some tools to set up shop with. They soon found out that I was a mechanic and pretty handy at repairing cooking vessels. One gave me part of an old jack-knife, which was beyond price at that time. Another gave me several darning needles to make drills of, and many useful articles. Cooking utensils were so scarce and the demand so great that I opened up a regular shop for the manufacture and repair of those articles. This, I think, had as much to do in saving my life as any one thing. It gave employment to my mind as well as exercise to my body. In addition I received more rations, and so I had more to eat.

I opened up my shop for the repair of buckets, cups, and spoons with the outfit of tools that I had at my residence on Tenth street. I added, from time to time, such tools as I could get, and soon found myself in possession of what was then considered a good outfit. I had two railroad spikes, one old jack-knife with the large blade broken off, so it was not more than one inch long, two darning needles which I had made drills of, one five-inch easy running file, one old back-spring of a knife which I made a punch with. I soon received a good patronage, had all the work I could do from morning until night, day after day. This gave me steady employment, and for my work I received a certain portion of corn meal from the boys that I engaged work from. It would take two weeks for a fellow to pay for making a bucket. He would give me each day for a certain number of days, two or three spoonfulls of meal, just as he thought he could spare it. In this way I soon had many fellows indebted to me and just as soon as they drew their rations they would come around and give me the amount due for that day. I soon accumulated a good supply of meal and beans and with this extra amount of rations and the exercise it gave to earn it, my health began to improve and I began to feel like myself once more. I now took hold of life with more determination to try and live through. The weather through the month of January was cold and damp most of the time. There would be days at a time that you could scarcely see a man on the move inside of the prison, only at roll call or time of drawing rations. They would spend the entire time in their dug-outs, trying to keep as warm as possible. Whenever there would come a warm day and the sun shone out clear for three or four hours in the afternoon, you could see hundreds of men doing skirmishing duty. They would go on the north side of the Branch and arrange themselves on the south side of the hill, facing the south. Then operations would commence. Each fellow would take off his clothes and search the seams for gray-backs. In this way they could get rid of the largest of them, when hostilities would cease until another favorable day came. I have seen a thousand or more engaged at a time trying to exterminate the pest. This was an every day occurrence when the weather was favorable.

The latter part of January, one cold damp evening, I received orders to report at the gate. I asked, "What do they want of me?" The guard said, "I dunno, that is the ordahs." I said, "I have not violated any prison rule that I know of, and

I can't think what they want of me." "Well," said he, "I have given you the ordahs and you had better go." I said, "I won't go. If you want me you can take me, but I will not go of my own accord." He insisted that I had better go. At last Mr. Ellis said to me, "I think you had better go, for if they want you they will come and take you, and it will only make matters worse for you." I studied over the matter for a minute when I said to Mr. Ellis, "I think you are a man of good judgment, and I will take your advice, and let the consequences be what they may." When I started for the gate I said to the boys, "Good-bye, if I never see you more." They said, "We hope nothing bad will happen you." Dave Scolstock said, "I am going with you to the gate and see what the trouble is." We walked up to the gate and stood there for a minute or two, when the officer asked if Long had come yet. I stepped out and said that I was the chap he sent for. "All right," he said. You can now imagine my feelings better then I can describe them. Moments seemed hours to me. At last he opened the gate, when I saw two boys from Illinois that I was acquainted with, who had been detailed to go outside and help bury the dead. The officer said to them, "Is that the fellow?" When they said, "He is," the officer pointing to me, said, "the boys have a pack of stuff they want to give to you." The older of the two, stepping forward, extended me his hand, which I clasped, and at the same time said, "We have here a pack of goods which we think will be of value to you." He stooped down and picked up a large roll of tin, and a good supply of rivets, handing them to me. They said, "We hope this will be the means of helping you through." I thanked them for their kindness, when the officer said, "You must get inside the stockade." Bidding my friends good-bye I walked inside of the stockade. Scolstock was still standing there. He said, "what in the world have you got?" I answered, "I am not able to tell you yet." He said, "Who gave it to you?" When I had told him we went down to the dug-out where the rest of the boys were. We found them discussing the "whys and wherefores" of my being taken out. They had about come to the conclusion that it was because I was engaged in working for the boys, and were about as greatly surprised at seeing me back so soon as I was in getting back. We unrolled the tin and found it was part of the roof of a car that had been wrecked a few days before. They gathered up a large lot of the tin and took it to Captain Wirz's headquarters, where they obtained permission to give it to me. I have bought many a box of tin since that day, but I am free to say that those few sheets of tin were worth more to me at that time than all I have purchased since. I now commenced the manufacture of buckets for cooking purposes, and I have no doubt that some of the boys are still living who used these buckets. I made one for myself which I brought through the lines when I got back to God's country.

There were no new prisoners received during the month of January. Those that did come in were some that had been held at other prisons for several months. It was a very long month to us. We could get no fresh news from our armies and did not know what had become of Sherman. It made us very restless, yet we reasoned in this way that if they had defeated Sherman there would be some new prisoners coming in, and as there were none, it was fair to presume that they had not defeated him. At last, February opened more pleasant, and we felt in better cheer, as we could take more exercise, and the boys began to sing patriotic songs, something we had not heard for weeks. One day we heard a big noise up at the railroad, and looking over that way we saw a sight that made our hearts sink within us. There were a thousand or more prisoners being arranged in hundreds preparatory to coming in the stockade. We looked one at the other and asked ourselves what it meant, had they really captured Sherman's army, and were they bringing it here. We asked one of the guards where they were from and he laughed and said, "That is some of your Uncle Billie's boys that you seem to think so much of." "You do not mean to say they are a part of Sherman's army do you?" "Certainly I do. Did we not tell you that we would soon have him in the same fix as you!" Pretty soon we saw them start for the stockade. We got as near the gate as we could, every fellow trying to learn first who they were. As soon as the gate opened and they began to file through we began to ask them questions. Almost every boy called out, "What command do you boys belong to?" You can imagine our relief when they said, "Banks'." The next word would be where are you from? They said from Cahaba, Alabama. "How long have you been prisoners?" Some said two months and others said four. At last I cornered a fellow from whom I learned that they were the odds and ends of several small prisons in Alabama, and had been taken while on different scouts from time to time until there were more at Cahaba than they could keep, hence they were sent up here. Among them was a Baptist preacher who belonged to a Chicago battery. He was brimful of patriotism, and was a fluent talker, and I think hated a rebel as bad as any man I ever saw. The first evening they were in it was given out that about dark this man, who was called by his prison friends "Old Baldy," would make a speech. About dark I saw a large crowd gathering about the center of the prison. I walked up there and soon he began to speak. He spoke about twenty minutes. I thought it was the best speech that I ever listened to in my life. He exhorted the boys to prove true to the old flag. Said he, "I tell you this blasted Rebellion cannot succeed. It was born in sin and cradled in iniquity, and it is going to pieces like a ship driven upon a rock. Bill Sherman is at this time cutting a swath through South Carolina forty miles wide." At this the boys began cheering, and after they had cheered until they were hoarse, some one started up "Rally round the flag, boys," when it was taken up all over the camp. The rebels became very much alarmed fearing that in our excitement we would make an attempt to force the stockade, but as no one went towards the stockade but rather went from it, there was no cause for them to fire on us. After the excitement abated the announcement was made that he would speak the next evening, but what he had said had put new life in the camp. There had not been as much stir in camp for weeks together, as there seemed to be this night. Everybody seemed cheered up. The old man had been a prisoner but a few days and was well posted in what was going on in our armies. I had the pleasure of meeting this old man here in old Antioch after the war was over, and many of our citizens no doubt will remember him. He preached one or two sermons in the Christian church while here. He was then on his way to Philadelphia to attend the general conference.

All the next day the boys were in good cheer. You could see groups gathered together all over the prison discussing the situation. Evening came, and all of the prisoners were anxious to hear what "Baldy" had to say. About sunset some one opened up by singing, "Rally 'Round the Flag, Boys." This was the signal, and in a short time two or three thousand prisoners collected around the place where the singing was going on. I noticed that several officers were in the perches with the guards, seeming as anxious as we were to hear what he had to say. At last he commenced his speech and as he progressed he warmed up until he made the prison fairly resound. He commenced at the beginning of the trouble between the North and the South, giving it in detail, step by step, until the present time. He told us how our armies had cut the rotten confederacy in two and were simply going where they pleased. "Why," said he, "the rebels are thoroughly whipped now, and would be glad to stop the war but a few of them are afraid they will be hung, and are continuing it in the hope that they can get a chance to leave the continent." At this the boys began cheering, which created great excitement. They acted as if they were attending an old fashioned Methodist camp-meeting. They would sing and fairly shout for joy, march round and round shaking hands while the speaker exhorted them to prove true to the Government and the old flag. At last the excitement got so great and his speech was so cutting that the rebels became excited and gave orders to stop the speech and disperse the crowd, or they would fire on the camp regardless of consequences. It required a good bit of work to get the boys to disperse and keep quiet. After everything was quiet the rebels sent in an officer, who said there should not be any more speeches made, and should there be any gathering of the prisoners as there had been this evening, it would be construed to mean that they meant to try and force the stockade and they would be fired upon without any further notice. Of course this settled the matter, but "Baldy" improved the time going over the ground and talking to the boys and cheering them up. He said, "I know they cannot keep us three months. As soon as spring opens up there will be a move all along the lines, and this cursed Confederacy will go up like a house on fire." His words acted like magic. The boys took courage and seemed to think that it was but a question of time until they would be released. They talked of home, and made many plans as to what they would do when they got back to God's country.

CHAPTER XV.

WE LEAVE ANDERSONVILLE AGAIN BUT ONLY FOR THREE DAYS—THE GUARD BECOME CONSIDERATE AND COL. GIBBS MAKES A SPEECH—ANOTHER EXCURSION—WE VISIT MACON BUT RETURN TO ANDERSONVILLE IMMEDIATELY—FUGITIVE CONFEDERATES FLEEING SOUTH—A SCARED LOT OF REBELS —CONFEDERATE MONEY LOSES ALL VALUE—A SIXTY-FIVE MILE MARCH—IN CAMP AT LAKE CITY, FLORIDA.

ALL through the month of February the weather was very fine with but few exceptions. There were no more prisoners came in after "Baldy's" squad, and we could hear nothing new, only the rebels would occasionally say that Lee had given Grant another drubbing. At last April came, and one day the first week in the month an order came to get ready to leave at once. This, of course, was good news and we were soon ready, and so the next evening an order came for one thousand to go over to the depot. Said the officer, "You will all go as fast as transportation can be obtained." We were soon at the railroad where we found a train of cars in waiting for us. The officers said they were ordered to take us South, probably to Florida, for exchange. We did not care where they took us, so we got away from Andersonville. We were soon all aboard, and away we go for Albany. We arrived at Albany along in the afternoon the next day, when we were ordered off the cars and lay near the depot for several hours. The officers seemed to be at a loss to know what to do with us. At last we got in line and marched through the town, crossed the river and went into camp for the night. We remained here for two or three days when orders came to return to Andersonville. The officers said that our folks would not receive us unless we were sent back to Vicksburg. We marched back to the railroad. It was very warm when we got back to Andersonville. We arrived there about noon, and were soon inside of the stockade, when the boys fixed up their huts as though they were going to stay all summer. The hot weather began to tell on the old prisoners, who had the scurvy so bad their joints began to swell and they could scarcely walk. I, myself, felt the effects of it more than I had at any time during my imprisonment. I began to think that if ever I got back to old Indiana I would have to start soon. After we got in the stockade an officer got in one of the perches and said that Colonel Gibbs would make us a speech late in the evening, when it was cool. Said he, "The Colonel will speak from this stand, and when the bugle sounds he requests that you will come up here and hear what he has to say." Some one yelled out, "Tell Colonel Gibbs and all the rest of your lying officers to go to h—l; we have heard enough of your rebel lies." These epithets did not seem to rile up the guards or officers as they used to. At the sound of the bugle a large body collected near the gate where they could hear the Colonel. He began by saying, "Prisoners. I hold in my hands an order from General Pillow, which was received at this camp this day, and it is for the removal of you to your lines. It will go into effect between this and the 18th of this month. You will be taken to Vicksburg for exchange. I want you to take as good care of yourselves as you can under the circumstances. Prisoners, I call on you for witnesses that during your long confinement, when you were being removed from one prison to another, have I ever said you were going home? It has often pained me to see you so badly deceived. I did not at that time, nor do I now, think it was right to so cruelly deceive you. It has often pained me more than I can express to you, to witness the horrors of this prison. Many months ago I resolved that I would never knowingly deceive one of you. Many of you will remember when you asked me about exchange I would say that it was not for me to say when an exchange would take place. If I had had the power I would have caused an exchange many months ago, or I would have made your condition different from what it has been. But I now speak from authority and can say that there will be no extending the time beyond the 18th, and it may be sooner." The Colonel made quite a lengthy speech. Be it remembered that Colonel Gibbs was the colonel who had commanded the guard at Andersonville for many months. It was he who testified at the trial of Captain Wirz and gave such damaging testimony. After the Colonel closed his speech there was much speculation as to whether it was genuine or not. Several of the old prisoners said, "I have often heard him asked about exchange, when he would say, 'That is not for me to say.'" Some said, "It is nothing but another rebel lie. They need these guards somewhere to help their forces and have taken this plan to deceive us again, but that is getting old and won't work any longer, and as soon as we see the guard is being diminished, we think we had better make an effort to force the stockade if half of us are killed. It will be better than staying here another summer, for more than that many of us will die if we do not get out soon." We found by walking over the camp that the speech had created a good bit of excitement. Many said, "I believe Gibbs is honest and knows what he says, and this war cannot last always. It must close sometime, and why not now as well as any time?" They would reason in this way: He did not say they were going to exchange us, but he said he had an order to take us to our lines, and no one has ever known Gibbs to tell us a lie. And it is certain that Sherman is making his way through South Carolina at will, and how do we know but what Grant has taken Richmond before this time, as there are no new prisoners coming in here? The boys finally made up their minds that they would wait and see if Gibbs was telling the truth.

The weather was very warm and my legs began to swell badly, so much so that it was with considerable pain that I could walk around, yet I took exercise every day, for I knew my only chance of getting out alive was by taking all the exercise I could, and thus baffle the disease. At last, on the evening of April 17th, an order came to get ready to move. We were not long in getting ready. Soon we passed outside of the gates, and away to the railroad and here we go for Macon.

There were three train loads of us and I was on the last train. We got to Macon just at day-light. The next morning when our train pulled up alongside of the other trains, which were laying on side-tracks, we asked how long they had been here. They said, "Several hours." "Why do you not get off the cars?" we asked. They said, "There seems to be some trouble and they do not know what to do with us." I saw a well off about two hundred feet from the track and asked the guard if I could go and get a drink of water. An officer was standing near and heard me ask. He said, "Certainly." I walked over to the well and while there a guard came up and I asked him what the trouble was. He said, "I do not know exactly." I saw he was considerably excited. I said, "Where are you going to take us?" "I do not know, but I think it is time that our officers were doing something for I am getting tired of this d—n business." I walked back to the cars, and just then I saw Captain Wirz coming along giving orders to the officers. He said, "We will go back to Andersonville, but will stop only to draw rations," when you could hear from a hundred at a time, "You old lying Dutch s— of b—, you are going to put us back in the stockade."

The trains moved back towards Andersonville in the same order they came. That threw the train that I was on in the rear. At the rear of our train was attached one passenger coach which was filled with rebel officers and among them was Captain Wirz. All went well until in the afternoon. Our trains ran very slow and kept as close together as it was safe to run. Along about two o'clock in the afternoon our train stopped to take wood and water, and it so happened that the car that I was on stopped on the crossing of a wagon road. We discovered a long train of negroes, white folks, mules and wagons all mixed up, and looking on the other side of our train, as far as we could see down the wagon road was a perfect jam of vehicles of every description. There were several darkies close to the road, when our boys called them up to the cars and commenced to ask questions. They said to the darkies, "Sambo, what's the trouble?" The darkies answered, "I dunno. Massa said we had better be going for the Yankee's am up at Columbia and specks they will be down here afore long, so we dun packed up and am going south clean away from them." "You don't say that our armies are at Columbia do you?" "Dat am hit, sure; dey done come last night and Massa is in a big hurry to get all de critters away 'fore they come and toat dem off." "Who is it that is commanding the Yankees?" "Massa says his name is General Wilson. He has lots of you-uns on horses and we done want to get away foo he gits down here." The guard noticing the darkies, walked up and ordered them away and refused to let them come near the cars. From this, on every wagon road we passed, we could see men, women and children going south. We now began to ask what it meant, when some of the last prisoners who had been brought to Andersonville said that General Wilson was in command of a large force of cavalry and mounted infantry and was operating in Alabama, and no doubt he was making his way for Andersonville and Macon, for, be it remembered, that the rebels had a stockade at Macon for officers only and kept a large number there all the time since they built the prison at Andersonville. Well do I remember seeing the officers taken from our train when we were on our way from Richmond to Andersonville almost one year before.

Just before we arrived at Andersonville our train stopped and I saw Captain Wirz step off the car. He had a newspaper in his hand. A rebel officer came walking up along the train and he and Wirz talked for a few minutes. We could see they were very badly excited. Soon the train moved on and when we came in sight of the stockade we fairly strained our eyes to see if we could see any of our boys inside. As we came near and could see better we saw no one inside the stockade, nor were there any guards in the perches. We said, "what does all this mean? Are they going to take us somewhere else?" Arrived at the station we saw no rebels there, but learned from our men who had been left to take care of the sick, who were unable to be moved, that there was a call for men to go for rations. While they were getting rations one of our boys who had remained to help the sick came to our car and related the following: "Early in the morning word was sent to the officer of the prison to destroy all the artillery and ammunition together with the muskets, and for the guards to disperse in every direction and not more than two of them go together, and keep in the woods as much as possible." He said, "There is no doubt but that some of Wilson's men are near here now and the rebels do not want to be caught guarding us. They have destroyed all the artillery in the forts, cut down the wheels of gun carriages, thrown their muskets in that deep well at Wirz's headquarters." Said he, "It was worth a month's imprisonment to have seen those scared devils. Their livers fairly turned white when they heard that there was some real live Yankees close by, and to encourage them we would halloa at them and tell them they had better git before Wilson's men got here if you do not want to try the strength of Georgia cotton, for if he comes here and finds you he will hang every mother's son of you." We noticed that our guards were very nervous and the officers seemed much excited.

At last Colonel Gibbs came along the train and said we would go to Albany and march across the country to Thomasville, where we would take the cars for Tallahassa or Lake City, Florida. Soon the signal was given and our train moved on south. Our boys seemed in good cheer. They indulged in singing patriotic songs and the guards were very kind to us now to what they had formerly been. We thumped and pounded along the road all night. The next morning we arrived at Albany and were marched through the town, crossed the river, and marched down near the Blue Springs where we went in camp and remained for two days. The weather was very hot. Some of the boys had got hold of some Confederate money, consisting of Richmond bills. They tried to buy beans with it, but the rebels refused to take it. This was the first time they had refused Richmond money and it created considerable excitement with the boys, and we said to the guards that we believed the reason was that Grant had taken the city. This they denied and said that Lee had given Grant a terrible licking, almost annihilating his army. We said, "What have you done with the prisoners you took?" They said, "Our authorities have concluded to parole all prisoners that we take as fast as taken, together with all old ones, so as to curtail expenses of keeping them." We said, "That looks rather thin." They said, "What do you think is being done with them?" "We do not believe you have taken very many, and if you have paroled any it is because you could not get them away. We think your rotten Confederacy is about used up." They said, "Not a bit of it." We said, "Then why were you fellows so badly scared at Andersonville the other day?" "Oh! we were not scared. We have concluded to abandon all of the prisons, as we have said, to reduce expenses." We said, "We guess your army is getting reduced in about the same proportion as your territory is being reduced." On the third morning after we had arrived at Albany, we started on the march. It is sixty-five miles to Thomasville. The weather was very hot, and our guards never had done any marching. The prisoners marched four abreast. This caused the guards to walk outside of the well-beaten track and was very hard marching for them. They could not make any better time than the prisoners and complained about as much. They had knapsacks to carry. We had gone but a short distance until one of the guards came up to me and said, "If you will carry my knapsack to-day, I will divide my rations with you when we go in camp to-night and will give you some tobacco." I looked at the fellow and said, "I think you are about as able to carry your traps as I am." He said, "That may all be so, but I never marched a day in my life and am not stout, nor am I well this morning, and if you will take it, should I not be able to keep up, I will get permission to take charge of you and we will take our time." I looked at the fellow. He seemed like a very nice young man. I said, "I will try it, and if I find it is too much for me I will hand it over to you." He took it off and strapped it on me. It was not very heavy. Now, in order for him to save his traps, it was necessary for him to watch me closer than it would have been otherwise. I tried to give him the slip two or three times during the first two or three hours I had his traps, but his eyes were on me and he would order me to my proper place, when I would make some excuse for getting out of my place. Along in the afternoon he complained of being very tired, and said he would be compelled to stop and take a rest. His Captain came along and he asked permission to stop and rest, also for me to be given to him and he would be responsible for me. He explained to the Captain what I was doing for him, and the Captain consented to his request. We walked outside of the road a few steps to a log and sat down. As soon as we were out of hearing he commenced to talk to me. He said his father had been very wealthy before the war commenced. He owned several hundred negroes, the most of whom had run off, and it was going to financially ruin him. He said that he had never done a day's work in his life, had not been in very good health. His father had not been in favor of the war from the start, and, said he, "I managed to keep out of the army until a few months ago, when I was conscripted and taken up to Andersonville to do duty. I am very tired of it and wish it was over." I said, "Do you not think that the war is about over?" He said, "I do not know, but there is something very strange about it. We cannot get our officers to say much about it, but I notice they are all the time talking about something when no one is near enough to hear what they say." I found him very talkative when we were by ourselves. We jogged along until night. It was quite dark when we came up to where they had gone in camp. Before we went inside of the guard line he took his knapsack and opened it and gave me half of his rations and some tobacco and said, "I want you to take it for me to-morrow."

I soon found my comrades and the next morning I looked

for my man but could not find him. I never saw him afterwards. We started early on the march. The roads were good and we made pretty good time—much better than we did when we marched over the same road in December. The rebel officers seemed to be in a great hurry to get somewhere. As for ourselves, it did not matter much. Anywhere was better than being cooped up at Andersonville. There was nothing of importance occurred on the march but every day we became more convinced that they were going to release us. The night before we got to Thomasville our friend Rood said that he was going to run the guard and do a little foraging off the country. He left his traps in our care and said if he could find anything to eat he would divide with us when he returned. A little after dark he slipped out of camp and started out in the country. He traveled from farm to farm all night but could find nothing. He did not leave the road very far. The next morning, a little after daylight, he came out near the road and about five miles from our camp. While he was standing near the road he saw a rebel soldier coming toward him. The soldier saw him about the same time. Rood started to run, when the soldier ordered him to stop, saying, at the same time, "I do not mean to hurt you in the least." Rood halted, when the rebel came up. He was a sergeant and said his folks lived about two miles further on the road towards Thomasville. He said, " I have permission to go home and wait till the rest come up." He asked Rood where he had been. Rood told him that he had been trying to find something to eat. He said, " Go with me and we will get something when we get to my home." They soon arrived at his home. Rood said the folks seemed very glad to see the soldier. They wanted to know what fellow this was and he told them it was a Yankee. Rood said the soldier asked them to prepare breakfast for them, which they did. The soldier's mother was very talkative and improved the time to the best advantage. She inquired of her son if he did not think the war was about over. He said he did not know, but was in hopes it was. The old lady said, "If I could only get all the Yankee coffee I could drink once more, I would be satisfied to die." She said, "I do hope Sherman will come down here, then I know I can get coffee." They talked very freely and Rood soon began to think they were not in sympathy with the rebellion. The old lady said, "I told them it was wrong, and they would find it out. Now I guess they see who was right." The folks gave Rood a good supply of corn bread, and meat, to bring to us. As we came up, Rood was sitting under a shade tree at the side of the road. He gave us some bread and meat, which was very acceptable. At that time our rations had been very small on the entire march. Rood said it was about five miles to Thomasville. We got there about two o'clock in the afternoon and got some rations—the first that had been given us since the morning before. The boys were very hungry and weak.

We heard the trains blowing at the railroad and were ordered to be ready in one hour to leave. We could see the officers were very much excited and seemed to be in a terrible hurry. Soon the word was given to start for the cars. We went aboard the train and started south. Of all the roads we had traveled over this was by all odds the worst. It was at times a torture to remain in the cars. The squeaking of the dry axles, the wheezing of the engine, all combined, made it terribly disagreeable. Then we would come to places in the road where the train would have to move very slow, owing to the bad condition of the road bed. Thus we pounded along for two or three days and nights. At last we arrived at Lake City. Here the same scenes were enacted as at Thomasville. The officers seemed to be at a loss to know what to do. We remained on the cars for several hours. The guard said that they were awaiting for orders from General Pillow. We were finally moved out about one-half mile from the town, near a large swamp, ordered off the cars and told to go in camp on the west side of the railroad. They then gave us some corn meal. Fires were soon burning all over the camp, the meal made into mush and eaten with a relish after a fast of forty-eight hours or nearly so. Soon a lot of officers came out with some blank rolls and ordered them filled out, and said as soon as they were completed we would be sent to Baldwin and there turned over, or rather, released.

CHAPTER XVI.

FIGHT AMONG THE GUARDS—THE GOOBERS VS. THE SANDLOPPERS—TAKEN TO BALDWIN—OFFICIALLY NOTIFIED OF OUR RELEASE AS PRISONERS—THE MARCH TO THE LINES OF THE UNION ARMY—A LAST LOOK AT THE REBEL SOLDIERS—SECRETING MY BUCKET, TOOLS, SPIKES AND TRINKETS.

A FEW hours after we had been in camp a regiment of the Florida coast guards came out to relieve the Georgia militia. Now the fun commenced. The Georgia fellows said, "We'uns have guarded the Yankees this far, and we'uns do not intend to let the Sandloppers have anything to do with 'uns." The Florida fellows said, "We don't want any Goobers down here." The Goobers was a name applied to the Georgia militia. You could not find a Georgia soldier without he had his pocket filled with peanuts, called in Georgia "goober peas." "Sandlopper" was a name applied to the Florida coast guards, probably from the fact that the country was very sandy and poor. Each party seemed to think more of the Yankee than they did of each other. They finally got to fighting, and it was our turn to enjoy the fun. They became so enraged that the fight became almost a general thing all over their camp. The officers had hard work to stop the fuss. They finally compromised by putting the Florida guards on the east and south of our camp, the Georgia fellows on the north and west sides. The Georgia fellows were to guard the first train out, the Florida fellows the second, and so on. There had been a detail of our boys made to assist in making out the rolls, which were being hurried through as fast as possible. At Lake City many citizens came out to see us. As soon as the rolls were completed orders were given for the first division to move. A train pulled up by the camp, when the boys went aboard and soon left for Baldwin. Soon another train arrived, which was quickly loaded and moved off. Thus it continued until the last train. I was on the last train.

We arrived at Baldwin when the sun was about one hour high. As we got off the train Colonel Gibbs was standing on top of a freight car and said he would like to talk to us a few minutes. Said he: "Prisoners, I have done all for you I can. I have no rations to give you. I am sorry to see you go without rations when I know you need them so bad, but it is not in my power to do more than I have done. I want you to keep together and not take to the swamps. You are released. We cannot take you further, and, no doubt, some of your men will reach Jacksonville to-night. Then your folks will know the situation, and will no doubt meet you with teams and assist you to get to your lines. I advise you to keep on the grade of the railroad. That is a direct route. You will meet scouts and see pickets on the way, but they have been notified that you are coming, and will not disturb you in the least."

The railroad had been torn up from Jacksonville to Baldwin by our men sometime before and the iron removed, so Baldwin was as far as the rebels could run trains out from Lake City. All the sick were removed from the cars and laid on the grass under the live oak trees. A few well prisoners stayed back to bring water to them and render all the assistance they could until our folks could get to them. The squad that I belonged to was composed of boys from different states. There were about thirty of us. We went out under a shade tree and held a little council. Gibbs said it was about five miles out to their last picket post. After we passed that post, said he, you will see no more Confederate soldiers. We took a vote as to whether we should try and get outside of the pickets before we camped or remain another night in the Confederacy. The question was put and carried unanimously that we would try and get to God's country before we camped. It was also agreed that we would not leave any of our squad, but would help the sick and the lame to make the trip. So here we go. The sun was not more than half an hour high. This was the hardest march we ever made. The road bed was nothing but a sand bank and was full of sand burrs. We were all bare-footed, and the sand burrs were as sharp as needles. The road was full of boys. As far as you could see either way you could see dozens at a time trying to extract the burrs from their feet. I presume this was about as motly a crowd as any one ever saw. There were but very few who had on a suit of clothes; most of them were bare headed; some had on pauts— no shirt or coat of any kind; some had on only a shirt. Many had been prisoners from twelve to twenty-two months and had long hair and matted beards. Their skins were black from the pine smoke, not having had any soap for twelve months to wash with. We made a pitiful sight, yet I presume there was not a happier set of men on God's green earth at that time. It was joy enough to know we were going to a land of plenty and where we would be permitted to see the glorious Stars and Stripes. Every little while you could hear the boys giving three cheers for some fancied reception they would receive when they got to God's country.

 Our squad moved forward as fast as we could until dark. We became very thirsty, but could find no water. We kept going until about nine o'clock, when the boys became so weak and thirsty they said they could go no farther unless they could get some water. We saw, over in a field, a light. As I was about the strongest one of the squad, I said I would go and see if any one was there who could tell us where we could get water. I started across the field and was soon near the fire, when I was halted by a sentinel who said, "who goes there?" I answered that I was a paroled prisoner and in search of water. He said, "all right, we have been notified of your coming; you can advance and we will not molest you in the least." I approached the fire where I found a Captain and twenty or thirty men who were doing picket duty. It was a company of Cavalry and their extreme out-post. The Captain said, "what do you want?" I told him we could find no water, and some of the boys could go no farther unless we could find some. He said there was none close at hand, "but," said he, "I have several men who have gone for water and as soon as they return you can have a drink." I said that some of my comrades were in need of it more than I. He said, " I will send a man over to the road and have the boys come out here, and by the time they get here, my men will be back with the water. Sit down and rest yourself." Soon the rest of the boys came out to the post, and in fifteen or twenty minutes the water squad came with the water, when the Captain said, "give these boys a drink." After we had all taken a drink, the officer said, "boys, I am sorry I can not give you anything to eat, but such is the fact. We used up all our rations for our supper and expect to go to camp for breakfast." We then asked how far it was to our pickets. He said " about eight miles. We are the out-post of our army, and you will not see any more pickets after you leave this post." " Then we are outside of your lines," I said. "Yes," he answered. We could scarcely control our feelings to know that we were once more outside of rebel authority, and I noticed the boys brighten up at that announcement. The officer said, "about one mile further down the road is a creek, and as soon as you cross it you will find good dry ground to camp on, and can get to the water handily. On this side the ground is wet and marshy. There is plenty of good wood to build fires with on that side, but you must be careful, for you have to cross a tressle bridge, and the timber is so thick that it will be very dark, and if you are not careful some of you will get hurt. Just as soon as you cross it you will get on good, firm ground." The officers or men never intimated to us that the war was over. If they knew it we could not detect it in their conversation, but to the contrary, they seemed very sanguine of succeeding in the end. I now think they knew the war was over, but were too proud to make the acknowledgment.

After we had rested we started on our journey, intending to stop for the rest of the night at the place the officer spoke of. Bidding our rebel friends good night, we started. After going about twenty steps, for some cause I turned and took a good look at the rebel squad, who were standing around their fire watching us as we were leaving them. They were the last armed rebels I ever saw, yet I have seen many since who were too big cowards to show it by carrying a musket or saber, although they were willing to hold secret meetings to plot treason, and to do all their cowardly natures would let them do to destroy the best government the sun ever shone upon. Such traitors we have nothing but contempt for. We can respect a brave man, if he is our enemy, but a sneaking, cowardly whelp we have no respect for under any circumstances. After trudging along for half an hour or so we came to a curve in the road. As soon as we came round it we could see hundreds of fires burning in the distance. Soon we came to the tressle work, and after crossing it we went into camp for the rest of the night. It tried one's faith to cross the bridge, as it was so dark we could not see any object. We had to get down on our hands and knees and crawl over it in that manner to prevent falling through between the ties. There being plenty of good dry wood, we soon had a big fire burning, and our boys could not be content with one fire for our squad, but started half a dozen or so. They said it was the first time they had found plenty of anything in the cursed Confederacy, and they intended to use all they could.

One of the boys was standing near me watching the fires. He turned to me and said, "I wish the whole Confederacy would burn as readily as do the piles of brush. What delight I would take in spreading the flames and witness the last dying embers of the cursed thing die out." I said, "We are free now I think, and you should not feel that way." Said he, "I cannot help it. I can never think of this country without it brings to my mind the horrors of Andersonville, and think how many of my comrades are left there in that sand bank, and to know, as we know, that they starved to death when there was plenty in sight. It makes me sick to think of it. If I could forget what I saw and felt there, I would be glad, but it is burned in my mind and can never be erased while I live. I am a Southerner. I was born and raised in Tennessee, and to know that our own people would use us as they have, is more than I can account for." Said I, "Perhaps they have seen their folly now and will do better after the war is over." "Well," said he, "I have fully made up my mind that some of them can't live in the same country that I do. I am determined to be avenged of the wrongs I and my family have received at their hands. I was driven from my home and had to hide in the mountains for weeks before I could get to the Union lines. My stock was all run off or killed by them. My fences were all burned. Wife and children insulted, and everything that they could do to annoy myself and family has been done, and I cannot rest until I am avenged."

While he was talking he became very much excited. The boys lay down on the ground near the fires to rest and sleep if they could, but I do not think there was much sleeping done that night, for all night men would come up who had stopped to rest and got behind their comrades. As they came in camp they would call for their comrades, and kept it up until they could find them. Some of the first that had stopped in camp, becoming rested, would start on the march. My squad adhered strictly to our pledge, and kept together. Every time I closed my eyes I could see, in imagination, the guards, or hear them calling out the time of night.

At last morning came. We went to the creek and took as good a wash as we could without soap. Returning to the fire we gathered up our traps and made ready to start. I had a bucket that I made at Andersonville, and all of my tools, such as they were. I do not think the entire outfit would weigh more than eight or ten pounds, yet it was quite a load to carry. I was thoroughly convinced that we were released, for this was the first morning for twelve months that we could not see or hear guards pacing around our camp. As daylight came, we could see no guards nor hear any hounds baying. It did not seem possible that we were free, yet we could see our boys going where they pleased and no one ordering them back in line. While we stood by our fire I said, "There can be no doubt but what we are free, and I believe I will leave my tools and bucket here as it is too heavy to carry." The boys gathered around me while I layed them out on a log, seeming to take a last look at the faithful friends of railroad spikes and other trinkets. At last, one of the boys said, "Let's wrap them up in this old rag and put them under the log so they may remain undisturbed for all time to come, for I do not believe that anybody will ever want to live in this God forsaken place." So we wrapped them up carefully and placed them under the side of the log, covering them over with leaves and laying a heavy chunk on them. This done, we started on our journey, towards God's country. If I had those faithful tools now, no reasonable price would buy them, but alas, they are gone but not forgotten, for to them, I think I owe my life.

We traveled on the railroad. The boys were thickly scattered all along the track. They had traveled until too tired to go farther, when they would lay down to rest. When rested they would get up and start once more. Yet they seemed happy. As the sun came up, the sand became so hot to our bare feet that we could scarcely travel through it, but our faces were toward the Promised Land and we were determined to press forward. The country through which we were traveling was very thinly timbered, almost a prairie, with now and then a clump of trees and occasionally a palmetto tree. The ground was covered with a thick coat of grass, which was at that time about knee high. We made pretty good time while it was cool in the morning, but our progress became slower as it got hotter. About 10 o'clock, as we were passing a nice grove of trees about ten rods from the road, some of the boys proposed that we go out there and rest. So out we go, and throw ourselves on the ground in the shade of the trees. We were O! so hungry. After resting a few minutes, the boys commenced to pull up the grass and weeds, chewing the roots to appease the cravings of their stomachs. We found some soft brush that we chewed, which seemed to stop the cravings of our appetites. All at once we heard a sound that startled every one and brought us to our feet.

CHAPTER XVII.

First View of the Stars and Stripes—The Grandest Sight of My Life—Providing for the Sick—News of the Assassination of Lincoln—Medicated Coffee—Getting Rid of the Graybacks—Arrival at Annapolis, Maryland.

"What is that," some one said. "It sounds like a steamboat whistle." I said, "I think it is a boat on the St. Johns river, and is coming to the landing at Jacksonville." While we were talking we heard it more distinctly. Some said it was the whistle of a railroad engine. I said, "it is too far to the right, for the railroad makes a curve just ahead of us, and it cannot be the whistle of a railroad engine." We started for the road, but had not gone far when we heard a shrill whistle, more to our left, when all exclaimed, "that is the cars coming out to meet us." Just before we left the track to go to the shade trees we had come to where the iron remained on the ties, not having been taken up. We had not gone far before we heard it more plainly. By the time we arrived at the track we could hear strains of music from a brass band, and could hear our boys cheering. We stopped to listen and we strained our eyes looking up the track in hopes of seeing the cars. Imagine our joy if you can. While we stood there the train came around the curve in the road, and the first thing we could see was the glorious old stars and stripes. There was a fellow standing on top of a box car holding them out to the breeze. I never saw the American flag look half so grand as it did at that time. There was a good band on the train playing National airs. We forgot that we were hungry or naked and commenced to cheer.

Reader, imagine our feelings if you can. I cannot find words to express them. I never saw such a time, nor do I ever expect to see another similar one. May that glorious old banner wave over the Land of the Free as long as time shall last, is the wish of one who was there. Men would cheer until they became so exhausted they would fall to the ground and could not get up until they were helped. This was one of the grandest days of my life. I felt that I had, to a certain extent, been repaid for the suffering that I had endured. The very sight of that old flag gave us new life. Upon the train were several officers in full uniform, nice and clean. How grand and noble they looked, to what the rebel officers did, dressed in their dirty gray, with old slouched hats and long hair. There was no comparison between the two in our estimation. We could not look or speak to one of them but what he would try to insult us or the cause in which we were engaged. Now it was different. The officers spoke kindly to us. The cars were moving along very slow, as it was not safe to run fast, as many of the boys were on the track. Several of the cars were supplied with tobacco cut in small pieces. As they moved along the officers would throw the tobacco out to the boys, and one officer standing on the car, said to us, as they passed by, to get into the shade and not try to walk any further, as they would take us all in on the train as fast as possible. Little did that officer know our anxiety to get where we could secure something to eat.

We could not be content to stay, but kept on the move.

The train went on as far as the rails were laid, where they unloaded some whiskey and provisions for the sick. The teams were on the wagon road, coming out to take the provisions to our sick at Baldwin, and several doctors went out, also, to take care of the sick and have them brought in to Jacksonville. As soon as they unloaded the provisions, the train started back. Before it got to my squad there had as many got aboard as could be accommodated. As they passed us the conductor said, "We will soon be back," but we could not be content to stay but kept on going.

We soon came to the thick timber and got out of the sand burrs by going to the side of the track. We got along very well there. We came to a small creek, and upon looking down the stream we saw smoke arising. Some of the boys said, let us go down there and see what it is. We did not go far until we smelled coffee, when one of the boys exclaimed, "my God, don't you smell the coffee?" When we got to the fire we found several soldiers there. It was the reserve picket post. They were from Massachusetts, and were one of the last regiments that State had furnished. Among them was an old soldier who had served all through the war. The post was in command of a lieutenant, who was away visiting some of the other posts at the time we came to them. As soon as we came up, the old soldier said, "boys, I suppose you are very hungry." "Yes," we said, "can you give us some coffee?" "I will make it as quick as possible." He turned to the other soldiers, who were engaged in conversation with the boys, and said, "come boys, lend a hand here, and let us get these fellows some coffee, and then we will talk with them." They soon had coffee boiling. O! how delicious it smelled. As soon as the coffee was made he said, "now boys, every one of you that has got anything to eat in his haversack bring it out here and let us divide it with the boys." Harversacks were soon brought forth and emptied of their contents, the old soldiers divided them with our boys. Oh, what a breakfast! Coffee and soft bread! Something I had not tasted for twelve months. The coffee was good and strong. It fairly made us drunk.

While we were eating we heard heavy firing down towards Jacksonville. I asked what they were firing for. "Do you not know that the President has been assassinated? These are minute guns on account of his death." I said, "Do you mean to say that President Lincoln has been killed?" "Yes," he said. I said, "I am sorry to hear that, for I was in hopes that he would live to see the close of the war." "Well, don't you know the war is over?" I said, "We have not heard it before." "Well," said he, "that is a fact. Lee and Johnson have surrendered, and all of the rebel troops east of the Mississippi River. Dick Taylor is trying to keep the strife up over in Texas, but we will soon close his career if he does not surrender." I said this is news to us. The soldiers seemed fairly surprised that we did not know about these great events which had taken place in the last few days. We told them that the Johnnies said Lee had given Grant a terrible drubbing and had almost annihilated his army. "Well, Lee has no army any more, and our forces are now occupying Richmond and Petersburg." It seemed like a dream to us as we walked back to the railroad. We said to each other, "Can that be possible? It does not seem that it can be so, but the soldiers would not have said so if it were not true."

Soon the train came back and stopped near us. We went aboard and were taken to the depot at Jacksonville. An officer said to me, "This train load will go up the river to the Live Oak Grove, where tents are prepared for you." I said, "I know where that is. I was here about fourteen months ago." He said, "You can go there through the city or you can go out this road, which is as near." I said, "I prefer to take the road." He then said, "You go ahead and the rest will follow." I started off and we soon reached the grove, where we found tents already prepared for us. They had been put up by the colored troops who were stationed there. Three or four of our officers came out to us and said that we would soon have some dinner. It was then about two o'clock in the afternoon. In a short time some one yelled out, "Here comes the ration wagon." Soon a large government wagon, drawn by four mules, drove up. The boys crowded up, expecting to get something to eat. Imagine our surprise when the fellow who was in the wagon said, "Get in line, and as you pass by the wagon I will hand you a piece of this soap." Some one said, "I thought you were going to give us something to eat?" "So we are, but we wash here before we eat, and I think from the looks of you fellows you need a good wash, so take this piece of soap and go for the river, and by the time you take a good wash there will be some rations here for you." We took the soap and went to the river. After being in the water twenty or thirty minutes we saw the wagon coming back. This time they gave us some bread and coffee, but the coffee was not good. They had put medicine in it to act as a physic. We took our ration, which was not large, and there was a good deal of grumbling. Some said they did not give us much more than the rebels did, but after awhile an officer came out and said that we would get more rations late in the evening. He said, "In your weak condition it will not do for you to have all your stomachs crave. Last night several of your comrades got to the city and were furnished by the citizens and soldiers all they could eat, and now some ten or fifteen are dead from the effects of eating too much. You must be careful for awhile, as we wish to see you all get home. You will be provided with clothing as soon as it can come up from Hilton Head, and as soon as you are able to stand the trip you will be sent North.

So now make yourselves as comfortable as possible under the circumstances. We are glad to see you, and want to do all for you we can. There are many blackberries now ripe here in the thickets. You can eat all you want, for they will do you good. Bathe as often as you wish. That will help you, and it will not be long until you can go home." In a few days the clothing came, and was issued out to us. When my squad went up to get ours, we told the fellow to roll them up so that we could carry them without getting them exposed to the gray-backs. When the last one got his clothing, we took them, holding them as far from our persons as possible. Going to the river we hung them on a brush, taking off our old ones and throwing them in the water. We then took a good bath, putting on our new clothes. We felt like new men. That was the last time that I ever saw a grayback. In about ten days we were notified to be ready to start North the next day. Early in the morning we went to the landing and went aboard a boat, which was soon out on the great deep. On arriving at Hilton Head we were put on a propeller and started for Annapolis, Maryland, where we arrived in due time.

CHAPTER XVIII.

CAMP CHASE, OHIO—MEETING OLD COMRADES—LONGINGS FOR HOME—A KIND-HEARTED OFFICER—FORWARDED TO INDIANAPOLIS—FURLOUGHED FOR THIRTY DAYS—HOME AT LAST.

THE next day after arriving at Annapolis I was walking through the camp when I heard some one call my name. I looked around, but could see no one that I knew. I started on again when I heard my name called a second time. I looked around and could see no one but a man dressed in citizens' clothes. I thought I would go to him and see who he was. When I got near him he called out, "well, old fellow, you do not seem to know your old friend since you have got in God's country." I now recognized him as one of the boys that run the guard at Blackshear, of whom I have spoken in a previous chapter. They had just landed that morning, and he was looking to see if he could find any one he knew. Our meeting was a great surprise to both of us. He said to me, "come down to the barracks and see the other boys." I went down there and we had a good time together. And here is where they related to me their experience in getting to our boats on the coast of Florida, of which I have spoken before.

I remained at Annapolis only five days, when with several hundred more, I was started for Camp Chase, Ohio. In the course of due time we arrived at Camp Chase. Here I was again surprised on entering the camp. Among the first boys I met was my old friend Fisher, and several of the Fifth Cavalry boys. They had got out on parole some months before, had been at home on furlough, and were now in camp waiting for their descriptive lists in order to be discharged from the service. We had a good time talking and making inquiries after friends. I asked Fisher how long he had been here. He said, "several weeks and we have to remain here until we are discharged. There is an order out," he said, " forbidding the furloughing of any of the men, but that they would be discharged as fast as the descriptive list could be had." He said to me, "you will have a good, long stay here before you get out." I said, " I am going home." " How will you get out?" I said, "you do not think this old rotten board fence will keep me here many days, do you?" "Well, supposing you get outside of the camp, what will you do?" "I will get aboard the train and go home. I have money and can pay my fare." He laughed at me and said, "things are not now like they were when you were here. Every train is guarded and all soldiers traveling without a pass are arrested, and you can not get a pass, so I guess you will have to stay awhile." I said, "I will get on the outside of that fence before a week and will march home. I guess they will not arrest me in the country." He laughed, and said, " I guess you had as well make up your mind to be contented and remain here for a few weeks." But I had set my face homeward, and there was no place like home for me at that time, so I set about looking for a chance to get out.

While going through the camp I saw a notice stuck up ordering all Indiana soldiers whose terms of service had expired to report to General Cox's headquarters. This was Thursday morning. I at once started for the General's headquarters. On arriving there I found two boys from the 29th and one from the 47th regiment. We took seats on a bench. At last a captain came to us and took our names, regiment, etc., and told us to report the next day at ten o'clock, which we did promptly. After waiting for more than two hours, an orderly came to us saying that they could not get our papers out that day, and we should report the next day at ten o'clock. We were on hand promptly at the appointed time and after waiting for a long time an officer came to the door and said they could do nothing for us that day. I was the nearest to him. I said, "I am sorry, as I wanted very much to get home." He looked at me and said, " how long since you were at home?" "Three years," I said. "How long have you been a prisoner?" "One year." " Well, you look like you ought to be at home." I saw by his talk that he was anxious that we should start for home. He said, "wait here for a few minutes and I will go and see the General." I could see the General from where I was standing. The officer approached him and they engaged in an earnest conversation for a few minutes. I could see that they were talking about us and were very earnest. Soon the General and the other officer came to the window and asked us a few more questions, which I answered promptly. The General turned to some clerks and said, "have these men's papers made out at once." Turning to the officer he said, " Captain, have these men go to their quarters at once, and get their traps ready to leave. Call a corporal to go with them to the Soldiers' Home. They will get their dinners there. You must hurry so they can take the 12:30 train for Indianapolis." We were soon at the quarters and commenced rolling up our blankets, when the boys gathered around us and wanted to know how we had managed to get a permit to go. I said, "There is an order there posted on that tree. Go and read it. If you are included in it, you can go as well as us." In a few minutes the corporal was at the quarters with our papers and said we must hurry in order to make the train. We bade the boys good-bye once more, and some of them for the last time this side of the Great Beyond, as we have never seen them since, and some of them have gone to answer to the roll-call beyond the river. We hurried to the Provost Marshal's office. The corporal handed him the papers. He glanced over them and said to the soldier, "take these men up to dinner. They are in a hurry, for the train will soon leave." We went to our dinners, but before we were half done eating, the officer called us, saying, "you must come; I can not hold the train longer." As we passed out of the gate he handed me a large envelope, at the same time saying, "take this and report to Major Dunn at Indianapolis." We were soon on the cars. It was a very pleasant afternoon, the very last of May. At twelve o'clock that night we arrived at Indianapolis. On going to the hotel the clerk said he would give us a bed, but it was too late for supper. Being very hungry, we started out; going to a restaurant we got our suppers. On going back to the hotel the clerk demanded $1.50 for our bed and breakfast, which we paid.

The next morning was Sunday. We walked over the city, saw many ex-soldiers and spent the day very pleasantly. Monday morning we reported to Major Dunn. When I handed him the papers, he looked at me and said, " You look like you had seen some hard service." I said, "About as hard as I care to see." He opened the envelope, looked over the papers and called the names. The two 29th boys were discharged. The 47th boy had something wrong with his discriptive list. The Major said, " I will give you a furlough home for thirty days. By that time I will get your papers all right and can give you a discharge. Looking up to me he said, " How does it come that you never received pay or clothing since your enlistment." I said, " I have received pay and clothing. Was paid the last time at Jacksonville, Florida, in April, 1864. Do not remember the paymaster's name." "Well, if that is so, I cannot discharge you. Your descriptive list does not state that you ever received pay or clothing from the day of your enlistment. I will give you a furlough home for thirty days. You can go home and rest and recruit up, which I think you need about as much as you need a discharge. At the expiration of your furlough you will report here, and I will have your papers ready." He wrote an order and handing it to me he said, "Take this, go over to the quarter-master, who will furnish you with transportation." I went over and got my transportation. At 1 o'clock we left for home, arriving at home about 9 o'clock that night, May 29th, 1865, just one month after I got to our lines.

So here I am, and my neighbors know what I have been since that time. I have tried to do my duty as an American citizen. I love the old flag. I love the brave boys who gave the best days of their lives to protect it. I love every American citizen who loves the old flag and is willing to give his life to protect it if need be. I can find no words to express my contempt for a disloyal man or woman. There is nothing so degraded in my eyes as a traitor to his flag.

My attention has been called to the fact that I have omitted to mention the recovery of the money taken from me by the rebel Provost-Marshal, at Richmond. It was finally returned to me through General Mulford, the United States exchange agent. When Richmond was captured, the register which the Provost Marshal kept was found, together with some $25,000 in money, a large number of watches, gold rings, pins, and other valuables taken from the prisoners. Several months after my return, Mr. Thomas Gibbs, then a resident of Mt.

Etna, Huntington county, but now living at Dora, Wabash county, saw an advertisement in the Baltimore *American*, over the signature of General Mulford, calling upon all prisoners who had turned over their valuables to the rebel Provost Marshal to inform him of the fact, and if their statements were verified by the register in his possession, and the property had been recovered, it would be forwarded to the owners. Mr. Gibbs having shown me this advertisement, I wrote to General Mulford, telling him the facts regarding my case, and in about ten days the amount surrendered by me to the Provost Marshal was forwarded to me by express at old Antioch.

CHAPTER XIX.

THE USE OF BLOOD-HOUNDS BEFORE THE WAR—HOW THE CONFEDERATE AUTHORITIES HUNTED THE PRISONERS WITH THESE BRUTES—INSTANCES OF THE REMARKABLE INSTINCT OF THE DOGS—REFUGEES OVERTAKEN AND TORN ALMOST TO PIECES—A DAY OF RECKONING.

THE young men and young women who are to-day filling important positions in life, know very little of the state of society before the war, especially in the South. The present differs from the past in a great many respects, and many things which were tolerated twenty-five years ago, and sanctioned, would now be condemned and suppressed. In the Southern States, then, every black man and woman was a slave, or in a condition little better than slavery. They were subject to all the abuse that any white man desired to heap upon them. They had no rights the white race were bound to respect. There was no redress for wrongs inflicted upon them in the courts. Even their testimony could not be received when whites were engaged in controversy, or in their own behalf. All slaves were held as chattels. The slaves were bought and sold just as we buy and sell horses in these days. A good, sound and healthy young man would command a good price—from $800, to $1500. In order to keep them subject to their masters, they were kept in ignorance as much as possible.

PRISONERS HUNTED DOWN WITH BLOOD-HOUNDS.

It was a crime for any one to teach them to read and write, punishable by a heavy fine and imprisonment. These slaves were always quartered near their master's residence, in small houses built for that purpose. All slaves must be in their quarters at certain hours in the evening. Should any be absent at roll call, they were punished the next day by receiving a certain number of lashes on their bare backs. But there was always a certain instinct that seemed to say, "I have just as good a right to my freedom as any one else." Hence, some took their chances to make their escape. To prevent this, and help to secure the re-capture of the fugitives, each planter kept a pack of blood-hounds which were trained to track the negroes in case of attempted flight. Many slaves, from mistreatment or some cause, would hide in the swamps, coming out of their places of refuge at night to get something to eat, and retiring to the swamps during the day. The dogs were very useful to hunt down the runaway slaves, and by reason of their long training, the rebel authorities found them equally useful in hunting down refugees and escaping prisoners during the war. They were of more real service to the Confederacy, in this direction, than many regiments of soldiers would have been. In all the histories of wars, I know of no civilized nation—except the so-called Confederacy—which ever resorted to such means as the use of dogs, to hunt down their enemies.

In this chapter I will tell my recollections of the blood-hounds that were kept at Andersonville for the purpose of hunting down escaping prisoners. There were several packs of hounds and other dogs kept for that purpose. One of the packs of a dozen or more was kept near the stockade. When not on duty they were kennelled in an old log house. A man had charge of them whose duty it was to make the rounds of the prison every night and morning, to see if any Yankee had gotten out. This man rode a small white horse part of the time, and part of the time a mule. He carried a carbine and a cow's horn scraped very thin. When all the prisoners were put inside the stockade at night he would go to the log house, open the doors, let out his dogs, mount his horse, give a blast on his horn, when all the dogs would start by making a circuit of the entire prison. If no one had escaped he would go to the house, give a few blasts on his cow's horn, when all the dogs would come up and enter their den. This man was a professional slave hunter before the war, I was informed, and was sent to Andersonville on account of his knowledge of the business in managing the dogs. This business was followed every day while I was at Andersonville, making the rounds in the morning before any one was allowed to go out, and again in the evening after all had been returned to the stockade. If any one had made an escape, as soon as the dogs would strike the trail they would set up a howl, when their keeper would follow them. It has always been a mystery to me how they could tell the trail of an escaping prisoner while there were several hundred paroled men on the outside, besides seven or eight thousand guards and patrols, who were continually scouting the country over, both day and night. If any one can tell how they knew the difference I would be glad to know it. I know, however, that they could tell, as but very few prisoners were ever able to make their escape from the prison on account of these dogs. They were feared more than the guards. The guards could be bribed or deceived, but the dogs never. All old prisoners recollect how the dogs would howl and what a noise they would make while in the house, and how anxious they seemed to be to start on their rounds when once turned loose. I have seen several boys who got out of different prisons and eluded the dogs by wading in water for miles. Then they would go on dry land and travel for days, but as sure as any white man or woman saw them they would soon hear the dogs coming on their trail. Be it remembered that almost every man that owned a slave also owned a pack of hounds to hunt runaway slaves. The hounds were used to hunt Yankees during the war. All prisoners remember how they would say to us, "Why are 'uns all come down heah to fight we'uns foah?" Our answer would be, "To preserve the Constitution and enforce the laws of our Government." They would then say, "Why are 'uns putting niggers in the field to fight we'uns foah?" We would always shut them up by asking, "Why are you hunting our men with dogs?" for as common as this practice was in the South, they did not like to talk about it. There is no doubt but what thousands of our men would have made their escape if it had not been for the dogs. Many a poor boy who sleeps the sleep that knows no waking at Andersonville would to-day be living if it had not been for these dogs. They deterred many from making the effort to escape. I did not like to take the risk of laying in the woods and swamps for weeks almost starved, possibly almost within hearing of friends, to be overtaken by these dogs. The guards could never have captured one man in ten had it not been for the assistance the dogs rendered them.

While we were at Millen some of the Fifth Indiana Cavalry made their escape in the following manner: They were in the first lot that went up to Millen from Savannah. They arrived at Millen late in the evening. It was quite dark when they went inside the stockade. The rebels placed a guard line through the center of the prison just on the opposite side of the creek from them. On going to the creek for water they discovered that they could get outside of the stockade. Where it crossed the creek, the logs were far enough apart to let a small man through. Several small boys belonging to the Fifth Cavalry availed themselves of this opportunity to go out, and as the start was made in the water on the inside of the prison, they thought they could keep in the water so far down the creek that the dogs would not strike their trail. So a little while after dark, four, I think, started, and succeeded in going out unobserved. They followed down the stream until they became so badly chilled they could not stay in the water any longer, when they took to the solid ground. They made good time, and at daylight they were several miles away from the prison. They then secreted themselves in the woods for the day. Starting out early in the evening they made good time, and when daylight came they were crossing a large farm, endeavoring to make the woods on the opposite side. While crossing this farm they were discovered, and soon heard the dogs coming on their trail. They started to run, but before they could gain a place of safety they were overtaken and badly scratched and bitten about the breast and arms. They were returned to the prison without any attention being given to their wounds.

I saw a man while I was at Andersonville, who tried to make his escape, was overtaken by the dogs and had one cheek almost torn off. His left arm was badly bitten. He said he used his left arm as a guard to keep the dogs from getting him by the throat while he was striking at them with a club which he had in his right hand. He said while he was thus engaged the rebels came up and ordered him to stop striking at the dogs, saying that if he did not they would shoot him.

Reader, you can now form some idea of the chance you had to make your escape when you recollect that every white man and woman in the South stood ready to assist in your re-capture should you be able to get outside of the prison pen. It was said that many of the dogs were brought to the South from Cuba during the Florida war to hunt the Indians in the swamps. If such was the case it certainly does not reflect much credit upon our people or any people who would resort to such measures. I want it understood that I do not complain of the cruelties of the service or of prison life while they were conducted on the principles of civilized warfare. What we complain of was the barbarities which the rebels practiced on us. We know war is cruel the best you can make of it, and then to add all the barbarities practiced upon its helpless prisoners that the imagination of man could conceive, is what we complain of as prisoners of our late war. There is not a civilized nation on the globe that ever practiced such gigantic outrages as were practiced by the rebel authorities who had charge of the Union prisoners. It would have been doing many a poor boy good service if they had done by them as the Spanish authorities did in Cuba a few years ago, drawn them up in line and shot them, instead of torturing them by the slow process of starvation and exposure. Who is to blame for these outrages? There certainly will be a reckoning. What a chapter this will make when it is written as it ought to be written, and as I believe it will be.

CHAPTER XX.

THE PRESENT OWNER OF ANDERSONVILLE—OFFICIAL REPORT OF UNITED STATES OFFICER AS TO ITS CONDITION WHEN TAKEN POSSESSION OF BY THE GOVERNMENT.

I HAVE often been asked as to the ownership of the land that the stockade at Andersonville was built on. In order to be able to give the correct answer, I wrote to the postmaster at Andersonville, Georgia, on the 18th of September, 1885, asking him who was the owner of the land at the time the stockade was built. In reply he says the land was owned by a white man by the name of B. B. Dykes. The owner at this time is a colored man by the name of George W. Kennedy. The population of Andersonville he reports as now about 500. Distance from Andersonville to Americus, eleven miles; to Albany, forty-seven miles; Thomasville, 100 miles; Macon, sixty miles. Macon is on the North. The other towns named are on the South. In order to further substantiate what I have said in regard to the horrible condition of the prisoners at Andersonville, I will here give the testimony of James M. Moore, Captain and Assistant Quartermaster, U. S. Army. The following is his report in full :

WASHINGTON, D. C., September 20, 1865.

GENERAL : — In accordance with special orders No. 19, Quartermaster General's office, dated June 30, 1865, directing me to proceed to Andersonville, Georgia, for the purpose of marking the graves of Union soldiers for future identification, and enclosing the cemetery, I have the honor to report as follows:

I left Washington, D. C., on the 8th of July last, for Andersonville, *via* Savannah, with mechanics and material for the purpose above mentioned. On my arrival at Savannah I ascertained there was no railroad communication whatever to Andersonville. The direct road to Macon being broken, and that from Augusta *via* Atlanta also in the same condition, I endeavored to procure wagon transportation, but was informed by the General commanding the department of Georgia that a sufficient number of teams could not be had in the State to haul one-half of my stores, and as the roads were bad and the distance more than four hundred miles, I abandoned all idea of attempting a route through a country difficult and tedious under more propitious circumstances. The prospect of reaching Andersonville at this time was by no means favorable and nearly one week had elapsed since my arrival at Savannah. I had telegraphed to Augusta, Atlanta and Macon, almost daily, and received replies that the railroads were not yet completed. At length on the morning of the 18th of July the gratifying telegram from Augusta was received announcing the completion of the Augusta & Macon road to Atlanta, when I at once determined to procure a boat and proceeded to Augusta by the Savannah River. The desired boat was secured and in twenty-four hours after the receipt of the telegram alluded to I was on my way with men and material for Augusta. On my arrival there, I found the railroad completed to Macon, and that from Macon to Andersonville having never been broken, experienced little difficulty in reaching my destination, where I arrived July 25th, after a tiresome trip occupying six days and nights.

At Macon, Major General Wilson detailed one company of

the 4th United States Cavalry and one from the 137th Regiment United States colored troops to assist me. A member of the former Company was killed on the 5th of August at a station named Montezuma, on the Southwestern railroad. The rolling stock on all the roads over which I traveled is in a miserable condition and very seldom a greater rate of speed was attained than twelve miles an hour. At the different stations along the route the object of the expedition was well known and not infrequently men wearing the garb of rebel soldiers would enter the cars and discuss the treatment of our prisoners at Andersonville, all of whom candidly admitted it was shameful and a blot on the escutcheon of the South that years would not efface. While encamped at Andersonville, I was daily visited by men from the surrounding country and had an opportunity of gleaning their feelings towards the Government and with hardly an exception found those who had been in the rebel army penitent and more kindly disposed than those who had never taken a part, and anxious again to become citizens of the Government they had fought so hard to destroy.

On the morning of the 26th of July the work of identifying the graves, painting and lettering of head boards, laying out walks, and enclosing the cemetery, was commenced, and on the evening of August 16th was completed with the exceptions hereafter mentioned. The dead were found buried in trenches on a site selected by the rebels, about three hundred yards from the stockade. The trenches varied in length from fifty to one hundred and fifty yards. The bodies in the trenches were from two to three feet below the surface, and in several instances, where the rain had washed away the earth, but a few inches. Additional earth was, however, thrown upon the graves, making them of a still greater depth. So close were they buried without coffins, or the ordinary clothing to cover their nakedness, that not more than twelve inches were allowed to each man. Indeed the little tablets marking their resting places, measuring hardly ten inches in width, almost touch each other. United States soldiers, while prisoners at Andersonville, had been detailed to inter their companions, and by a simple stake at the head of each grave, which bore a number corresponding with a similar numbered name upon the Andersonville hospital record, I was enabled to identify and mark with a neat tablet similar to those in the cemeteries at Washington, the number, name, rank, regiment, company and date of death, of twelve thousand four hundred and sixty-one graves, there being but four hundred and fifty-one that bore the sad inscription, "unknown." One hundred and twenty thousand feet of pine lumber were used in these tablets alone. The cemetery contained fifty acres, and has been divided by one main avenue running through the center, and subdivided into blocks and sections in such a manner that with the aid of the record which I am now having copied for the Superintendent, the visitor will experience no difficulty in finding any grave. A force of men are now engaged in laying out walks and cleaning the cemetery of stumps and stones preparatory to planting trees and flowers. I have already commenced the manufacture of brick and will have a sufficient number by the 1st of October to pave the numerous gutters throughout the cemetery, the clay in the vicinity of the stockade being well adapted to the purpose of brickmaking. Appropriate inscriptions are placed through the grounds, and I have endeavored as far as my facilities would permit, to transfer this wild, unmarked and unhonored graveyard into a fit place of interment for the Nation's gallant dead.

At the entrance gate, the words, "National Cemetery, Andersonville, Ga.," designate this city of the dead. On the morning of the 17th of August, at sunrise, the stars and stripes were hoisted in the center of the cemetery, when a National salute was fired and several National songs sung by those present. The men who accompanied me, and to whom I am indebted for the early completion of my mission, worked zealously and faithfully from early in the morning until late at night, although suffering intensely from the effects of the sun. Unacclimated as they were, one after another was taken sick with the fever incident to this country, and in a brief period my force of mechanics was considerably lessened, obliging me to obtain others from the residents in different parts of the State. All my men, however, recovered with the exception of Eddy Watts, a letterer, who died on the 16th of July, of typhoid fever, after a sickness of three weeks. I brought his body back with me and delivered it to his family in this city. Several of the 4th United States Cavalry, detailed by General Wilson, died of the same fever, shortly after joining their command at Macon.

Andersonville is situated on the Southwestern railroad, sixty miles from Macon. There is but one house in the place except those erected by the so-called Confederate Government as hospitals, officers' quarters, and commissary and quartermaster's buildings. It was formerly known as Anderson, but since the war the ville has been added. The country is covered mostly with pines and hemlocks and the soil is sandy, sterile and unfit for cultivation, and unlike the sections of country a few miles north and south of this place, where the soil is well adapted to agricultural purposes, and cotton as well as corn are extensively raised. It is said to be the most unhealthy part of Georgia and was probably selected as a depot for prisoners on account of this fact. At mid-day the thermometer in the shade reaches frequently one hundred and ten degrees, and in the sun the heat is almost unbearable. The inhabitants of this sparsely settled locality are, with few exceptions, of the most ignorant class, and from their haggard and sallow faces, the

Twelve Months in Andersonville. 185

effects of chills and fever are distinctly visible. The noted Prison Pen is fifteen hundred and forty feet long and seven hundred and fifty feet wide. The dead line is seventeen feet from the stockade and the sentry boxes are thirty yards apart. The inside stockade is eighteen feet high, the outer one twelve feet, and the distance between the two is one hundred and twenty feet. Nothing has been destroyed. As our exhausted, emaciated, and enfeebled soldiers left it, so it stands to-day, as an inhumanity unparalleled in the annals of war. How men could survive as well as they did in this pen, exposed to the rays of an almost tropical sun by day, and drenching dews by night, without the slightest covering, is wonderful. The ground is filled with holes where they had burrowed in their efforts to shield themselves from the weather, and many a poor fellow, in endeavoring to protect himself in this manner was smothered to death by the earth falling in upon him. The stories told of the sufferings of our men while prisoners here have been substantiated by hundreds and the skeptic who will visit Andersonville even now and examine the stockade, with its black oozey mud, the cramped and wretched burrows, the dead line, and the slaughter house, must be a callous observer, indeed, if he is not convinced that the miseries depicted of this prison pen are no exaggerations.

JAMES M. MOORE,
Captain and Assistant Quartermaster.

Brevet Major General M. C. MEIGS,
Washington, D. C.

CHAPTER XXI.

THE TRIAL OF WIRZ—HIS EFFORTS TO SHIFT THE RESPONSI-
BILITY—THE CHARGES AND SPECIFICATIONS—OVERWHELM-
ING EVIDENCE OF GUILT—THE SENTENCE AND EXECUTION.

CAPTAIN HENRY WIRZ, the infamous commandant at Andersonville, died, as he deserved, by the hand of the hangman. At the close of the rebellion, General Wilson, commander of the Federal cavalry forces, learned that he was still at Andersonville, and sent a squad of cavalry from Macon, Ga., under Captain Noyes, of the 4th regiment, to arrest him. Wirz knew resistance was useless, but claimed immunity from punishment by reason of the terms granted at the surrender of Johnson. His protest was of no avail, however. Even had the Government permitted him to escape, it is almost certain he would have met a violent death at the hands of some of the prisoners whom he had maltreated in the days of his despotic power. The day of his arrest, he wrote the following letter to General Wilson:

ANDERSONVILLE, Ga., May 7, 1865.

GENERAL:—It is with great reluctance that I address you these lines, being fully aware how little time is left you to attend to such matters as I now have the honor to lay before you, and if I could see any other way to accomplish my object, would not intrude upon you. I am a native of Switzerland,

and was, before the war, a citizen of Louisiana, and by profession, a physician. Like hundreds of others I was carried away by the excitement and joined the Southern army. I was very severely wounded at the battle of Seven Pines, near Richmond, Va., and have nearly lost the use of my right arm. Unfit for field duty, I was ordered to report to Brevet Major General John H. Winder, in charge of the Federal prisoners of war, who ordered me to take charge of a prison in Alabama. My health failing me, I applied for a furlough, and went to Europe from which I returned in February, 1864. I was then ordered to report to the commandant of the military prison at Andersonville, who assigned me to the command of the interior of the prison. The duties I had to perform were arduous and unpleasant, and I am satisfied that no man can, or will, justly blame me for things that happened here and which were beyond my power to control. I do not think that I ought to be held responsible for the shortness of rations, for the over crowded state of the prison, which was of itself a prolific source of fearful mortality, for the inadequate supply of clothing, want of shelter, etc. Still I now bear the odium, and men who were prisoners have seemed disposed to wreak their vengeance upon me for what they have suffered—I, who was only the medium, or I may better say, the tool, in the hands of my superiors. This is my condition. I lost all my property when the Federal army besieged Vicksburg. I have no money at present to go any place, and even if I had, I know of no place where I can go. My life is in danger, and I most respectfully ask of you help and relief. If you will be so generous as to give me some sort of a safe conduct, or what I should greatly prefer, a guard to protect myself and family against violence, I should be thankful to you, and you will not be giving to one who is unworthy of it. My intentions are to return with my family to Europe as soon as I can make the arrangements. In the meantime I have the honor, General, to remain, very respectfully,

Your obedient servant,

HENRY WIRZ, Captain, C. S. A.

Major General J. H. WILSON, Commanding, Macon, Ga.

The trial of Wirz was held at Washington. The prisoner was brought North *via* Chattanooga, Nashville and Cincinnati, and so bitter was the public feeling that, although accompanied by a strong guard, it was necessary to smuggle him through in disguise to escape the vengeance of ex-prisoners and the friends of those who had died in captivity. So execrated was the man that even his fellow countryman, the Swiss Consul-General at Washington, refused to be the custodian of funds raised to conduct his defense before the Court-Martial.

The Court-Martial detailed to try the prisoner consisted of Major General Lew Wallace, of Indiana, President; Brevet Major Generals Mott and Geary; Brigadier Generals Fessenden, Bragg and L. Thomas; and Colonels Ballier, Allcock and Stibbs. The Commission convened August 23d, 1865, and the taking of testimony continued until the 1st of October. Colonel Chipman was the Judge Advocate, and the culprit was defended by Lewis Schade, a prominent Washington attorney, together with three assistant counsel. Over two thousand pages of testimony were taken, and so completely was the truth of the charges established that the Government closed the case before all the evidence offered was heard. The following is an abbreviated copy of the charges and specifications upon which Wirz was tried:

CHARGE I.—That Henry Wirz maliciously, willfully and traitorously, in aid of the then existing rebellion against the United States, at divers times on or before and between the 1st day of March, 1864, and the 10th day of April, 1865, combined, confederated and conspired with John H. Winder and others to injure the health and destroy the lives of soldiers in the military service of the United States, then held as prisoners of war in the military prisons of the so-called Confederate States, to the end that the armies of the United States might be weakened and impaired, in violation of the laws and customs of war. That the said Wirz subjected prisoners to torture and great suffering by confining them in unhealthy and unwholsome quarters; by exposing them to the inclemency of winter and the burning suns of summer; by furnishing them with insufficient and unwholesome food, he being fully clothed with authority of the so-called Confederate Government, and in duty bound to treat, care and provide for such prisoners according to the laws of war; by neglecting to furnish the prisoners with tents, barracks and other shelter; by ordering the confiscation of the clothing, blankets, etc., of the prisoners; by refusing to furnish food to sustain the lives of the prisoners, or wood to cook their scanty rations or for warming purposes; by compelling the prisoners to subsist on unwholesome food in quantities inadequate to sustain life; by compelling the prisoners to use unwholesome water reeking with the filth and garbage of the prison and prison guard, and the offal and drainage of the cook-house, whereby the prisoners became greatly reduced in bodily health and strength, their minds impaired, their intellects broken, and over ten thousand permitted to languish and die for want of proper care and treatment; by leaving the bodies of the dead until they became corrupt and loathsome, among the emaciated sick and languishing living, thereby increasing the unwholesomeness of the prison, and causing the sickness and death of prisoners to the number of one thousand; by subjecting prisoners to cruel, unusual and infamous punishments upon slight, trivial and fictitious pretense, such as binding prisoners closely together with large chains around their necks and feet, placing them in an instrument of torture known as the "stocks," without the power to change position and without food and water, thereby causing the death of thirty prisoners; by the establishment of a "dead line," which was in many places an imaginary line, and in many other places marked by insecure and shifting strips of board, nailed upon the top of small and insecure posts, instructing the prison guard to fire upon and kill prisoners who might touch, fall upon, pass over or under or across the said "dead line," thereby causing the death of about three hundred prisoners; by keeping ferocious and blood-thirsty beasts, dangerous to human life, called blood-hounds, to hunt down, seize, tear, mangle and maim the bodies and limbs of fugitive prisoners, whereby about fifty prisoners lost their lives; by the use of poisonous and impure vaccine matter, for the pretended purpose of preventing small-pox, by reason of which about one hundred prisoners lost the use of their arms and about two hundred lost their lives.

The finding of the Commission on this awful charge, after amendment, was "GUILTY."

CHARGE II. — This charge embraced personal acts of brutality perpetrated by Wirz. Twelve distinct specifications were alleged, on ten of which the finding was "*guilty.*" These specifications were as follows: 1. July 9th, 1864, with a revolver in his hands, shooting and mortally wounding a prisoner, from the effects of which injuries death followed in twenty-four hours. 2. September 20th, 1864, jumping upon, stamping, kicking and bruising a prisoner with the heels of his boots, causing his immediate death. 3. June 13th, 1864, shooting and mortally wounding a prisoner, with a revolver, causing his immediate death. 4. August 20th, 1864, confining a prisoner in the stocks, in consequence of which cruel treatment, maliciously and murderously inflicted, the prisoner died in ten days. 5. February 1st, 1865, confining a prisoner in the stocks, and causing death in seven days. 6. July 20th, 1864, binding the necks and feet of prisoners together with heavy chains, compelling them to carry large iron balls on their feet, from the effects of which one of the sufferers died in five days. 7. May 15th, 1864, ordering a rebel soldier to fire on an unarmed and helpless prisoner, thereby causing his immediate death. 8. July 1st, 1864, ordering a guard to fire upon a helpless prisoner, causing his death. 9. July 1st, 1864, causing the blood-hounds to pursue, attack, wound, and tear to pieces, a prisoner, from which injuries death followed in six days. 10. July 27th, 1864, commanding a sentinel to fire upon a helpless prisoner, causing immediate death.

There was no lack of proof of the charges preferred against Wirz, or of the atrocities perpetrated by and under the authority of this monster. The evidence was overwhelming, that, by his orders, prisoners had been beaten until they died from their injuries; that they had been confined in the stocks until death ended their suffering; that they had been shot down in cold blood; that they had been torn and mangled by blood-hounds; that Wirz himself had inflicted punishment, such as shooting prisoners, knocking them down and kicking and stamping them. Nearly two hundred ex-prisoners gave their testimony, and in all the annals of crime history furnishes hardly a parallel to the damning character established for this brutal wretch. In addition to the testimony of the prisoners, Colonel Gibbs, the confederate commander of the troops stationed at Andersonville, testified that Wirz had sole control of the prison and prisoners. The surgeons in charge of the hospital testified as to his utter indifference to the condition of the sick, and the meager supplies furnished. Wirz had even refused to allow them to carry in vegetables to stop the scurvy, although a plentiful supply could have been secured, as there had been a fair crop raised in the vicinity.

In answer to the charges, Wirz put in pleas in bar to the effect: 1. That the war being over, and the country at peace, he could not legally be tried by a Court Martial. 2. That he was entitled to immunity by the terms of the surrender of the confederate army. The objection in the first paragraph of the answer was overruled, and in answer to the second, Captain Noyes, who made the arrest, declared that no terms or promises of protection had been given the prisoner at the time of his surrender. Wirz then entered a plea of not guilty; denying any knowledge of a conspiracy to destroy the lives of prisoners; denying that he was an accomplice of Winder or any other person for such a purpose; denying his responsibility for the over-crowded condition of the stockade, scanty prison fare, lack of shelter, awful mortality, etc.; and denying each and every act of cruelty alleged against him personally.

The sentence of the Court Martial was death by hanging. President Johnson approved the finding. and General C. C. Augur was charged with its execution. On the 10th day of November, 1865, the sentence was carried into effect in the Old Capitol Prison at Washington. Although Rev. Fathers Wheelan, Boyle and Hamilton were permitted to visit the prisoner up to the last moment for the purpose of giving him spiritual consolation, his body was, by order of that stern but just official, Secretary of War Stanton, refused Christian burial. Infamous as were his crimes, he met his fate without flinching. Jeff Davis, whose tool Wirz was, lives to this day, and from his comfortable home in Mississippi we occasionally hear his lamentations over "The Lost Cause." Truly, justice was blind when the subordinate only was punished and the principal allowed to go free.

Only Wirz, of all the brutal officers who were placed over

the prisoners, was punished. John H. Winder died the first day of January, 1865. Adjutant Ross was burned up in a hotel at Richmond a few years after the war. The others disappeared, no one knows where, well knowing that should they ever meet some of the prisoners whom they had so cruelly mistreated, their lives would have paid the penalty.

CHAPTER XXII.

FIXING THE RESPONSIBILITY—WHAT THE CONFEDERATE ARCHIVES DISCLOSE—WHY THERE WAS NO EXCHANGE OF PRISONERS—THE TREATMENT ACCORDED REBEL PRISONERS IN THE NORTH—THIRTEEN THOUSAND MARTYRS BURIED IN THE ANDERSONVILLE NATIONAL CEMETERY—THE DISEASES FROM WHICH THEY DIED, AND THE STATES FROM WHICH THEY ENLISTED.

IF proof were wanting of the truth of my statement of the horrors to which the prisoners were subject, the letter of Wirz, to General Wilson, furnishes it an abundance. It admits the scanty food, crowded condition of the stockade, lack of clothing, want of shelter and fearful mortality. That Jeff. Davis and the rebel authorities knew of the suffering and misery in the rebel prison pens does not admit of a doubt. That they permitted and encouraged the barbarities practiced on helpless prisoners, is equally clear. Wirz, as he declared, was their tool—a merciless and cruel one—conscious that his course was fully in accord with the sentiments of those in higher authority.

It has been urged, by rebel sympathisers, that the Confederate authorities were powerless to properly care for the prisoners; that their treasury was bankrupt to purchase supplies; that their country was impoverished to such an extent as to afford only a meager support for their armies in the field. In short, that the inhuman treatment of prisoners could not be helped, and, therefore, the Confederate authorities should not be held responsible. Out upon such lies! Even these lies afford no explanation of:—(1.) The location of the Andersonville stockade in a pestilential swamp, only a few rods removed from healthy ground with plenty of water and shade. (2.) The crowding of 35,000 men on sixteen acres of ground when there were thousands of acres of land, unoccupied, on every side. (3.) Depriving the prisoners of the privilege of securing fuel, without cost or labor to the Confederacy, from the abundant forests in the immediate vicinity of the stockade. Nor are the excuses made as to the inability of the rebels to secure supplies, valid, as witness the fact that the rebel soldiers always had provisions to sell the prisoners who were is possession of money.

By all the laws of civilized war, it was incumbent upon the rebel Government to treat its prisoners humanely. The South boasted of its chivalry, and yet no tribe of savages was ever guilty of greater barbarity. The tortures inflicted upon their captives by the Indians were not more cruel or more dreadful than fell to the lot of the men of the North, who, by the fortunes of war, fell into the hands of their own countrymen who were engaged in fighting the battles of a slave oligarchy. The man who excuses the treatment of the prisoners, is the meanest kind of a traitor—an enemy to the Union and a foe of humanity.

The capture of the archives of the Confederacy furnishes the most conclusive evidence that the condition of the Andersonville prison pen was fully known to the rebel authorities. Isaiah H. White, Chief Surgeon of the Hospital, over his own signature, called attention to the fact that when the stockade was built the outside limit of the number of prisoners for whom there was room was ten thousand. In August, 1864, he wrote a long report to General Winder, which was published after the war, in which he called attention to the crowded condition of the prison; lack of hospital accommodations; absence of vegetables necessary to prevent the scurvy; the drainage of the garrison camps into the stream which furnished water for the stockade; lack of clothing and proper medicines for the sick, and the fact that there were but twelve surgeons to look after the health of over thirty-one thousand prisoners. His report had no effect, however, and at the beginning of September he was succeeded as chief Surgeon by Doctor Stevenson, a man who was openly charged, at the trial of Wirz, by Doctor Thornburg, one of the hospital surgeons, with having embezzled about $80,000 of the hospital fund. The testimony of this same Stevenson as to the condition of the stockade reveals that he forbade General Winder and other officers from entering the stockade except when in the best of health, so filthy and pestilential was its condition. Doctor Bates, another rebel surgeon, testified that green corn was taken away from the patients and prisoners and the latter severely punished for buying it. These documents also disclose that during the month of August, 1864, Colonel Chandler, of Mississippi, Confederate Inspector of Military Prisons, visited Andersonville, and he, too, made a report, which was brought into court at the trial of Wirz, and which bore the indorsement of the War Department of the Confederate Government as filed in October. In this report Colonel Chandler denounced the condition of Andersonville prison as "a disgrace to the Confederacy as a Nation," and severely criticised General Winder. To these criticisms General Winder replied by impugning Chandler's veracity. This led to a demand by Colonel Chandler for a court of inquiry, but his request was refused on the ground that officers could not be spared from the field for that purpose! Here is direct evidence of knowledge of the condition of the prisoners by the Confederate Government, and the fact is patent that there were no steps taken for their betterment.

Two pertinent inquiries will arise in the mind of every careful reader: (1.) What object had the Confederate authorities in exterminating the prisoners? (2.) Why was there not an exchange of prisoners?

In answer to the first inquiry: The deliberate cruelty was practiced in the hope that the desperate suffering in the rebel prison pens—reports of which were beginning to be heard in the North—would create such a sentiment as to demand a cessation of hostilities in the interest of humanity. If the people of the loyal States could be made to believe that the fifty thousand Union prisoners in captivity must perish unless the war should cease, the rebels believed it would raise a great cry for peace to reinforce the copperheads and rebel sympathizers of the North in their demands for a compromise. Failing in this, a secondary object was to cripple the Union army, in case of an exchange, by returning to it a lot of diseased and broken-down soldiers—" miserable wretches," as Robert Ould, the Rebel Commmissioner of Exchange, called them—unfit for service, in exchange for the well-fed rebels who were cared for in the Northern prisons, who were then in prime condition for field service, and who would prove a valuable reinforcement to the Confederate army.

As to the second inquiry: There was no general exchange of prisoners the latter part of the war for the sole reason that the rebels refused to concede that the black man was no longer property. The Federal Government desired an exchange, and General B. F. Butler, United States Commissioner of Exchange, addressed a long letter to Robert Ould, the Confederate Commissioner, in August, 1864. In this letter

General Butler declared his Government ready provided that all enlisted soldiers and officers could be exchanged alike. Here was the stumbling block. The South refused to treat the black men in the United States service as soldiers, and held that white officers over them were criminals. It claimed the right to reduce to a state of slavery, free men, prisoners of war, who had once been in bondage, but had been emancipated by the proclamation of President Lincoln; and, by advertisement in Southern newspapers, called upon the former owners of black men regularly enlisted in the Federal army, who had been captured, to come forward and claim "their property." Because the Government of the United States insisted that every soldier who wore the blue—black as well as white—should be equally entitled to the privilege of exchange; that officers in colored regiments should have the same treatment as officers in white regiments; the rebel authorities declined an exchange. The United States was honorably bound to protect the rights of the colored soldiers and their white officers, and because it refused to discriminate against them, no agreement could be arrived at. The scenes of Andersonville, Belle Isle, Florence, etc., were among the last dreadful pictures of the woe brought upon this Nation by the terrible crime of human slavery.

I am rejoiced to know that the confederate prisoners who were captured and lodged in the military prisons of the North were kindly treated. I have acquaintances who served as guards at northern prisons, and they tell me the prisoners fared as well as the soldiers who guarded them. The prison discipline was rigid of necessity, but the Johnnies did not lack for food, clothing or shelter. The sick were cared for properly and the mortality of the prisoners were but little, if any higher, than the mortality of men kept in confinement in penal institutions the world over. Nor have I ever heard, from responsible rebel sources, any complaint of inhumanity such as disgraced the cause of the Southern Confederacy.

In writing this, the story of my personal experience in Andersonville, I have endeavored to avoid any exhibition of vindictiveness. Twenty years of peace have not been without their effect in toning down the just resentment which every survivor of Andersonville feels at the barbarity to which himself and comrades were subject, but thrice twenty years cannot obliterate the remembrance of the horrors of the place. With all these scenes rising fresh before my eyes, it has been a difficult task to write with the moderation which I had hoped, but of one thing my readers can rest assured: *I have written only the truth.* I could not have drawn a milder picture had I been on the witness stand to answer "under the pains and penalties of perjury."

Of the fifty-two members of the 13th Indiana who entered the stockade, thirteen died while prisoners at Andersonville. How many died in other prisons, how many went to premature graves from the effects of that confinement, or how many still linger in this life the victims of diseases brought on by their sufferings, I have no means of determining. I know that thirteen thousand as brave soldiers as ever followed the Stars and Stripes—six hundred of them the sons of the Hoosier State—laid down their lives at Andersonville, martyrs to the grand cause of Freedom and National Supremacy.

APPENDIX.

The total number of prisoners received at Andersonville during its use as a prison was 45,613. The records show that 18,000 of this number were admitted to the hospital for treatment, and the death register contains the names of nearly 13,000 prisoners who died. The principal causes of death were diarrhea and dysentery, 6,400; scurvy, 3,800; gangrene, 700; fevers, 406; gun wounds, 155; phthsis, 137; rheumatism, 83; small pox, 68; sunstroke, 52. Of the remaining two thousand, many different forms of disease are named, but the majority were wantonly murdered, and no report made. The hospital records alone give the cause of the death of 443 prisoners as "unknown."

The recapitulation of deaths by States is as follows:

Alabama,	15
Connecticut,	315
Delaware,	45
District Columbia,	14
Illinois,	850
Indiana,	594
Iowa,	174

Kansas, ...	5
Kentucky,	436
Louisiana,	1
Maine, . . .	233
Maryland, . .	194
Massachusetts,	768
Minnesota, . . .	79
Michigan,	630
Missouri, ...	97
New Hampshire,	124
New Jersey, . . .	170
New York, . .	2572
North Carolina,	17
Ohio, ...	1030
Pennsylvania, .	1811
Rhode Island, .	74
Tennessee.	738
Vermont, . .	212
Virginia, .	288
Wisconsin,	244
U. S. Army. .	399
U. S. Navy, . . .	100
Civilians, . .	166
Unknown,	517
Total, . . .	12,912

The following is a list of Federal prisoners from Indiana and Ohio who died and were buried at Andersonville, from the organization of the Prison in February, 1864, to the surrender of the Confederate army in May, 1865. Compiled from the Prison Hospital Register kept by the Confederate Surgeons, White, Stevenson and Clayton:

Appendix.   III

INDIANA.

A

No. of Grave.	Name.	Co. Regt.	Date of Death.
571.	Allen, Jessie, corporal,	K, 116th Inf.	April 15, '64
1917.	Adkins, George	D, 6th Cav	June 14, '64
3991.	Andrews, E. L	K, 6th Cav.	July 26, '64
4270.	Anderson, D.	E, 76th Inf.	July 29, '64
5680.	Ault, J. W.	D, 40th Inf.	Aug. 14, '64
6921.	Alexander, S.	D, 93d Inf.	Aug. 26, '64
7124.	Alexander, J. D.	K, 5th Cav.	Aug 28, '64
9292.	Auburn, C.	H, 65th Inf.	Sept. 19, '64
9445.	Adkins, J. F.	H, 2d Cav.	Sept. 21, '64
9584.	Adams, H.	A, 35th Inf.	Sept. 23, '64
9643.	Allen, D. B., sergeant.	29th Inf.	Sept. 24, '64
9759.	Alfred, W. J.	K, 117th Inf.	Sept. 25, '64
10473.	Allyn, D.	K, 88th Inf.	Oct. 7, '64
10793.	Atland, C	C, 32d Inf	Oct. 12, '64
11186.	Albin, I.	D, 89th Inf.	Oct. 19, '64
12183.	Austin, Alfred	K, 5th Inf	Nov. 27, '64
12513.	Amick, W.	B, 93d Inf	Jan. 23, '65

B

313.	Bash, David	C, 117th Inf.	April 2, '64
576.	Bee, Thomas	Cavalry	April 16, '64
596.	Bock, Samuel	I, 75th Inf	April 17, '64
838.	Brown, T.	D, 66th Inf	May 1, '64
1514.	Barry, Henry	D, 84th Inf	May 31, '64
1603.	Boley, A. J.	C, 66th Inf.	June 4, '64
1759.	Barra, John	H, 65th Inf.	June 9, '64
2016.	Burnett, Wm.	G, 6th Cav	June 15, '64
2191.	Buckhart, E.	F, 27th Inf	June 19, '64
2222.	Brasier, S., musician	I, 19th Inf	June 20, '64
2299.	Baumgardner,	D, 44th Inf	June 22, '64
2458.	Barrett, E.	I, 42d Inf	June 25, '64
2874.	Bowman, John	C, 42d, Inf.	July 4, '64
3044.	Bruce, J. W.	M, 5th Cav	July 8, '64

Appendix.

No. of Grave.	Name.	Co. Regt.	Date of Death.
3359.	Broughton, D.	K, 7th Inf.	July 15, '64
3366.	Bricker, J.	C, 68th Inf	July 15, '64
4027.	Barton, J. F.	G, 52d Inf.	July 26, '64
4035.	Balinger, Robt.	I. 39th Inf.	July 26, '64
4251.	Bonly, James	C, 81st Inf.	July 29, '64
4479.	Baker, J.	G, 9th Inf.	Aug. 1, '64
4563.	Baker, D. W.	B, 13th Inf	Aug. 2, '64
4948.	Bayer, F.	H, 129th Inf.	Aug. 7, '64
5089.	Brenton, J. W.	I, 29th Inf.	Aug. 8, '64
5993.	Bowlin, Wm.	G, 53d Inf.	Aug. 8, '64
5220.	Barton, E.	G, 2d Cav.	Aug. 10, '64
5275.	Busick, W. A., corporal	F, 101st Inf.	Aug. 10, '64
5442.	Bryer, P.	K, 81st Inf.	Aug. 12, '64
5590.	Bohens, Philip	A, 79th Inf	Aug. 14, '64
5690.	Baker, J. P.	H, 7th Cav	Aug. 15, '64
5794.	Boom, W. P.	F, 31st Inf.	Aug. 15, '64
5981.	Barton, George	F, 130th Inf.	Aug. 17, '64
6163.	Brookers, J. M	E, 112th Inf.	Aug. 19, '64
6410.	Brown, J. M.	F, 66th Inf.	Aug. 22, '64
6518.	Bartholomew, I.	A, 99th Inf.	Aug. 22, '64
7370.	Bamgroover, J. A.	H, 101st Inf.	Aug. 31, '64
7794.	Barnes, Thomas M.	C, 5th Cav.	Sept. 4, '64
8314.	Babbitt, W. H.	I, 29th Inf.	Sept. 10, '64
8397.	Bassinger, H.	C, 14th Inf.	Sept. 10, '64
8519.	Boyd, W. F.	F, 125th Inf.	Sept. 12, '64
9098.	Bortley, S.	I, 88th Inf.	Sept. 18, '64
9548.	Bray, T. E.	K, 79th Inf.	Sept. 23, '64
9708.	Brown, J., sergeant,	A, 1st Cav.	Sept. 24, '64
9777.	Birch, T. A.	L, 58th Inf.	Sept. 26, '64
9793.	Bozell, J. F.	B, 40th Inf.	Sept. 26, '64
9846.	Bixter, D.	B, 5th Inf.	Sept. 27, '64
10350.	Blackaber, W. H	I, 42d Inf.	Oct. 5, '64
10909.	Benton, L.	H, 30th Inf.	Oct. 14, '64
11559.	Bennett, R. N.	D, 72d Inf.	Oct. 27, '64
11604.	Bemis, J. M., sergeant,	F, 87th Inf.	Oct. 28, '64
11919.	Brown, D.	B, 128th Inf.	Nov. 8, '64

Appendix. V

No. of Grave.	Name.	Co. Regt.	Date of Death.
11930.	Bailey, George	A, 72nd Inf	Nov. 8, '64
12019.	Bennett, A.	G, 29th Inf	Nov. 15, '64
12128.	Booth, J	E, 32nd Inf	Nov. 22, '64
12294.	Bennett, C.	H, 6th Inf	Dec. 15, '64
12486.	Barrey, H	I, 66th Inf	Jan. 19, '65
12504.	Balstrum, J.	F, 93d Inf	Jan. 22, '65
12596.	Branson, E	A, 57th Inf	Feb. 6, '65

C

301.	Charles, James	G, 6th Inf.	April 1, '64
625.	Connell, P.	M, 6th Cav	April 19, '64
634.	Claycome, S. A., sergeant,	G, 66th Inf.	April 20, '64
1117.	Cox, Joseph, sergeant,	B, 42d Inf.	May 15, '64
1146.	Carter, Henry	C, 2d Cav.	May 16, '64
1172.	Curry, J. W.	F, 30th Inf.	May 17, '64
1463.	Currier, Wm.	K, 87th Inf	May 30, '64
1523.	Crest, J. D.	F, 31st Inf.	May 31, '64
2254.	Carpenter, O. C., corporal.	D, 29th Inf	June 21, '64
2307.	Cottrell, M. sergeant,	G, 6th Cav	June 22, '64
2776.	Cooley, A	C, 38th Inf.	July 2, '64
3043.	Clark, W.	C, 82d Inf.	July 8, '64
3922.	Connolly, D.	I, 9th Inf	July 25, '64
4234.	Curry, W. F.	I, 4th Cav.	July 29, '64
4192.	Cox, S.	E, 66th Inf.	July 28, '64
4917.	Clifford, H. C	I, 7th Cav	Aug. 6, '64
5262.	Courtney, J. F.	L, 2nd Cav	Aug. 10, '64
5654.	Collar, E	G, 130th Inf	Aug. 14, '64
5660.	Crews, E. M	A, 5th Cav	Aug. 14, '64
5901.	Clark, A	A, 54th Inf	Aug. 16, '64
6203.	Chrichfula, S.	A, 93d Inf.	Aug. 19, '64
6477.	Croane, J. J	C, 22d Inf.	Aug. 22, '64
6646.	Cornelius, E.	B, 58th Inf	Aug. 23, '64
6926.	Carnahan, A. W. sergeant	E, 6th Inf.	Aug. 26, '64
7383.	Carpenter, S.	I, 66th Inf.	Aug. 31, '64
7726.	Callings, W.	F, 120th Inf.	Sept. 3, '64
7737.	Cramer, A	H, 30th Inf.	Sept. 3, '64

VI   *Appendix.*

No. of Grave.	Name.	Co. Regt.	Date of Death.
7899.	Cheney, James	I, 7th Cav	Sept. 5, '64
8051.	Crampton, R.	I, 101st Inf	Sept. 6, '64
8108.	Crazen, J	G, 53d Inf	Sept. 7, '64
8133.	Crager, J.	C, 13th Inf.	Sept. 8, '64
8144.	Cooper, J	E, 80th Inf	Sept. 8, '64
9294.	Christman, J. E	G, 6th Cav	Sept. 19, '64
9535.	Collins, G.	F, 56th Inf	Sept. 22, '64
9980.	Connett, Daniel	F, 130th Inf.	Sept. 28, '64
10084.	Conel, J.	D, 13th Inf	Sept. 30, '64
10905.	Callen, M	B, 35th Inf.	Oct. 13, '64
11423.	Cafer, J. H.	K, 87th Inf.	Oct. 24, '64
11631.	Cummings, J. W.	F, 93d Inf	Oct. 28, '64
12062.	Clark, M	B, 101st Inf	Nov. 17, '64
12173.	Cannon, A	F, 42d Inf.	Nov. 16, '64
12213.	Cregs, Wm.	F, 5th Cav	Dec. 3, '64
12415.	Collins, W. A., sergeant	G, 5th Inf.	Jan. 8, '65
12559.	Calvert, G. F.	I, 8th Cav.	Jan. 30, '65

D

426.	Drummond, J. H.	F, 65th Inf.	April 7, '64
508.	Davis, J. M	I, 65th Inf.	April 12, '64
964.	Darker, Wm.	C, 12th Inf.	May 8, '64
2205.	Denny, John	E, 44th Inf.	June 19, '64
3157.	Detrich, C.	K, 29th Inf.	July 11, '64
3419.	Dusan, J.	D, 6th Inf.	July 16, '64
4021.	Develin, E.	B, 35th Inf.	July 26, '64
4029.	Decer, P.	K, 32nd Inf	July 26, '64
4124.	Dill, C. P	F, 42nd Inf.	July 27, '64
5255.	Davis, K.	D, 13th Inf.	Aug. 10, '64
5367.	Dunben, M	E, 36th Inf.	Aug. 11, '64
5420.	Delup, Z. S.	D, 13th Inf.	Aug. 12, '64
5681.	Dallinger, W. C	E, 38th Inf.	Aug. 14, '64
6147.	Denton, Philip.	D, 81st Inf.	Aug. 19, '64
6234.	Downey, S. M.	I, 116th Inf.	Aug. 25, '64
6944.	Dowell, W. S	C, 6th Inf.	Aug. 26, '64
9236.	Diver, O.	F, 19th Inf.	Sept. 19, '64

Appendix. VII

No. of Grave.		Co. Regt.	Date of Death.
9638.	Dunlap, W.	A. 30th Inf.	Sept. 24, '64
10010.	Downs, J. R.	I, 5th Cav.	Sept. 29, '64
10435.	Dane, Andrew	I, 36th Inf.	Oct. 6, '64
10446.	Dignon, L.	B, 35th Inf.	Oct. 7, '64
10916.	Dawson, L. F.	I, 29th Inf.	Oct. 14, '64
10954.	Dial, R.	B, 1st Cav.	Oct. 14, '64
12087.	Daffendal, P. H.	D, 58th Inf.	Nov. 18, '64
12172.	Davenport, J.	I, 6th Cav.	Nov. 24, '64
12236.	Delasement, F. sergeant	B, 14th Inf.	Dec. 6, '64
12533.	Duckworth, J.	F, 85th Inf.	Jan. 27, '65
12545.	Dawley, J.	I, 73rd Inf.	Jan. 27, '65
12580.	Dawson, J.	D, 124th Inf.	Feb. 3, '65

E

916.	Evans, G. H.	A, 1st Cav.	May 6, '64
917.	Edwards, G. H. musician	G, 6th Inf.	May 7, '64
1083.	Ellis, H. C.	D, 6th Cav.	May 14, '64
1279.	Evans, W.	I, 75th Inf.	May 22, '64
1346.	Eskridge, Oakley	D, 29th Inf.	May 24, '64
1994.	Edwards, J. W.	G, 38th Inf.	June 15, '64
2481.	Essenthal, F.	D, 5th Cav.	June 25, '64
4075.	Eaton, W. H.	B, 58th Inf.	July 27, '64
4953.	Ecker, J.	I, 39th Inf.	Aug. 17, '64
5076.	Evans, J.	I, 6th Cav.	Aug. 8, '64
7917.	Ells, D.	I. 20th Inf.	Sept. 5, '64
11320.	Elston, F.	B, 9th Inf.	Oct. 22, '64
11429.	Estelle, E. W. sergeant	L, 2d Cav.	Oct. 24, '64
11712.	Eldridge, E.	38th Inf.	Nov. 1, '64
11774.	Earl, D. corporal	B, 2nd Cav.	Nov. 3, '64
12285.	Emmons, W.	D, 5th Inf.	Dec. 14, '64

F

1482.	Frecks, F.	D, 35th Inf.	May 30, '64
1808.	Fitter, B.	I, 66th Inf.	June 10, '64
2143.	Fike, Tobias	D, 30th Inf.	June 18, '64
3014.	Fitzgerald, I.	D, 30th Inf.	July 7, '64

Appendix.

No. of Grave.	Name.	Co. Regt.	Date of Death.
3458.	Fescher, D.	E, 32nd Inf.	July 17, '64
3637.	Fuget, W	C, 3rd Cav.	July 20, '64
8379.	Fields, N.	F, 6th Cav.	Sept. 10, '64
8547.	Fenton, I	D, 72nd Inf.	Sept. 12, '64
8766.	Farward, S.	I, 8th Cav.	Sept. 14, '64
9847.	Forshua, W.	H, 25th Inf.	Sept. 27, '64
10509.	Farmingham, W. C.	K, 14th Cav.	Oct. 8, '64
11311.	Fanier, F	I, 6th Cav.	Oct. 22, '64
11526.	Fish, C	H, 2nd Cav.	Oct. 26, '64
12012.	Falkerson, J. sergeant	B, 93rd Inf.	Nov. 14, '64
12144.	Francis, F. musician	93rd Inf.	Nov. 24, '64
12320.	Frass, John, sergeant.	D, 6th Cav.	Dec. 24, '64
12728.	Felnick, H.	F, 10th Inf.	March 4, '65

G

No. of Grave.	Name.	Co. Regt.	Date of Death.
98.	Graham, Wm	G, 6th Inf.	March 22, '64
322.	Gladman, H.	B, 110th Inf.	April 2, '64
1048.	Goodwin, Wm.	M, 2nd Cav.	May 12, '64
1165.	Grimes, F. O.	I, 66th Inf.	May 17, '64
1215.	Garver, John	F, 29th Inf.	May 19, '64
1312.	Gullsen, Wm	L, 7th Cav.	May 23, '64
1594.	Griffin, William.	I, 6th Cav.	June 3, '64
2337.	Gray, D. L.	I, 22nd Inf.	June 22, '64
2386.	Guthrie, W. B.	C, 80th Inf.	June 24, '64
2418.	Gillard, Wm.	C, 120th Inf.	June 24, '64
3573.	Gibbon, W. T.	I, 128th Inf.	July 19, '64
4179.	Gould, Wm	E, 66th Inf.	July 28, '64
4273.	Gilbert, H. A. sergeant.	K, 2nd Cav.	July 29, '64
4847.	Galliger, Wm	B, 7th Inf.	July 31, '64
4901.	Gerard, H.	G, 35th Inf.	Aug. 6, '64
6189.	Goodwin, I	F, 20th Inf.	Aug. 19, '64
6398.	Gordon, W. M.	G, 74th Inf.	Aug. 21, '64
6493.	Goodridge, E. corporal.	H, 91st Inf.	Aug. 22, '64
7298.	Grass, C.	H, 32nd Inf.	Aug. 30, '64
7321.	Gray, H. F.	H, 2nd Cav.	Aug. 30, '64
7608.	Gerber, I.	C, 30th Inf.	Sept. 3, '64

Appendix. IX

No. of Grave.	Name.	Co.	Regt.	Date of Death.
8546.	Galliger, P.	C,	58th Inf.	Sept. 12, '64
8791.	Gaham, William	K,	35th Inf.	Sept. 14, '64
9112.	Green, S	E,	72d Inf.	Sept. 18, '64
9114.	Gillan, J.	F,	29th Inf.	Sept. 18, '64
10782.	Griswold, Thomas	F,	2d Cav.	Oct. 12, '64
11409.	Gordon, J. W.	D,	13th Inf.	Oct. 24, '64
11581.	Greenwood, W.	C,	3d Cav.	Oct. 28, '64
12216.	Grant, H. G.	G,	5th Cav.	Dec. 3, '64
12398.	Garnet, T.	E,	6th Inf.	Jan. 5, '65
12483.	Green, William	E,	39th Inf.	Jan. 19, '65

H

630.	Hollar, John	I,	5th Cav.	April 19, '64
879.	Herrick, William	F,	80th Inf.	May 4, '64
1953.	Hall, L. S.	C,	117th Inf.	June 14, '64
2118.	Hilliard, J.	D,	116th Inf	June 17, '64
2130.	Hodges, J.	C,	7th Inf.	June 18, '64
2379.	Hustin, James	B,	74th Inf.	June 23, '64
2392.	Hodges, S.	F,	9th Inf.	June 24, '64
2629.	Humphrey, I.	C,	3d Cav.	June 28, '64
2768.	Hendricks, J.	C,	2d Cav.	July 2, '64
2768.	Higgins, M. P.	C	3d Cav.	July 2, '64
2793.	Hodges, W. J.	F,	5th Cav.	July 2, '64
2812.	Hillman, H.	G,	65th Inf.	July 3, '64
2974.	Hamilton, James	K,	7th Cav.	July 7, '64
3289.	Hine, S	A,	68th Inf.	July 14, '64
3507.	Hodgen, J. W.	G,	80th Inf.	July 18, '64
4487.	Hanger, L. S.	A,	65th Inf.	July 1, '64
3362.	Hart, J. R.	H,	83th Inf.	Aug. 11, '64
5678.	Hittle, B.	L,	6th Cav.	Aug. 14, '64
5695.	Helville, N. C.	F,	20th Inf.	Aug. 15, '64
5872.	Heah, Jacob	G,	20th Inf.	Aug. 16, '64
6076.	Hearne, John	F,	5th Cav.	Aug. 18, '64
6198.	Hershton, A.	M,	4th Cav.	Aug. 19, '64
6491.	Hendricks, I.	H,	129th Inf,	Aug. 22, '64
7031.	Hartsock, I.	A,	30th Inf.	Aug 27, '64

Appendix.

No. of Grave.	Name.	Co.	Regt.	Date of Death.
7790.	Hunter, J. M.	F,	42d Inf.	Sept. 4, '64
7837.	Hammond, G. W., sergeant	D,	65th Inf.	Sept. 4, '64
7903.	Halfree, J. A.	A,	32d Inf.	Sept. 5, '64
7971.	Hamilton, P. S.	E,	7th Inf.	Sept. 6, '64
8091.	Hughes, W. H., corporal	D,	81st Inf.	Sept. 7, '64
8347.	Hart, A.	A,	7th Inf.	Sept. 10, '64
8541.	Haff, M.		Battery 4	Sept. 12, '64
8681.	Hunter, H.	F,	42d Inf.	Sept. 13, '64
8778.	Haynes, W.	G,	30th Inf.	Sept. 14, '64
8836.	Higgins, John W.	C,	3d Cav.	Sept. 15, '64
8967.	Holloway, J.	M,	5th Cav.	Sept. 16, '64
9023.	Hubbner, F.	E,	4th Cav.	Sept. 18, '64
9329.	Hurst, R. V., corporal	B,	36th Inf.	Sept. 20, '64
9429.	Higgins, W. E.	H,	53d Inf.	Sept. 21, '64
9911	Haghton, J.	D,	2d Cav.	Sept. 28, '64
9933.	Harrington, O.	I,	30th Inf.	Sept. 28, '64
10123.	Hoffman, J.	C,	80th Inf.	Oct. 1, '64
10293.	Hunsler, W. H., sergeant	E,	38th Inf.	Oct. 4, '64
10522.	Hoagler, N. C	E,	39th Inf.	Oct. 8, '64
10613.	Harris, W. C.	D,	13th Inf.	Oct. 10, '64
10820.	Hector, E.	D,	13th Inf.	Oct. 12, '64
11231.	Haskins, H.	A,	99th Inf.	Oct. 20, '64
11243.	Hasfle, J., musician	F,	1st Cav.	Oct. 21, '64
11790.	Hill, R.	D,	14th Inf.	Nov. 4 '64
12249.	Hamilton, D.	B,	13th Inf.	Dec. 9, '64
12536.	Hall, H. H.	E,	2d Cav.	Jan. 27, '65

I

6414.	Ihn, C.	B,	129th Inf.	Aug. 22, '64
8963.	Igo, T., corporal	E,	4th Cav.	Sept. 16, '64

J

670.	Johnson, Isaac	C,	5th Cav.	April 22, '64
1931.	Jennings, C., corporal	I,	6th Cav.	June 14, '64
2212.	Jackson, John	C,	22d Inf.	June 20, '64
2353.	Jones, William M.	D,	63d Inf.	June 23, '64

Appendix.

No. of Grave.	Name.	Co.	Regt.	Date of Death.
3311.	Jasper, William	I,	38th Inf.	July 10, '64
5245.	Judd, Henry, sergeant	D,	2d Cav.	Aug. 10, '64
6172.	Julerso, H.	D,	2d Cav.	Aug. 19, '64
6311.	Jones, H. C.	C,	5th Cav.	Aug. 20, '64
7100.	Jones, A.	I,	88th Inf.	Aug. 28, '64
9948.	Johnson, J.	A,	7th Cav.	Sept. 28, '64
12517.	Jones J.	C,	120th Inf.	Jan. 24, '65
12799.	Johnson, H.	C,	40th Inf.	March 19, '65

K

417.	Kistner, George	B,	42d Inf.	April 7, '64
618.	Kinnan, A.	G,	56th Inf.	April 18, '64
858.	Ketcham, G. W., sergeant	I,	5th Cav.	May 3, '64
1908.	Kelso, E. O.	C,	3d Cav.	June 13, '64
2036.	Kelley, John, sergeant		5th Cav.	June 15, '64
2407.	Kennedy, Amos	H,	2d Cav.	June 24, '64
2527.	Kanga, J.	E,	74th Inf.	June 26, '64
3047.	Kennedy, J. W. corporal	I,	3d Cav.	July 8, '64
4024.	Keyes, William	E,	72d Inf.	July 26, '64
5149.	Keiler, W. J., sergeant	H,	4th Cav.	Aug. 9, '64
5253.	Kecher, T.	I,	29th Inf.	Aug. 10, '64
5722.	Kern, W.	H,	25th Inf.	Aug. 15, '64
6596.	Kelley, John	C,	32d Inf.	Aug. 23, '64
7085.	Kames, J.	F,	128th Inf.	Aug. 28, '64
8621.	King, D.	A,	81st Inf.	Sept. 13, '64
10689.	Keller, I.	B,	49th Inf.	Oct 11, '64
12278.	Kuling, I.	A,	79th Inf.	Dec. 12, '64
12587.	Keef, P., corporal	C,	10th Cav	Feb. 4, '65

L

1041.	Lewis, J.	H,	6th Inf.	May 12, '64
1239.	Lawrence, R. J.	G,	30th Inf	May 20, '64
1261.	Lower, N. G.	I,	116th Inf	May 21, '64
2615.	**Lewis, James**	F,	65th Inf	June 28, '64
2745.	Luff, C.	I,	58th Inf	July 1, '64
3029.	**Lewis, J.**	C,	3d Cav.	July 7, '64

Appendix.

No. of Grave.	Name.	Co.	Regt.	Date of Death.
3767.	Lannon, J. S.	F,	128th Inf.	July 22, '64
3890.	Lawrence, D.	A,	80th Inf.	July 24, '64
4548.	Lyons, Wm.	A,	35th Inf.	Aug. 2, '64
5014.	Lee, John	C,	3d Cav.	Aug. 8, '64
5585.	Lawson, Wm.	A,	75th Inf.	Aug. 14, '64
5616.	Lawyer, James	B,	80th Inf.	Aug. 14, '64
6775.	Lyons, Wm.	E,	1st Cav.	Aug. 25, '64
7162.	Lowery, D.	G,	2d Cav.	Aug. 29, '64
8607.	Lunger, A.	M,	7th Cav.	Sept. 12, '64
9256.	Liggett	G,	52d Inf.	Sept. 10, '64
10508.	Lewis, R.	C,	7th Cav.	Oct. 8, '64
11152.	Lash, J.	B,	101st Inf.	Oct. 18, '64
11715.	Lakin, A.		7th Cav.	Nov. 1, '64
12250.	Lawrence, B. T.	D,	42d Inf	Dec. 9, '64

M

130.	McCarty, John	D,	66th Inf.	March 23, '64
5.	Moodie, Z.	K,	119th Inf.	March 31, '64
631.	Mullen, James	G,	6th Cav	April 19, '64
746.	Masters, Wm.	C,	65th Inf.	April 26, '64
841.	Milton, John	C,	18th Inf	May 1, '64
903.	Mytinger, Wm.	F,	117th Inf.	May 5, '64
954.	Milburn, J.	K,	6th Inf.	May 8, '64
1090.	Moore, Peter	I,	6th Inf	May 14, '64
1405.	Miller, Jacob	E,	74th Inf	May 27, '64
1516.	Martin, George, sergeant	C,	3d Cav.	May 31, '64
1860.	Merritt, H	G,	30th Inf.	June 12, '64
2240.	Mitchell, J. J	D,	30th Inf.	June 20, '64
2397.	Milliken, S. L	G,	1st Cav.	June 24, '64
2511.	Moneyhon, P.	D,	38th Inf.	June 26, '64
2608.	Marsh, J	D,	88th Inf.	June 28, '64
3387.	Mank, E.	E,	80th Inf.	July 16, '64
3633.	Marlit, J.	H,	80th Inf.	July 20, '64
3884.	Mulchy. J.	A,	35th Inf.	July 24, '64
4010.	Mercer, John	F,	12th Inf	July 26, '64
4388.	Malsby, F.	A,	14th Cav.	July 31, '64

Appendix.

No. of Grave.	Name.	Co. Regt.	Date of Death.
4959.	McDall, R.	A, 19th Inf	Aug. 7, '64
5562.	Manihan, J.	D, 38th Inf	Aug. 13, '64
5618.	Mageson, J.	A, 7th Cav	Aug. 14, '64
5703.	Mensome, S., sergeant	E, 42d Inf	Aug. 15, '64
5713.	Monroe, S.	F, 33d Inf.	Aug. 15, '64
5767.	Montgomery, R.	F, 80th Inf	Aug. 15, '64
5863.	Michael, S.	I, 7th Cav.	Aug. 16, '64
6461.	Mitchell, J. H.	I, 30th Inf	Aug. 22, '64
6521.	Monroe, H. J. sergeant.	G, 44th Inf.	Aug. 22, '64
6566.	Matthews, M.	K, 42d Inf.	Aug. 23, '64
7043.	Milsker, J.	D, 5th Cav.	Aug. 27, '64
7233.	Matheny, N., sergeant	A, 42d Inf.	Aug. 29, '64
7272.	McQueston, J. O.	B, 13th Inf.	Aug. 30, '64
7510.	Myers, A.	E, 29th Inf.	Sept. 1, '64
7820.	Moore, G. corporal.	F, 101st Inf.	Sept. 4, '64
7973.	Mine, John N.	H, 2d Cav.	Sept. 6, '64
8007.	Miller, W. W.	B, 101st Inf.	Sept. 6, '64
8176.	McCoy, W. sergeant.	B, 66th Inf.	Sept. 8, '64
8389.	Murphy, J.	E, 9th Inf.	Sept. 10, '64
8651.	McElvain, J.	E, 93d Inf.	Sept. 15, '64
8925.	Myers, J.	D, 143d Inf.	Sept. 16, '64
9575.	Morrison, J.	B, 4th Cav.	Sept. 23, '64
9600.	Miller, J.	G, 7th Cav.	Sept. 23, '64
9856.	Murgu, A.	D, 35th Inf.	Sept. 27, '64
10231.	Monay, G. W.	E, 7th Inf.	Oct. 2, '64
10245.	McFarney, J.	B, 93d Inf.	Oct. 3, '64
10394.	Maples, H.	H, 29th Inf.	Oct. 6, '64
10891.	Murphy, F.	B, 35th Inf.	Oct. 13, '64
10995.	McDonald, I.	B, 74th Inf.	Oct. 16, '64
11166.	Mills, Milton	D, 26th Inf.	Oct. 18, '64
11271.	Mitchell, I.	K, 7th Inf.	Oct. 21, '64
11585.	McCarty, A.	A, 7th Inf.	Oct. 28, '64
11665.	McBeth, I. C.	K, 28th Inf.	Oct. 30, '64
11680.	Murphy, F.	C, 35th Inf.	Oct. 31, '64
11746.	McCarty, A.	A, 7th Inf.	Nov. 2, '64
11857.	McCarty, I.	A, 6th Inf.	Nov. 6, '64

Appendix.

No. of Grave.	Name.	Co.	Regt.	Date of Death.
11946.	Miller, F. B.	C,	30th Inf.	Nov. 10, '64
12548.	Madlener, L.	K,	12th Inf.	Jan. 27, '65
12563.	McFall, I.	A,	30th Inf.	Jan. 31, '65
12624.	Manifold, W.	I,	6th Cav.	Feb. 9, '65
12639.	Montgomery, W.	G,	5th Cav.	Feb. 17, '65
12769.	Maloy, I.	G,	5th Cav.	Feb. 28, '65

N

No. of Grave.	Name.	Co.	Regt.	Date of Death.
2007.	Noosman, G.	G,	117th Inf.	June 15, '64
3205.	Newcomb, George	A,	22d Inf	July 12, '64
3519.	Nucha, S.	I,	3d Cav.	July 18, '64
4627.	Napper, W. H., sergeant	I,	6th Inf.	Aug. 3, '64
6528.	Norton, N. A.	B,	38th Inf.	Aug. 23, '64
10187.	Note, John H.	F,	39th Inf.	Oct. 1, '64
12226.	Nichols, J.	G,	38th Inf	Dec. 5, '64
9494.	Newberry, M.	L,	7th Cav.	Sept. 21, '64

O

No. of Grave.	Name.	Co.	Regt.	Date of Death.
342.	O'Neil, Thomas	G,	6th Inf.	April 2, '64
1874.	Oliver, John, corporal		42d Inf	June 12, '64
2778.	Oliver, H. H.	M,	5th Cav.	July 2, '64
5226.	Oliver, J.	K,	120th Inf.	Aug. 10, '64
5361.	Osborn, J.	E,	73d Inf.	Aug. 11, '64
7863.	Oliver, J.	D,	19th Inf.	Sept. 5, '64
7911.	O'Connor, Thomas	B,	5th Cav.	Sept. 5, '64
10940.	Olinger, E.	A,	65th Inf.	Oct. 14, '64
12544.	Ortell, M.	G,	35th Inf.	Jan. 27, '65
12590.	Ousley, W. J.	A,	7th Inf.	Feb. 5, '65

P

No. of Grave.	Name.	Co.	Regt.	Date of Death.
287.	Peache, Cyrus	D,	66th Inf.	April 1, '64
559.	Pashby, John	C,	6th Cav.	April 15, '64
1249.	Packer, Samuel B.	G,	6th Cav.	May 20, '64
3434.	Pavy, W.	A,	123d Inf.	July 17, '64
3738.	Palmer, A.	F,	42d Inf.	July 21, '64
4068.	Parker, E. sergeant	A,	29th Inf.	July 27, '64

Appendix. XV

No. of Grave.		Co. Regt.	Date of Death.
4171.	Park, John	B, 129th Inf.	July 28, '64
4551.	Pettis, H.	C, 53d Inf.	Aug. 2, '64
4553.	Pruitt, H. C.	K, 7th Cav.	Aug. 2, '64
5627.	Prentice, J. M.	K, 22d Inf.	Aug. 15, '64
6159.	Penab, Alexander	B, 38th Inf.	Aug. 19, '64
6278.	Patterson, E.	G, 4th Cav.	Aug. 20, '64
6874.	Parten, D. R.	F, 65th Inf.	Aug. 26, '64
7710.	Plough, J. W. sergeant	D, 89th Inf.	Sept. 3, '64
8661.	Pratt, Wm.	F, 29th Inf.	Sept. 13, '64
9196.	Plumer, A.	D, 2d Cav.	Sept. 18, '64
9705.	Pope, I. T. sergeant	G, 5th Cav.	Sept. 24, '64
9709.	Patterson, N. S.	G, 93d Inf.	Sept. 24, '64
10128.	Packett, T. C. sergeant	F, 39th Inf.	Oct. 1, '64
11880.	Pangburn, sergeant	B, 20th Inf.	Nov. 6, '64
12572.	Potts, I.	H, 99th Inf.	Feb. 2, '65
12588.	Phepps, A.	D, 30th Inf.	Feb. 2, '65

R.

872.	Remy, John	B, 66th Inf.	May 4, '64
944.	Reed, R.	F, 57th Inf.	May 7, '64
1065.	Remcett, L.	H, 65th Inf.	May 13, '64
1440.	Ryan, Martin	B, 35th Inf.	May 28, '64
1558.	Roll, N. C.	F, 117th Inf.	June 2, '64
1696.	Reese, L.	I, 116th Inf.	June 7, '64
2140.	Robinson, L.	I, 7th Inf.	June 18, '64
4039.	Rogman	I, 38th Inf.	July 26, '64
4165.	Reiggs, K. N.	K, 39th Inf.	July 28, '64
4406.	Richardson, I.	I, 35th Inf.	July 31, '64
5180.	Rowlings, J. W.	F, 117th Inf.	Aug. 9, '64
5259.	Rains, G. D.	G, 4th Cav.	Aug. 10, '64
5454.	Ritter, Benjamin	K, 29th Inf.	Aug. 12, '64
5542.	Ralph, G.	F, 68th Inf.	Aug. 13, '64
6247.	Roundbush, Daniel	B, 6th Inf.	Aug. 20, '64
6383.	Redyard, A.	F, 65th Inf.	Aug. 21, '64
6707.	Rawlings, E., sergeant	C, 66th Inf.	Aug. 21, '64
9547.	Riggs, L.	E, 19th Inf.	Aug. 23, '64

No. of Grave.	Name.	Co.	Regt.	Date of Death.
6754.	Russell, J.	K,	7th Inf.	Aug. 24, '64
7677.	Ringold, I.	I,	7th Cav.	Sept. 3, '64
8488.	Russmore, E.	C,	2d Cav.	Sept. 11, '64
8577.	Redman, N. E.	F,	80th Inf.	Sept. 12, '64
9521.	Richardson, John	D,	86th Inf.	Sept. 21, '64
10829.	Reeves, William	F,	42d Inf.	Oct. 13, '64
11416.	Rierdon, M. D.	Bat.	5th Cav.	Oct. 24, '64
11451.	Rutger, W., corporal	D,	44th Inf.	Oct. 25, '64
11935.	Russell, W. H.	C,	13th, Inf.	Nov. 9, '64
12454.	Robinson, R.	G,	8th Inf.	Jan. 14, '65
12523.	Richardson, E.	E,	127th Inf.	Jan. 26, '65

S

No. of Grave.	Name.	Co.	Regt.	Date of Death.
86.	Smiley ——	I,	65th Inf.	March 21, '64
129.	Stein, Thomas	D,	66th Inf.	March 23, '64
205.	Stouts, ——	I,	65th Inf.	March 28, '64
768.	Sanderson, H.	G,	6th Cav.	April 27, '64
817.	Sears, I.	I,	65th Inf.	April 30, '64
901.	Shick, Eli	C,	20th Inf.	May 5, '64
1039.	Smith, M. C., corporal	Battery 24		May 12, '64
1331.	Smith H.	A,	86th Inf	May 24, '64
2447.	Stafford, J. W.	I,	68th Inf.	May 25, '64
1400.	Sapp, A. J.	H,	44th Inf.	May 26, '64
1430.	Swindle, T. O., sergeant	A,	82d Inf.	May 28, '64
1501.	Smith, L.	A,	116th Inf.	May 31, '64
1611.	Schroder, W.	A,	42d Inf.	June 4, '64
1690.	Sparks, L. D.	D,	66th Inf.	June 7, '64
1732.	Search, C.	D,	5th Cav.	June 8, '64
2079.	Shigley, T. W.	H,	10th Inf.	June 17, '64
2083.	Stinit, D.	L,	6th Cav.	June 17, '64
2218.	Smudley, W.	E,	5th Cav.	June 20, '64
2318.	Swain, J. W.	A,	30th Inf.	June 22, '64
2420.	Snow, J.	G,	5th Cav.	June 24, '64
2625.	Sattershwait, A.	I,	82d Inf	June 28, '64
2740.	Smith, J.	H,	65th Inf.	July 1, '64
2799.	Stanchley, Wm.	K,	5th Cav.	July 2, '64

Appendix. XVII

No. of Grave.	Name.	Co. Regt.	Date of Death.
2923.	Stofer, L sergeant	B, 29th Inf.	July 5, '64
3416.	Spencer, M.	K, 80th Inf.	July 16, '64
4014.	Shields, J.	F, 128th Inf.	July 26, '64
4054.	Smith, J. W.	G, 38th Inf.	July 27, '64
4062.	Smith, H.	H, 79th Inf.	July 27, '64
4088.	Schneider, S. A.	3d Cav.	July 27, '64
4229.	Sollman, C., sergeant	D, 35th Inf.	July 29, '64
4418.	Stevens, M.	M, 6th Cav.	July 31, '64
4630.	Snider, D.	K, 117th Inf	Aug. 3, '64
4799.	Summersvolt, V.	A, 29th Inf.	Aug. 5, '64
5254.	Scott, B.	D, 9th Inf.	Aug. 10, '64
5418.	Smith, Samuel E.	C, 9th Inf.	Aug. 12, '64
5513.	Shoemaker, E. W.	I, 5th Cav.	Aug. 13, '64
5514.	Sims, S.	B, 101st Inf.	Aug. 13, '64
5571.	Sackett, I.	G, 6th Cav.	Aug. 14, '64
5611.	Stockman, L. M.	E, 68th Inf.	Aug. 14, '64
5884.	Standish, M.	B, 66th Inf.	Aug. 16, '64
5977.	Stockhoff, G.	I, 19th Inf.	Aug. 17, '64
6044.	Stout, H.	G, 7th Inf.	Aug. 18, '64
6736.	Sipe, J.	A, 82d Inf.	Aug. 24, '64
6830.	Strong, L.	F, 9th Inf.	Aug. 25, '64
7120.	Spellman, J.	F, 80th Inf.	Aug. 28, '64
7264.	Shaver, F.	I, 129th Inf.	Aug. 30, '64
7683.	Snyder, L.	A, 6th Cav.	Sept. 3, '64
7822.	Sanders, D.	I, 7th Inf.	Sept. 4, '64
8058.	Suthien, J. H.	E, 63d Inf.	Sept. 7, '64
8107.	Starkey, I.	I. 6th Cav.	Sept. 7, '64
8262.	Sizeman, I.	B, 123d Inf.	Sept. 9, '64
8313.	Stagewald, J. M., sergeant	K, 22d Inf.	Sept. 10, '64
8623.	Suillenbarger, F.	I, 21st Inf.	Sept. 13, '64
8666.	Sylvanus, J. J.	G, 35th Inf.	Sept. 13, '64
8727.	Shoel, J. P.	B, 30th Inf.	Sept. 14, '64
8910.	Storm, L. M., sergeant	A 6th Inf	Sept. 16, '64
9093	Simmons, J.	I, 84th Inf.	Sept. 18, '64
9252.	Sharp, D. M.	E, 13th Inf.	Sept. 19, '64
9546.	Sharpless, W.	G, 43d Inf.	Sept. 23, '64

Appendix.

No. of Grave.	Name.	Co.	Regt.	Date of Death.
9623.	Smith, S. B.	F,	17th Inf.	Sept. 24, '64
9807.	Skeets, W.	A,	65th Inf.	Sept. 26, '64
10790.	Smith, George	D,	131st Inf.	Oct. 12, '64
10949.	Smith, I.	I,	39th Inf.	Oct. 14, '64
11006.	Sloat, G. W., sergeant	B,	44th Inf.	Oct. 16, '64
11187.	Seigferd, G. H.	I,	4th Cav.	Oct. 19, '64
11427.	Sweltzer, J.	G,	2d Cav.	Oct. 24, '64
11842.	Shaw, W. R.	B,	99th Inf.	Nov. 5, '64
11969.	Shoe, G. W.	E,	74th Inf.	Nov. 12, '64
11984.	Steamer, F.	F,	29th Inf.	Nov. 13, '64
12113.	Scarff, F.	D.	6th Cav.	Nov. 21, '64
12381.	Starke, M. S.	D,	73d Inf.	Jan. 2, '65
12492.	Saltz, H. C.	F,	4th Cav.	Jan. 20, '65
12582.	Smith, D. H.	H,	12th Cav	Feb. 3, '65
12645.	Sides, G.	A,	66th Inf	Feb. 8, '65
12666.	Smure, C.	G,	2d Cav.	Feb. 17, '65
12724.	Stewart, E. B.	E.	38th Inf	March 3, '65
12809.	Staley, G. W	A,	72d Inf	March 24, '65

T

518.	Tenher, James	I,	117th Inf	April 13, '64
3778.	Tunblora, B.	B,	65th Inf	July 22, '64
3791.	Thompson, J.	C,	6th Cav	July 22, '64
4733.	Tooley, G. W	H,	42d Inf	Aug. 4, '64
5065.	Truman, L. H., sergeant	G,	6th Cav	Aug. 8, '64
5403.	Taylor, N	I,	63d Inf	Aug. 12, '64
6509.	Tooley, W. R., corporal,	H,	42d Inf	Aug. 22, '64
6719.	Todd, T.	B,	6th Inf	Aug. 24, '64
7096.	Thomas, H. D.	I,	42d Inf	Aug. 28, '64
7442.	Taylor, George H	M,	4th Cav	Sept. 1, '64
8495.	Trumble, D. A.	A,	30th Inf	Sept. 11, '64
8525.	Taylor, E	I,	25th Inf	Sept. 12, '64
10219.	Tasnahet, Charles, sergeant	E,	31st Inf	Oct. 2, '64
10438.	Thomas, M		2d Cav	Oct. 6, '64
12337.	Tucer, B., citizen,			Nov. 26, '64
12609.	Terhune, C	A,	9th Cav	Feb. 7, '65

Appendix.

No. of Grave.	Name.	Co.	Regt.	Date of Death.

U

| 10356. | Underwood, F. | C, | 7th Cav. | Sept. 5, '64 |
| 10769. | Upton, F. M. | A, | 52d Inf. | Oct. 12, '64 |

V

1717.	Volt, S.	K,	6th Cav.	June 8, '64
5363.	Venome, James	K,	30th Inf.	Aug. 11, '64
6250.	Vanose, J.	B,	93d Inf.	Aug. 20, '64
7691.	Verhouse, D.	A,	42d Inf.	Sept. 3, '64

W

135.	Windinger, J.	G,	117th Inf.	March 24, '64
886.	Walters, J. H., corporal	G,	6th Cav.	May 5, '64
934.	Williams, A.	G,	6th Inf.	May 7, '64
1194.	Wright, Samuel	I,	6th Cav.	May 18, '64
1776.	White, P.	C,	6th Cav.	June 9, '64
1812.	Wise, Eli	D,	88th Inf.	June 10, '64
1918.	Warren, E.	H,	65th Inf.	June 14, '64
2107.	Williams, F.	F,	38th Inf.	June 17, '64
2242.	West, E.	H,	7th Cav.	June 20, '64
2363.	Woodward, W. W.	A,	29th Inf.	June 23, '64
2417.	Wilson, J. N.	G,	75th Inf.	June 24, '64
2467.	Warden, I.	B,	44th Inf.	June 25, '64
2554.	Warren, E.	I,	37th Inf.	June 27, '64
2670.	Ward, J.	F,	79th Inf.	June 29, '64
2900.	Wyn, W. E.	D,	13th Inf.	July 5, '64
2929.	Wislake, I.	I,	116th Inf.	July 5, '64
2934.	Wicks, L.	H,	6th Cav.	July 6, '64
3837.	Weltz, Ira, sergeant	B,	4th Cav.	July 23, '64
4528.	Whitehead, J.	I,	29th Inf.	Aug. 2, '64
4639.	Winship, James	K,	36th Inf.	Aug. 4, '64
4826.	Witt, T.	D,	125th Inf.	Aug. 5, '64
5399.	Wade, C.	K,	81st Inf.	Aug. 12, '64
5547.	Waynin, J. H.	I,	4th Cav.	Aug. 13, '64
6000.	West, S. N. corporal	B,	7th Inf.	Aug. 17, '64
6132.	Washburn, R. H.	A,	6th Cav.	Aug. 19, '64

Appendix.

No. of Grave.	Name.	Co.	Regt.	Date of Death.
6405.	Winders, A	I,	120th Inf.	Aug. 21, '64
6524.	Wagner, M.	I,	5th Cav.	Aug. 25, '64
7184.	Winters, F. W	C,	84th Inf	Aug. 29, '64
7191.	Wagoner, E.	A,	42d Inf.	Aug. 29, '64
7349.	Witzgall, John	D,	2d Cav.	Aug. 31, '64
8943.	Weibel, Charles	F,	13th Inf.	Sept. 16, '64
9228.	White W	E,	7th Inf.	Sept. 19, '64
9316.	Watkins, J.	A,	81st Inf.	Sept. 20, '64
6418.	Wellington, H.	I,	129th Inf.	Sept. 21, '64
9501.	Wilson, J. B.	E,	6th Inf.	Sept. 21, '64
9020.	Williams, J. A. sergeant	C,	38th Inf	Sept. 28, '64
9908.	Wagner, F.	D,	7th Inf.	Sept. 29, '64
10643.	Ward, J.	G,	29th Inf.	Oct. 11, '64
11141.	Whitehead, N. B.	L,	5th Cav.	Oct. 18, '64
11424.	White R. B	D,	6th Inf.	Oct. 24, '64
11602.	Walters, J.	I,	5th Inf.	Oct. 28, '64
12708.	Winebrook, P	B,	35th Inf	Nov. 18, '64
12316.	Werper, J.	E,	32d Inf.	Dec. 20, '64
12341.	White, J.	A,	7th Inf.	Dec. 26, '64
12402	Wells, J. M	D,	13th Inf.	Jan. 16, '65
12497.	What, J.	B,	93d Inf.	Jan. 21, '65
12737.	Wade, W	M,	10th Cav.	March 6, '65

Y

5055.	Younce, Charles A.	I,	7th Cav.	Aug. 8, '64
5838.	Yorker, Daniel	B,	28th Inf	Aug. 16, '64

Z

1540.	Zuet, J.	H,	65th Inf.	June 1, '64

Appendix.

OHIO.

A

No. of Grave.	Name.	Co.	Regt.	Date of Death.
251.	Arthur, George	B,	7th Inf.	March 30, '64
789.	Arrousmith, W. R.	K,	45th Inf.	April 28, '64
1118.	Ames, George	K,	100th Inf.	May 14, '64
1550.	Allen, W.	B,	45th Inf.	June 1, '64
1569.	Allinger, D.	C,	51st Inf.	June 2, '64
1724.	Anderson, D.	B,	111th Inf.	June 8, '64
1779.	Augustus, T.	K,	89th Inf.	June 9, '64
1805.	Akers, A. A.	F,	94th Inf.	June 10, '64
2040.	Aldridge, C. W.		33d Inf.	June 15, '64
2935.	Adam, Miller	I,	103d Inf.	July 5, '64
3046.	Anderson, R.	C,	93d Inf.	July 8, '64
3197.	Aldbrook, C. W.		60th Inf.	July 12, '64
3485.	Arthur, I. C.	A,	89th Inf.	July 17, '64
3852.	Armbrish, A.	A,	21st Inf.	July 24, '64
3932.	Almond, A.	A,	72d Inf.	July 25, '64
4529.	Arnold, Charles	G,	9th Cav.	Aug. 2, '64
4990.	Ailes, G. T.	I,	20th Inf.	Aug. 7, '64
5048.	Andrews, Samuel G.		———	Aug. 8, '64
6422.	Adams, E.	C,	2d Cav.	Aug. 22, '64
7429.	Allen, A. B.	C,	121st Inf.	Aug. 31, '64
7482.	Alward, A.	B,	135th Inf	Sept. 1, '64
7436.	Arthur, J.	I,	69th Inf.	Sept. 3, '64
7843.	Arne, I.	D,	64th Inf.	Sept. 4, '64
9818.	Alown A.	D,	34th Inf.	Sept. 26 '64
10393.	Andrews, I. R.	K,	63d Inf.	Oct. 6, '64
10425.	Adams, I.	I,	122d Inf.	Oct. 6, '64
10874.	Allen, James C.	F,	94th Inf.	Oct. 13, '64
11198.	Andermill, John	K,	24th Inf.	Oct. 20, '64
12495.	Allen, J. W.	G,	1st Inf.	Jan. 20, '65
12846.	Akers, J. W.	B,	4th Inf.	April 24, '65

B

No. of Grave.	Name.	Co.	Regt.	Date of Death.
188.	Baiel, W. T.	F,	45th Inf.	March 27, '64
207.	Bodin, Thomas		44th Inf.	March 28, '64
517.	Blackwood, I. H.	I,	92th Inf.	April 12, '64
791.	Beaver, George E.	B,	111th Inf.	April 23, '64
829.	Beeman, Richard	E,	125th Inf.	May 1, '64
861.	Biddinger, M., musician	K,	94th Inf.	May 3, '65
952.	Branigan, James	F,	82d Inf.	May 8, '64
1094.	Biangy, T.	B,	70th Inf.	May 14, '64
1212.	Botkins, A. S	G,	45th Inf	May 19, '64
1226.	Black, G. W.	F,	99th Inf.	May 20, '64
1366.	Bates, L. B.	A,	1st Cav.	May 25, '64
1368.	Bodkin, W.	K,	45th Inf.	May 25, '64
1376.	Baldwin, N.	F,	9th Cav.	May 26, '64
1385	Bowers, James	A,	89th Inf.	May 26, '64
1468.	Boyd, H. I.	H,	7th Inf.	May 30, '64
1602.	Boman, John	C,	2d Inf.	June 4, '64
1609.	Bryan, R.	C,	16th Inf.	June 4, '64
1781.	Balcomb, D.	F,	19th Inf.	June 9, '64
1919.	Brownles, John	I,	7th Inf.	June 14, '64
1937.	Brooks, J.	I,	135th Inf.	June 14, '64
1970.	Bothin, W. J	F,	45th Inf.	June 15, '64
1993.	Bartholomew, E. W	C,	205th Inf	June 15, '64
2065.	Belding, F.	D,	105th Inf	June 16, '64
2067.	Brookheart, W.	I,	45th Inf	June 16, '64
2087.	Benor, H	E,	100th Inf	June 17, '64
2110.	Bishop, S	K,	49th Inf	June 17, '64
2170.	Berry, J. C	E,	90th Inf.	June 19, '64
2264.	Beers, A	A,	45th Inf	June 20, '64
2292.	Burnham, W	K,	1st Art	June 21, '64
2415.	Bird, I.	A,	45th Inf	June 24, '64
2492.	Bratt, G.	G,	21st Inf.	June 26, '64
2599.	Broughfman, I	C,	39th Inf.	June 28, '64
2696.	Brandon, John	F,	15th Inf.	June 30, '64
3053.	Barnes, V. H	H,	92d Inf	July 9, '64
3245.	Brown, Charles	D,	23d Inf	July 13, '64

Appendix. XXIII

No. of Grave.	Name.	Co.	Regt.	Date of Death.
3299.	Burns, M. G.	B,	111th Inf	July 13, '64
3608.	Brackneck, H	A,	7th Cav	July 19, '64
3656.	Bogart, John	G,	9th Inf	July 20, '64
3706.	Bontrell, C	G,	6th Inf	July 21, '64
3756.	Butch, O	I,	45th Inf	July 22, '64
3831.	Bowman, S	K,	15th Inf	July 23, '64
4073.	Brockway, M	D,	2d Art	July 27, '64
4279.	Boyle, W. H	H,	11th Inf	July 30, '64
4684.	Britton, B. H	H,	125th Inf	Aug. 4, '64
4968.	Berdy, M. J.	D,	45th Inf	Aug. 7, '64
5138.	Buckle, J. J	E,	126th Inf	Aug. 9, '64
5219.	Brabham, George	B,	9th Cav	Aug. 10, '64
5498.	Baldwin, George	G,	9th Cav	Aug. 13, '64
5653.	Bonestine, W. H	I,	107th Inf.	Aug. 14, '64
5656.	Burna, J. M.	K,	121st Inf.	Aug. 14, '64
5758.	Balmet, J.	I,	19th Inf.	Aug. 15, '64
5771.	Brutch, E	I,	10th Cav.	Aug. 15, '64
5819.	Bond, S. T	B,	123d Inf.	Aug. 16, '64
5825.	Boyle, H	B,	130th Inf.	Aug. 16, '64
5937.	Bower, F.	I,	61st Inf.	Aug. 17, '64
5985.	Birch, L. T.	H,	31st Inf.	Aug. 17, '64
6008.	Bowman, A	E,	104th Inf.	Aug. 17, '64
6020.	Bright, N	E,	6th Inf.	July 17, '64
6152.	Brown, G. S.	F,	111th Inf	Aug. 18, '64
6839.	Buren, T. J	A,	89th Inf.	Aug. 25, '64
7280.	Barrett, S. C.	F,	26th Inf.	Aug. 30, '64
7283.	Bell, A.	B,	70th Inf.	Aug. 30, '64
7484.	Baxter, P. D.	D,	121st Inf.	Sept. 1, '64
7490.	Brenning, C.	G,	14th Inf	Sept. 1, '64
7529.	Brown, W.	G,	26th Inf.	Sept. 1, '64
7806.	Bear, E.	A,	33d Inf.	Sept. 4, '64
7983.	Bender, C.	C,	54th Inf.	Sept. 6, '64
7993.	Brown, M.	F,	110th Inf.	Sept. 6, '64
7994.	Barnes, T. S.	B,	31st Inf.	Sept. 6, '64
8363.	Benear, W. A.	F,	135th Inf.	Sept. 10, '64
8376.	Barston, G. H.	F,	135th Inf.	Sept. 10, '64

XXIV   *Appendix.*

No. of Grave.	Name.	Co.	Regt.	Date of Death.
8476.	Brenner, N.	F,	60th Inf.	Sept. 11, '64
8496.	Barnes, A.	G,	36th Inf.	Sept. 11, '64
8508.	Blythe, C.	I,	1st Inf.	Sept. 12, '64
8509.	Brinhomer, J.	C,	65th Inf.	Sept. 12, '64
8676.	Brown, H. H.	A,	41st Inf.	Sept. 13, '64
8693.	Bell, James	B,	135th Inf.	Sept. 14, '64
8872.	Buckley, J. G.	A,	126th Inf.	Sept. 15, '64
8939.	Blessing, C.	F,	9th Inf.	Sept. 16, '64
9287.	Baker, W. C.		94th Inf.	Sept. 19, '64
9446.	Brookover, George	B,	135th Inf.	Sept. 21, '64
9473.	Brace, J. R.	C,	123d Inf.	Sept. 21, '64
9625.	Bradley, A.	A,	101st Inf.	Sept. 24, '64
9679.	Blackman, S.	G,	72d Inf.	Sept. 24, '64
9897.	Birchfield, Eli		14th Inf.	Sept. 27, '64
9949.	Beant, H. T.	D,	34th Inf.	Sept. 28, '64
10120.	Brewer, D. C.	K,	43d Inf.	Oct. 1, '64
10199.	Brown, E. N.	E,	21st Inf.	Oct. 2, '64
10281.	Brum, W. H.	B,	20th Inf.	Oct. 4, '64
10591.	Briggs, F.	G,	17th Inf.	Oct. 16, '64
11072.	Baymher, L. G.	A,	153d Inf.	Oct. 17, '64
11307.	Boles, G.	H,	112th Inf.	Oct. 22, '64
11308.	Bunker, J.	K,	11th Inf.	Oct. 22, '64
11313.	Burns, M.	K,	12th Inf.	Oct. 22, '64
11626.	Bricker, J. J.	H,	126th Inf.	Oct. 28, '64
11920.	Bumgardner, Joel	C,	3d Inf.	Nov. 8, '64
11939.	Barber, B.	D,	10th Cav.	Nov. 9, '64
12296.	Bissel, J.	E,	2d Inf.	Dec. 16, '64
12383.	Beckley, G.	F,	102d Inf.	Jan. 3, '65
12524.	Barnes, E. H.	D,	2d Inf.	Jan. 26, '65
12641.	Bower, A.	F,	37th Inf.	Feb. 12, '65
12772.	Bowens, W.	A,	100th Inf.	March 13, '65

C

5.	Carpenter, W.	D,	92d Inf.	March 4, '64
458.	Copeland, G.	A,	1st Inf.	April 9, '64
561.	Coates, George	I,	7th Cav.	April 15, '64

Appendix.

No. of Grave.	Name.	Co.	Regt.	Date of Death.
563.	Campbell, James	H,	7th Cav.	April 15, '64
723.	Callaway, Wm.	F,	7th Cav.	April 25, '64
763.	Coleman, G.	A,	101st Inf.	April 27, '64
911.	Chapman, G.	A,	75th Inf.	May 1, '64
928.	Crosser, M.	B,	111th Inf.	May 7, '64
965.	Corby, W. C.	B,	111th Inf.	May 8, '64
1269.	Cruat, Wm.	C,	82d Inf.	May 21, '64
1291.	Collins, Thomas	G,	21st Inf.	May 22, '64
1521.	Capeheart, H.	I,	7th Inf.	May 31, '64
1587.	Clark, H. S.	E,	62d Inf.	June 3, '64
1631.	Conklin, Wm.	B,	121st Inf.	June 5, '64
1679.	Clark, D. V.	B,	111th Inf.	June 6, '64
1900.	Childers, Wm.	B,	89th Inf.	June 13, '64
1945.	Crocker, George	A,	1st Art.	June 14, '64
1992.	Christy, W.	K,	89th Inf.	June 15, '64
2017.	Curtis, N.	D,	45th Inf.	June 15, '64
2025.	Careahan, G. M.	F,	65th Inf.	June 15, '64
2101.	Caldwell, J.	D,	15th Inf.	June 17, '64
2162.	Cornelius, L. C.	C,	89th Inf.	June 19, '64
2207.	Cochrane, James	G,	22d Inf.	June 25, '64
2468.	Church, E.	G,	2d Inf.	June 25, '64
2578.	Combston, J.	I,	7th Cav.	June 27, '64
2983.	Cameron, H.	C,	69th Inf.	July 6, '64
3002.	Callahan, H.	B,	34th Inf.	July 7, '64
3241.	Caynee, George M.	D,	89th Inf.	July 13, '64
3307.	Canard, J. Q. A.	G,	14th Inf.	July 13, '64
3356.	Cruer, J. W.	B,	60th Inf.	July 15, '64
3541.	Cole. B.	A,	82d Inf.	July 18, '64
3578.	Collins, T.	I,	15th Inf.	July 19, '64
3604.	Cook, L. B.	C,	2d Cav.	July 19, '64
3617.	Clark, J. C.	H,	31st Inf.	July 20, '64
3774.	Clayton, D. J.	D,	9th Cav	July 22, '64
3937.	Cover, L.	B,	49th Inf.	July 25, '64
4128.	Clayton, J.	G,	89th Inf.	July 28, '64
4342.	Conway, J.	A,	103d Inf.	July 30, '64
4493.	Cordray, J. J.	G,	89th Inf.	Aug. 1, '64

XXVI   *Appendix.*

No. of Grave.	Name.	Co.	Regt.	Date of Death.
4865.	Cahili, J. N.	C,	90th Inf.	Aug. 6, '64
5105.	Charles, F.	A,	10th Inf.	Aug. 9, '64
5451.	Collyer, J.	G,	11th Inf.	Aug. 12, '64
5548.	Chandler, M.	E,	124th Inf.	Aug. 13, '64
5922.	Clark, James	I,	89th Inf.	Aug. 17, '64
6022.	Cline, K.	B,	111th Inf.	Aug. 17, '64
6108.	Church, George E.	C,	14th Inf.	Aug. 18, 64
6188.	Chambers, R. S.	A,	89th Inf.	Aug. 19, '64
6258.	Copir, S. A.	C,	33d Inf.	Aug. 20, '64
6281.	Conklin, J. R.	I,	45th Inf.	Aug. 20, '64
6562.	Craig, D.	D,	2d Inf.	Aug. 23, '64
7483.	Caswell, G.	C,	21st Inf.	Sept. 1, '64
7486.	Coons, David	C,	57th Inf.	Sept. 1. '64
7495.	Crooks, J. M.	K,	92d Inf.	Sept. 1, '64
7695.	Chard, C. W.	H,	2d Inf.	Sept. 3, '64
7800.	Cregg, I.	K,	49th Inf.	Sept. 4, '64
7835.	Cline, M.	E,	2d Inf.	Sept. 4, '64
7919.	Clark, George	D,	60th Inf.	Sept. 5, '64
7998.	Cloker, J. W. S., major		40th Inf.	Sept. 6, '64
8130.	Cummins, W. S.	I,	35th Inf.	Sept. 8, '64
8454.	Cattlehock, T.	A,	35th Inf.	Sept. 14, '64
8457.	Campbell, W. C.	1,	5th Inf.	Sept. 11, '64
8694.	Chapin, James	F,	135th Inf.	Sept. 14, '64
8701.	Crooke. W. B.	B,	135th Inf.	Sept. 14, '64
8810.	Clarke, J. R.	F,	135th Inf.	Sept. 15, '64
9243.	Constein, W.	C,	98th Inf.	Sept. 19, '64
9288.	Cambrlet, A. J.	H,	123d Inf.	Sept. 19, '64
9452.	Campbell, Samuel	G,	74th Inf.	Sept. 21, '64
9476.	Cadwell, A. T.	F,	3d Inf	Sept. 21, '64
9491.	Clay, O.	D,	122d Inf.	Sept. 21, '64
9662.	Oort, W.	D,	11th Inf.	Sept. 24, '64
9770.	Cummings, A.	E,	6th Cav.	Sept 25, '64
9772.	Clark, S.	H,	24th Inf.	Sept. 26, '64
9895.	Conner, J. B.	G	9th Cav.	Sept. 27, '64
9971.	Castable, I.	A,	51st Inf.	Sept. 28, '64
10381.	Cotes, Rufus		2d Cav.	Oct. 5, '64

Appendix. XXVII

No. of Grave.	Name.	Co. Regt.	Date of Death.
10796.	Colts, R. E.	C, 2d Inf.	Oct. 12, '64
10834.	Cepp, J.	I, 14th Inf.	Oct. 13, '64
10968.	Carey, A.	E 21st Inf.	Oct. 16, '64
11103.	Carter, J. B.	I, 89th Inf	Oct 18, '64
11224	Craven, A. J.	C, 15th Inf.	Oct. 20, '64
11262.	Cromwell, W. H.	H, 59th Inf.	Oct. 21, '64
11403.	Cutsdagner, W. J.	D, 95th Inf.	Oct. 24, '64
11540.	Crominberger, I. C.	I, 23d Inf.	Oct. 27, '64
11567.	Cantright, L.	F, 57th Inf.	Oct. 27, '64
11587.	Chapin, J. A.	F, 185th Inf.	Oct. 28, '64
11618.	Clark, H M.	A. 21st Inf.	Oct. 28, '64
11641.	Clingan, A. P.	K, 26th Inf.	Oct 30, '64
11766.	Cohyen, J. H.	K, 6th Inf.	Nov. 3, '64
12082.	Cahill, William	A, 51st Inf.	Nov. 18, '64
12385.	Calvington, R.	C, 72d Inf.	Jan. 3, '65
12435.	Chambers, J. C.	C, 15th Inf.	Jan. 11, '65
12691.	Crampton, A.	C, 79th Inf.	Feb. 22, '65
12798.	Conover, S.	B, 175th Inf.	March 19, '65

D

690.	Davis, William E.	H, 7th Inf.	April 23, '64
930.	Downing, George	C, 45th Inf.	May 7, '64
981.	Dumar, R.	D, 45th Inf	May 9, '64
1267.	Dugan, Thomas	B, 1st Cav.	May 21, '64
1629.	DeRush, Samuel	F, 94th Inf	June 5, '64
1748.	Davis, I.	F, 7th Inf.	June 5, '64
2251.	Decker, B. F.	B, 111th Inf.	June 21, '64
2296.	Dumas, J. P.	H, 2d Inf.	June 21, '64
2351.	Douglas, W.	F, 24th Inf.	June 23, '64
2674.	Davis, B.	B, 22d Inf.	June 30, '64
2909.	Davis, G. H.	E, 45th Inf.	July 5, '65
2973.	Dandelion, T.	Ind. 3d Cav.	July 7, '64
3703.	Dodson, L.	H, 7th Cav.	July 21, '64
3802.	Dille, Charles	I, 23d Inf.	July 22, '64
4455.	Dodge, ——.	I, 2d Inf.	Aug. 1, '64
4501.	Diecy, C.	C, 26th Inf.	Aug. 2, '64

Appendix.

No. of Grave.	Name.	Co.	Regt.	Date of Death.
4772.	Denton, John	E,	7th Cav	Aug. 5, '64
5020.	Desselbem, M	I,	1st Inf	Aug. 8, '64
5268.	Dorson, L.	I,	12th Inf	Aug. 10, '64
5299.	Doty, E. E.	H,	41st Inf	Aug. 11, '64
5368.	Dyke, F.	K,	5th Cav	Aug. 11, '64
5465.	Donley, James	F,	1st Cav.	Aug. 13, '64
5620.	Davis, W. H.	D,	33d Inf.	Aug. 14, '64
6043.	Decker, J	B,	111th Inf	Aug. 18, '64
6223.	Duvant, B.	D,	95th Inf	Aug. 20, '64
6312.	Downer, A. P	B,	52d Inf.	Aug. 20, '64
6708.	Dougherty, W. H	H,	15th Inf.	Aug. 24, '64
7229.	Dildine, J	K,	33d Inf.	Aug. 29, '64
7376.	Deming, W	B,	111th Inf.	Aug. 31, '64
7419.	Daley, S	D,	33d Inf.	Aug. 31, '64
7427.	Dick, Charles	G,	53d Inf.	Aug. 31, '64
7431.	Davis, G. W.	G,	21st Inf	Aug. 31, '64
7479.	Drake, M	D,	59th Inf	Sept. 1, '64
7500.	Doran, James	A,	60th Inf	Sept. 1, '64
7609.	Ditto, John	A,	51st Inf	Sept. 2, '64
7631.	DeMastoris, J	B,	54th Inf	Sept. 2, '64
8034.	Davison, P. S	K,	21st Inf	Sept. 6, '64
8483.	Donley, M.	G,	59th Inf.	Sept. 11, '64
8498.	Drake, J. F	C,	185th Inf.	Sept. 11, '64
8779.	Diver, J.		4th Inf.	Sept. 14, '64
8820.	Davere, J	D,	49th Inf.	Sept. 15, '64
9293.	Diver, J.	H,	123d Inf.	Sept. 19, '64
9605.	Decker, S	C,	12th Inf	Sept. 23, '64
9702.	Dobson, J. R.	H,	90th Inf.	Sept. 25, '64
9849.	Duffy, G.	C,	45th Inf	Sept. 27, '64
10212.	Dunbar, J.	F,	122d Inf.	Oct. 1, '64
10113.	Divan, J.	F,	135th Inf	Oct. 1, '64
10130.	Duncan, A.	K,	49th Inf.	Oct. 1, '64
10190.	Dunhand, Jas	H,	8th Cav.	Oct. 1, '64
10424.	Dewitt, Joseph.	G,	65th Inf.	Oct. 6, '64
10596.	Dibble, F.	H,	101st Inf	Oct. 10, '64
11017.	Diper, O.	I,	128th Inf	Oct. 16, '64

Appendix. XXIX

No. of Grave.	Name.	Co.	Regt.	Date of Death.
11102.	Danton, W. H.	E,	105th Inf.	Oct. 18, '64
12159.	Donahue, P.	K,	72d Inf.	Oct. 25, '64
12254.	Drith, C.	K,	83d Inf.	Dec. 4, '64
12675.	Dunken, T.	K,	20th Inf.	Feb. 19, '65
12738.	Deputy, W.	H,	21st Inf.	Feb. 6, '65

E

327.	Elijah, Baker	B, 45th Inf.	April 2, '64
341.	Evalt, E. J.	M, 10th Inf.	April 12, '64
1047.	Eppart, Samuel	B, 9th Inf.	May 12, '64
2221.	Earles, Wm.	G, 4th Cav.	June 20, '64
3376.	Ellis, Charles	B, 29th Inf.	July 16, '64
4504.	Elliott, W.	F, 20th Inf.	Aug. 1, '64
5304.	Evans, Samuel	C, 33d Inf.	Aug. 11, '64
5349.	Eastman, J.	C, 18th Inf.	Aug. 11, '64
5717.	Evans, Charles	D, 1st Art.	Aug. 15, '64
5887.	Ensley, William	F, 135th Inf.	Aug. 16, '64
6015.	Eckhart, J.	B, 2d Inf.	Aug. 17, '64
7448.	Elmann, A.	F, 28th Inf.	Sept. 1, '64
8981.	Entulin, B. C.	K, 104th Inf.	Sept. 17, '64
11051.	Evans, W.	I, 51st Inf.	Oct. 17, '64
11169.	Evans, E. M.	I, 20th Inf.	Oct. 19, '64
11542.	Elha, D.	A, 8th Inf.	Oct. 25, '64
11654.	Ewing, D.	D, 135th Inf.	Oct. 30, '64
12321.	Ellerman, N.	K, 39th Inf.	Dec. 22, '64

F

75.	Falman, A.	H, 82d Inf.	March 20, '64
176.	Fairbanks, Alf.	A, 45th Inf.	March 26, '64
246.	Ferris, Joseph	H, 2d Cav.	March 30, '64
311.	Foster, A. M.	A, 100th Inf.	April 2, '64
572.	Frayer, Daniel	I, 99th Inf.	April 5, '64
636.	Facer, William	K, 111th Inf.	April 20, '64
830.	Fisher, Charles	C, 3d Cav.	May 1, '64
1054.	Free, M.	Bat. 22d	May 13, '64
1381.	Freenough, George	3d Cav.	May 26, '64

Appendix.

No. of Grave.	Name.	Co.	Regt.	Date of Death.
1786.	Fraiser, James	E,	2d Inf.	June 10, '64
2457.	Fry, W. L.	H,	123d Inf.	June 25, '64
2479.	Fenton, J. M.	I,	35th Inf.	June 25, '64
2761.	Finlan, James	K,	18th Inf.	July 2, '64
4231.	Fry, Jacob	I,	99th Inf.	July 29, '64
4317.	Fitch, E. P.	G,	40th Inf.	July 30, '64
4337.	Fulkinson, H.	E,	2d Inf.	July 30, '64
4651.	Fife, J.	E,	33d Inf.	Aug. 3, '64
4868.	Fling, T. I.	A,	27th Inf.	Aug. 6, '64
5249.	Ferce, R. S.	C,	2d Inf.	Aug. 10, '64
5626.	Falk, W.	D,	82d Inf.	Aug. 14, '64
5864.	Fullerston, W.	K,	18th Inf.	Aug. 16, '64
6212.	Foreman, A.	E,	64th Inf.	Aug. 19, '64
6308.	Fisher, D.	I,	89th Inf.	Aug. 20, '64
6891.	Futen, John H.	F,	82d Inf.	Aug. 26, '64
7873.	Franks, R. L.	E	122d Inf.	Sept. 5, '64
7976.	Forney, W. O.	D,	123d Inf.	Sept. 6, '64
9158.	Firman, V.		Cav.	Sept. 18, '64
9225.	Ferguson, H.	D,	3d Cav.	Sept. 19, '64
9530.	Fowler, C.	A,	100th Inf.	Sept. 22, '64
9557.	Finch, C.	B,	——	Sept. 23, '64
9976.	Franklinberg, C.	G,	72d Inf.	Sept. 28, '64
10045.	Farshay, A.	F,	116th Inf.	Sept. 29, '64
10915.	Freeley, P.	G,	10th Inf.	Sept. 14, '64
11819.	Flowers, W. T.	D,	116th Inf.	Nov. 5, '64
11914.	Forrest, Wm.	K,	21st Inf.	Nov. 8, '64
12108.	Fargrove, M. B.	F,	135th Inf.	Nov. 21, '64
12427.	Fike, W. P.	H,	95th Inf.	Jan. 9, '65
12637.	Fusselman, J.	H,	20th Inf.	Feb. 11, '65
12781.	Foults, M.	D,	183d Inf.	March 15, '65

G

197.	Grilling, Daniel	A,	13th Inf.	March 27, '64
245.	Gardner, A.	H,	100th Inf.	March 30, '64
386.	Grestcaust, S.	G,	6th Cav.	April 2, '64
611.	Gillinghar, B.	I,	7th Cav.	April 18, '64

Appendix. XXXI

No. of Grave.	Name.	Co. Regt.	Date of Death.
681.	Godfrey, Amos	C, 45th Inf.	April 23, '64
693.	Greek, Samuel	C, 100th Inf.	April 23, '64
906.	Gibson, Collins	H, 40th Inf.	May 5, '64
1465.	Greer, R. J.	C, 6th Cav.	May 29, '64
2152.	Gillanni, J.	K, 35th Inf.	June 27, '64
2926.	Garner, C.	K, 1st Cav.	July 5, '64
3130.	Goff, P. E.	K, 19th Inf.	July 10, '64
3251.	Gaunt, Wm.	I, 14th Inf.	July 13, '64
3327.	Gibson, R.	B, 40th Inf.	July 15, '64
3962.	Ginging, P. S.	E, 21st Inf.	July 25, '64
4037.	Gillett, G. W.	G, 6th Inf.	July 26 '64
4242.	Gilbert, J.	B, 19th Inf.	July 29, '64
4301.	Grafton, D.	D, 118th Inf.	July 30, '64
4383.	Graham, J. W.	C, 31st Inf.	July 31, '64
4445.	Goffy, P.	G, 113th Inf.	Aug. 1, '64
4655.	Gragrer, H.	H, 125th Inf.	Aug. 3, '64
4802.	Greer, G. G.	D, 49th Inf.	Aug. 5, '64
4902.	Granbaugh, F.	E, 85th Inf.	Aug. 6, '64
6023.	Gordon, Wm.	B, 45th Inf.	Aug. 17, '64
675.	Gallager, James	F, 38th Inf.	Aug. 13, '64
6207.	Green, E.	D 4th Cav.	Aug. 19, '64
6346.	Gordon, W.	G, 10th Inf.	Aug. 21, '64
6408.	Greff, A. G.	E, 13th Inf.	Aug. 22, '64
6486.	Gates, H.	G, 13th Inf.	Aug. 22, '64
6821.	Grooves, L.	C, 12th Inf.	Aug. 25, '64
7111.	Gilland A.	F, 27th Inf.	Aug. 28, '64
8380.	Goodrich, J. S.	A, 9th Inf.	Sept. 10, '64
8367.	Ganold, L.	A, 60th Inf.	Sept. 10, '64
9566.	Gould, J. M	A, 124th Inf.	Sept 23, '64
9813.	Graft, P.	20th Bat.	Sept. 26, '64
9927.	Galbraith, J. S.	H, 6th Cav.	Sept. 28, '64
11218.	Gaither, I.	B, 60th Inf.	Oct. 20, '64
11850.	Gardner, G.	K, 1st Inf.	Nov. 1, '64
12033.	Glissin, A.	M, 2d Cav.	Nov. 15, '64
12064.	Gillenbuck, I.	B, 77th Inf.	Nov. 17, '64
12109.	Goodbrath, C.	G, 28th Inf.	Nov. 21, '64

XXXII   *Appendix.*

No. of Grave.	Name.	Co. Regt.	Date of Death.
12560.	Griffith, J. H.	C, 58th Inf.	Jan. 31, '65
12842.	Gassler, P.	A, 64th Inf.	April 22, '65

H

No. of Grave.	Name.	Co. Regt.	Date of Death.
35.	Hall, J. W.	A, 4th Inf.	March 9, '64
295.	Hochenburg, N.	C, 45th Inf.	April 1, '64
420.	Hanny, W. T.	A, 45th Inf.	April 7, '64
424.	Hill, J.	I, 7th Cav.	April 7, '64
437.	Henry, James	I, 7th Cav.	April 8, '64
464.	Haner, Jacob	B, 45th Inf.	April 9, '64
527.	Hickcox, M. R.	B, 2d Cav.	April 13, '64
580.	Holdman, F.	D, Bat 1	April 16, '64
748.	Hanning, Mark	I, 7th Cav.	April 20, '64
31.	Heaton, Amos	F, 45th Inf.	April 20, '64
758.	Harvey, Charles	E, 76th Inf.	April 26, '64
875.	Henry, G. W.	E, 95th Inf.	May 4, '64
949.	Hawkins, W. W.	G, 103d Inf.	May 3, '64
1129.	Hudsonpilfer, R. L.	I, 7th Cav.	May 15, '64
1129.	Hudson, R. L.	I, 7th Cav.	May 15, '64
1132.	Hank, George B.	I, 7th Inf.	May 16, '64
1354.	Hind, George	H, 103d Inf.	May 25, '64
1390.	Holloway, G. W.	C, 1st Inf.	May 28, '64
1524.	Harrison, J.	I, 21st Inf.	May 31, '64
1666.	Hazlett, William	K, 2d Inf.	June 6, '64
1822.	Hull, S.	E, 21st Inf.	June 10, '64
1979.	Harris, E. D.	I, 99th Inf.	June 15, '64
2029.	Hengle, John	C, 1st Cav.	June 15, '64
2185.	Humphreys, W.	C, 45th Inf.	June 19, '64
2263.	Hanley, C.	F, 15th Inf.	June 20, '64
2300.	Henderson, S. W.	H, 40th Inf	June 22, '64
2369.	Howard, J., musician	D, 70th Inf.	June 23, '64
2607.	Hander, L. C.	E, 92d Inf.	June 23, '64
2424.	Hayford, A. E	E, 125th Inf	June 24, '64
2997.	Harrington, S. J	I, 103d Inf.	June 28, '64
2671.	Hurles, I.	C, 126th Inf.	June 30, '64
2775.	Hulburt, O.	H, 114th Inf.	July 2, '64

Appendix.

No. of Grave.	Name.	Co.	Regt.	Date of Death.
2842.	Hadison, J.	B,	111th Inf.	July 3, '64
3185.	Hall, T.	H,	2d Inf.	July 11, '64
3388.	Hudson, Wm.	G,	74th Inf.	July 16, '64
3420.	Hunt, W. H.	G,	113th Inf.	July 16, '64
3736.	Harman, L.	F,	9th Inf.	July 21, '64
4030.	Hansbury, E. A.	G,	6th Inf.	July 26, '64
4408.	Hindershot, John	D,	45th Inf.	July 31, '64
4411.	Harris, J.	E,	1st Inf.	July 31, '64
4506.	Hartman, H.	K,	73d Inf.	Aug. 1, '64
4599.	Harrison, J. M.	H,	105th Inf.	Aug. 3, '64
4993.	Hendrickson, O.	F,	19th Inf.	Aug. 7, '64
5293.	Hollibaugh, J. A.	E,	23d Inf.	Aug. 11, '64
5296.	Hatfield, G. W.	K,	126th Inf.	Aug. 11, '64
5396.	Holman, A.	K,	68th Inf.	Aug. 12, '64
5554.	Honnihill, T. R	G,	9th Inf.	Aug. 13, '64
5636.	Hany, B. T.	C,	89th Inf.	Aug. 14, '64
5813.	Hicks, F.	H,	40th Inf.	Aug. 16, '64
5853.	Hibbett, Wm.	D,	21st Inf.	Aug. 19, '64
5858.	Hoit, P.	B,	116th Inf.	Aug. 16, '64
6058.	Hamm, E. J.	K	———	Aug. 18, '64
6123.	Higgins, I. W.	C,	14th Inf.	Aug. 18, '64
6774.	Houser, W. R.	K,	89th Inf.	Aug. 18, '64
6522.	Hicks, I.	D,	11th Inf.	Aug. 23, '64
6625.	Hughes, Henry	A,	33d Inf.	Aug. 23, '64
6639.	Henrix, E.	H,	34th Inf	Aug. 23, '64
6647.	Hartman, I.	K,	2d Inf.	Aug. 23, '64
6798.	Herrig, N.	D,	7th Cav.	Aug. 25, '64
6802.	Hine, T. E.	D,	2d Cav.	Aug. 25, '64
7022.	Hull, O.	B,	89th Inf.	Aug. 27, '64
7388.	Hubbell, W. A.	A,	23d Inf.	Aug. 31, '64
7446.	Hurdnell, O.	C,	72d Inf.	Sept 1, '64
7825.	Holly, V. H.	B,	100th Inf.	Sept. 4, '64
7946.	Hughes, I.	E,	12th Inf.	Sept. 5, '64
8060.	Herbolt, Daniel	F,	115th, Inf	Sept 7, '64
8067.	Harper, I. H.	I,	60th Inf.	Sept. 7, '64
8284.	Halshult, A	C,	12th Inf.	Sept. 9, '64

XXXIV   *Appendix.*

No. of Grave.	Name.	Co.	Regt.	Date of Death.
8481.	Hechler, John	G,	36th Inf.	Sept. 11, '64
8696.	Hitchcock, G.	G,	34th Inf.	Sept. 14, '64
8725.	Hifner, G.	C,	86th Inf.	Sept. 14, '64
9189.	Hoyt, R.	K,	7th Inf.	Sept. 18, '64
9210.	Hart, E.	H,	10th Inf.	Sept. 19, '64
9538.	Hall, S.	F,	126th Inf	Sept. 20, '64
9415.	Hood, F.	F,	13th Inf.	Sept. 21, '64
9510.	Hamilton, J.	A,	13th Inf.	Sept. 22, '64
9582.	Hoover, J.	K,	18th Inf.	Sept. 23, '64
9622.	Hurley. J. C.	C,	124th Inf.	Sept. 23, '64
10094.	Holmes, Wesley	F,	135th Inf.	Sept. 30, '64
10207.	Harrison, J.	A,	2d Cav.	Oct. 2, '64
10208.	Holcomb, L.	I,	2d Inf.	Oct. 2, '64
10225.	Harkins, M.	D,	60th Inf.	Oct. 2, '64
10390.	Hinton, Wm.	A,	72d Inf.	Oct. 5, '64
10492.	Hererlin, B.		32d Inf.	Oct. 7, '64
10518.	Herbert, Wm.	I,	4th Inf.	Oct. 8, '64
10524.	Homich, C.	D,	110th Inf	Oct. 8, '64
10647.	Herman, R.	F,	135th Inf.	Oct. 11, '64
11029.	Hillyard, J.	F,	98th Inf.	Oct. 16, '64
11032.	Hubber, D.	A,	5th Inf.	Oct. 16, '64
11053.	Heymers, B.	G,	2d Inf.	Oct. 17, '64
11209.	Hannard, J. B.	C,	123d Inf.	Oct. 20, '64
11228.	Hoyt, W. B.	A,	29th Inf.	Oct. 20, '64
11335.	Henderson, D.	H.	122d Inf	Oct. 23, '64
11588.	Hintz D.	B,	1st Inf.	Oct. 28, '64
11592.	Hutchins, G. W.	A,	125th Inf.	Oct. 28, '64
11696.	Hutchins, J. W.	A,	153d Inf	Oct. 31, '64
11856.	Hayner, B.	A,	135th Inf.	Nov. 6, '64
11938.	Hatfield, A. G	E,	114th Inf.	Nov. 9, '64
12353.	Hume, J. A.	F,	32d Inf.	Dec. 29, '64
12371.	Haines, N. S.	E.	72d Inf.	Jan. 1, '65
12404.	Hill, W. L.	A,	54th Inf.	Jan. 6, '65
12416.	Hill, E. P.	G,	89th Inf.	Jan. 13, '65
12512.	Hagerman, R.	B,	33d Inf.	Jan. 23, '65
12569.	Hart, H. C.	C,	2d Inf.	Feb. 1, '65

Appendix.

No. of Grave.	Name.	Co.	Regt.	Date of Death.
12611.	Hagerly, D. G.	E,	72d Inf.	Feb. 7, '65
12743.	Holtz, W.	I,	101st Inf.	March 7, '65

I

1280.	Irving, Ester	H,	114th Inf.	May 22, '64
1967.	Ingler, Wm.	C,	31st Inf.	June 14, '64
7489.	Imboden, J.	E,	44th Inf	Sept. 1, '64
8744.	Irwin, A.	I,	1st Inf.	Sept. 14, '64
10700.	Idold, A.	C,	7th Cav.	Oct. 11, '64
12579.	Isham, D.	G,	89th Inf.	Feb. 3, '65

J

354.	Justice, G. W.	B,	45th Inf	April 2, '64
1637.	Johnson, J. H.	D,	98th Inf	June 5, '64
3590.	Jacobs, P. O.	E,	45th Inf.	July 19, '64
3754.	Jones, R	C,	45th Inf.	July 22, '64
3903.	Jones, S.	B,	111th Inf	July 24, '64
4381.	Jewell, I.	F,	99th Inf.	July 31, '64
5120.	Johnson, J. W.	H	89th Inf	Aug. 9, '64
5508.	Johnson, M	C,	126th Inf.	Aug. 13, '64
5583.	Jones, H.	G,	40th Inf.	Aug. 14, '64
5624.	Jewell, W. A.	G,	106th Inf.	Aug. 14, '64
5839.	Jolly, G.	K,	21st Inf.	Aug. 16, '64
6265.	Jeffries, H.	I,	36th Inf.	Aug. 20, '64
6810.	Jones, John	G,	40th Inf.	Aug. 25, '64
7308.	Johnson, E.	I,	124th Inf.	Aug. 30, '64
7861.	Jones, R. W.	F,	118th Inf.	Sept. 5, '64
7947.	Jacobs, H.	F,	26th Inf.	Sept. 6, '64
8647.	Jenkins, Wm		3d Bat.	Sept. 13, '64
8757.	Johnson, D.	B,	43d Inf.	Sept. 14, '64
8760.	Johnson, I.	A,	51st Inf.	Sept. 14, '64
9306.	Jordon, A.	G,	103d Inf.	Sept. 20, '64
9700.	Jones, I. B.	M,	3d Inf.	Sept. 25, '64
9744.	Johnson, I. B	C,	2d Inf.	Sept. 27, '64
9850.	Jones, Wm	B,	84th Inf	Sept. 25, '64
11014.	Jones, S. D.	F,	135th Inf	Oct. 16, '64

No. of Grave.	Name.	Co.	Regt.	Date of Death.
11203.	Jennings, John	K,	24th Inf.	Oct. 20, '64
11942.	Jones, G. L.	G,	125th Inf	Nov. 9, '64
12126.	Jarvitt, W.	A,	15th Inf.	Nov. 22, '64
12231.	Johnson, A. S.	I,	45th Inf	Dec. 6, '64
12335.	Jones, W. H.	C,	2d Inf.	Dec. 23, '64
12428.	Jackson, S.	E,	72d Inf.	Jan. 10, '65

K

No. of Grave.	Name.	Co.	Regt.	Date of Death.
13.	Kiger, J. H.	E,	45th Inf	April 9, '64
765.	Kinney, John	E,	67th Inf.	April 27, '64
830.	Kelley, Josiah	C,	45th Inf.	May 1, '64
2406.	Knowlton, E.	B,	6th Cav.	June 24, '64
416.	Kimble, S.	A,	98th Inf.	Aug. 1, '64
4714.	Knight, J.	E,	21st Inf.	Aug. 4, '64
5381.	Kelley, E.	D,	21st Inf.	Aug. 12, '64
5448.	Knidler, J. W.	H,	33d Inf.	Aug. 12, '64
5576.	Kelley, H.	I,	1st Inf.	Aug. 14, '64
6195.	Kelsey, John	I,	3d Inf.	Aug. 19, '64
7177.	Kennedy, S. J. B.	E,	45th Inf.	Aug. 29, '64
7424.	Kelley, G.	E,	15th Inf.	Aug. 31, '64
9377.	Kelley, William	C,	46th Inf	Sept. 20, '64
9436.	Kerr, J. H.	C,	122d Inf	Sept. 21, '64
9680.	Kapp, J.	E,	54th Inf.	Sept. 24, '64
10139.	Killar, J.	D,	15th Inf.	Oct. 1, '64
10607.	Kirby, A.	A,	4th Cav.	Oct. 10, '64
10853.	Keanshoff, L.	I,	28th Inf.	Oct. 13, '64
11055.	Kerr, A.	I,	13th Inf.	Oct. 17, '64
11732.	Kingkade, S.	C,	18th Inf.	Nov. 2, '64
12661.	Kennedy, J.	K,	70th Inf.	Jan. 16, '65
12746.	Kaler, J.	B,	70th Inf.	March 8, '65
12802.	Karch, J.	B,	183d Inf.	March 20, '65

L

No. of Grave.	Name.	Co.	Regt.	Date of Death.
834.	Lowry, James	I,	49th Inf.	May 1, '64
935.	Lewis, Frank	D,	103d Inf	May 7, '64
1286.	Larme, Charles	K,	45th Inf	May 22, '64

Appendix. XXXVII

No. of Grave.	Name.	Co. Regt.	Date of Death.
1364.	Larkin, Joseph	1st Art	May 25, '64
1470.	Logan, Frank	F, 89th Inf	May 30, '64
1645.	Logan, H.	E, 6th Cav	June 4, '64
1828.	Leonard, John	A, 21st Inf	June 11, '64
2173.	Lever, H. B.	C, 2d Inf.	June 19, '64
2372.	Tisure, Samuel	A, 7th Inf.	June 23, '64
2426.	Lemons, M.	E, 89th Inf	June 24, '64
3495.	Lutz, M.	C, 14th Inf.	July 18, '64
3497.	Love, John	E, 96th Inf.	July 18, '64
3649.	Linsay, J.	D, 21st Inf.	July 20, '64
4097.	Lyon, L. L.	E, 1st Art.	July 27, '64
4354.	Law, S. S.	I, 124th Inf.	July 31, '64
4262.	Lawson, J.	E, 2d Inf.	July 29, '64
4641.	Lucas, J.	H, 89th Inf.	Aug. 3, '64
4628.	LeGrand, D.	B, 111th Inf.	Aug. 3, '64
4692.	Long, John	H, 45th Inf.	Aug. 4, '64
5195.	Lightfoot, Wm.	G, 9th Cav.	Aug. 10, '64
5246.	Latta, W. H.	H, 89th Inf.	Aug. 10, '64
5449.	Lehigh, W.	B, 22d Inf.	Aug. 12, '64
5665.	Lamphare, G. W.	K, 125th Inf.	Aug. 14, '64
5676.	Larison, A.	D, 63d Inf.	Aug. 14, '64
6060.	Lowe, G. H.	C, 72d Inf.	Aug. 18, '64
6314.	Leasure, Isaack	K, 122d Inf.	Aug. 21, '64
7123.	Leasure, F.	K, 45th Inf	Aug. 28, '64
7744.	Linway, J.	H, 2d Inf.	Sept. 3, '64
8016.	Lambert, James	A 89th Inf.	Sept. 6, '64
8739.	Lickliter, Henry	B, 135th Inf.	Sept. 14, '64
8874.	Lindsley, A. K.	K, 99th Inf.	Sept. 16, '64
9336.	Leonard, T. M.	H, 12th Inf.	Sept. 20, '64
9518.	Lovely, John	K, 100th Inf.	Sept. 20, '64
9361.	Lawyer, J. B.	L, 89th Inf	Sept. 20, '64
7419.	Lefarer, W. G., citizen, Gardener, Athens county.		
10039.	Laley, ——	28th Inf.	Sept. 29, '64
11161.	Lepe, A.	K, 7th Inf.	Oct. 19, '64
11190.	Lantz, A. W.	A, 45th Inf.	Oct. 20, '64
11344.	Lochner, M.	E, 72d Inf.	Oct. 23, '64

Appendix.

No. of Grave	Name	Co.	Regt.	Date of Death
11440	Loughlin, M. W.	I,	1st Inf.	Oct. 24, '64
11400	Lips, F.	H,	2d Inf.	Oct. 26, '64
11516	Lane, D.	D,	91st Inf.	Nov. 4, '64
12007	Lay, John	K,	123d Inf.	Nov. 19, '64
12201	Lohmeyer, H.	K,	35th Inf.	Nov. 30, '64
12297	Livengood, C. R.	G,	35th Inf.	Dec. 16, '64
12515	Longstreet, W F	A,	31st Inf.	Jan. 26, '65
12668	Lewis, D.	A.	7th Inf.	Jan 28, '65
12828	Little, William	D.	175th Inf	April 7, '65

M

66	Metcalf, Milo R	E,	100th Inf.	March 19, '64
86	Malsbray, Asa	A,	40th Cav.	March 22, '64
113	Moore, T. J.	D,	2d Inf.	March 23, '64
141	McKeever James	G,	8th Inf.	March 24, '64
165	Mickey, Samuel	E,	45th Inf.	March 26, '64
215	Murphy, John	B,	7th Cav.	March 28, '64
412	Mitchell, J.	F,	120th Inf.	April 7, '64
444	McKindry, M	I,	7th Inf.	April 9, '64
575	Malone, R. J.	H,	40th Inf.	April 16, '64
880	McCormick, J. W. E	B,	33d Inf.	May 4, '64
984	Musser, D.	B,	45th Inf.	May 9, '64
995	Meek, David	K,	111th Inf.	May 10, '64
1362	McKnight, H	G,	11th Inf.	May 21, '64
1253	McMunny, George	G,	21st Inf.	May 22, '64
1630	Moore, Charles	H,	19th Inf.	June 5, '64
1840	Masters, Samuel	I,	17th Inf.	June 11, '64
1930	Martin, G.	F,	105th Inf.	June 14, '64
2075	McCliny, B.	I,	7th Cav.	June 17, '64
2139	Maloney, A.	H,	4th Inf.	June 13, '64
2150	Mitchell, W. H.	D,	31st Inf.	June 18, '64
2290	Massey, J. C.	A,	33d Inf.	June 21, '64
2471	Mullin, J	K,	65th Inf.	June 25, '64
2657	McCloud, A.	G,	35th Inf.	June 29, '64
2682	Miller, T.	A,	4th Cav.	June 30, '64
2743	McFarland, L	I,	2d Inf.	July 1, '64

Appendix. XXXIX

No. of Grave.	Name.	Co. Regt.	Date of Death.
2806.	McInnes, A . . .	B, 45th Inf	July 3, '64
2873.	Moriatt, Joseph	K, 5th Inf. . .	July 4, '64
2991.	Mitchell, James	D, 17th Inf	July 7, '64
3104.	Malone, L. B.	L, 7th Cav.	July 10, '64
3123.	Mitchell, C.	K, 1st Inf.	July 10, '64
3137.	Minchell R.	C, 45th Inf.	July 10, '64
3290.	Mahin, B.	I, 51st Inf.	July 13, '64
3491.	Master, J.	A, 13th Inf	July 17, '64
3718.	Miller, E.	E, 4th Inf.	July 21, '64
4040.	Marshall, T.	G, 21st Inf.	July 26, '64
4199.	Myer, C. . . .	I, 21st Inf. . .	July 29, '64
4252.	Meek, J.	E, 19th Inf.	July 29, '64
4298.	McKell, M. J.	D, 89th Inf.	July 30, '64
4361.	Mooney, James	D, 50th Inf.	July 31, '64
4421.	Morris, C. E.	H, 11th Inf.	July 31, '64
4101.	McCann, A.	C, 36th Inf.	Aug. 3, '64
4657.	Maher, P.	E, 7th Inf.	Aug. 3, '64
4789.	Martin, D. . . .	L, 3d Cav.	Aug. 5, '64
5738.	McCabe, H.	C, 12th Inf.	Aug. 15, '64
5777.	Manson, W.	G, 9th Inf.	Aug. 15, '64
5883.	McIntosh, D.	D, 50th Inf.	Aug. 16, '64
6026.	Manahan, Thomas	D, 21st Inf.	Aug. 18, '64
6040.	McKee, James	A, 51st Inf.	Aug. 18, '64
6055.	McHugh, W. S.	D, 2d Inf.	Aug. 18, '64
6063.	McClair, P. M.	A, 27th Inf.	Aug. 18, '64
6478.	McCabe, J.	C, 66th Inf.	Aug. 22, '64
6841.	McCormick, W. P.	G, 2d Inf.	Aug. 25, '64
6855.	McSorley, D.	F, 49th Inf.	Aug. 26, '64
6862.	McCoy, J. B.	A, 93d Inf.	Aug. 26, '64
6920.	McDell, William	K, 89th Inf.	Aug. 26, '64
7108.	McDonald, J.	H, 99th Inf.	Aug. 28, '64
7183.	Mason, J.	D, 45th Inf.	Aug. 28, '64
7186.	More, John H.	D, 60th Inf.	Aug. 28, '64
7515.	Myers, L. H.	B, 135th Inf.	Sept. 1, '64
7896.	Morris, J.	A, 105th Inf.	Sept. 5, '64
8021.	Meek, Robert	K, 111th Inf.	Sept. 6, '64

Appendix.

No. of Grave.	Name.	Co.	Regt.	Date of Death.
8044.	Myers, A.	I,	51st Inf.	Sept. 6, '64
8236.	Moor, D. D.	A,	2d Inf.	Sept. 9, '64
8385.	Maymer, R.	D,	68th Inf.	Sept. 10, '64
8408.	McCabe, J.	C,	70th Inf.	Sept. 11, '64
8482.	Morens, H.	A,	51st Inf.	Sept. 11, '64
8688.	Moore, T. H.	C,	59th Inf.	Sept. 13, '64
8726.	Miller, Samuel	F,	135th Inf.	Sept. 14, '64
8838.	Mackrill, R.	I,	50th Inf.	Sept. 15, '64
8885.	Manlig, S.	A,	60th Inf.	Sept. 16, '64
9039.	Miller, C.	I,	28th Inf.	Sept. 17, '64
9096.	McMillan, J. F.	A,	123d Inf.	Sept. 18, '64
9241.	McComb, J. S.	K,	14th Inf.	Sept. 19, '64
9348.	Maxwell, P.	A,	12th Inf.	Sept. 20, '64
9659.	Manley, J.	M,	7th Inf.	Sept. 24, '64
9867.	Mitchell, R. C.		10th Cav.	Sept. 27, '64
10064.	Morgan, R. O.	H,	12th Cav.	Sept. 30, '64
10081.	McIntosh, Wm.	I,	23d Inf.	Sept. 30, '64
10106.	Morais, Wm.	F,	135, Inf.	Sept. 30, '64
10517.	Montgomery, J.	G,	2d Inf.	Oct. 8, '64
10563.	Myer, L., blacksmith,	A,	1st Inf.	Oct. 9, '64
10936.	Martin, F.	A,	10th Cav.	Oct. 14, '64
11156.	McElroy, John	B,	92d Inf.	Oct. 18, '64
11200.	Martin, W.	A,	15th Inf.	Oct. 20, '64
11341.	McQuilkin, F.	I,	1st Inf.	Oct. 23, '64
11400.	Mark, J.	B,	135th Inf.	Oct. 24, '64
11811.	Miller, J.	I,	135th Inf.	Nov. 4, '64
12050.	Moore, R. F.	C,	101st Inf.	Nov. 16, '64
12054.	Mills, G. W.	F,	60th Inf.	Nov. 16, '64
12184.	Morrison, J. H.	B,	21st Inf.	Nov. 28, '64
12535.	McDonald, H. H.		Citizen,	Jan 27, '65
12717.	Millholland, R	B,	183d Inf.	March 1, '65
12872.	McGrath, D.	G,	115th Inf.	March 15 '65
12875.	Martin, M.	B	135th Inf	March 16, '65

N

| 983. | Neal, John | C, | 45th Inf | May 9, '64 |
| 2328. | Nash, C. D. | B, | 45th Inf | May 22, '64 |

No. of Grave.	Name.	Co. Regt.	Date of Death.
2183.	Niver, Edward	I, 3d Cav.	June 19, '64
4994.	Nelson, J.	K, 1st Cav.	Aug. 7, '64
5897.	Neff, B.	H, 95th Inf.	Aug. 16, '64
7103.	Nelson, Thomas	1st Cav.	Aug. 28, '64
10584.	Nelder, S.	G, 89th Inf.	Oct. 10, '64
11012.	Nott, J.	H, 153d Inf.	Oct. 16, '64
11448.	Norman, G. L.	B, 135th Inf.	Oct. 25, '64
12815.	Norris, E. J.	K, 102d Inf.	March 25, '65

O

2245.	Ostrander, E. W.	A, 100th Inf.	June 20, '64
2442.	Ott, C.	C, 51st Inf.	June 25, '64
4552.	O'Neil, James	F, 126th Inf.	Aug. 2, '64
11349.	O'Brien, John	D, 2d Inf.	Oct. 23, '64
12024.	O'Connor, F.	C, 103d Inf.	Nov. 15, '64
12247.	Oliver, J.	C, 122d Inf.	Dec. 8, '64
12429.	Olinger, J.	F, 63d Inf.	Dec. 10, '64
12805.	Ornig J. B.	I, 101st Inf.	April 17, '65

P

65.	Pussey, James	H, 45th Inf	March 19, '64
9.	Price, Barney	I, 45th Inf.	April 5, '64
724.	Parker, Wm. E.	H, 45th Inf.	April 25, '64
913.	Penny, A.	C, 59th Inf.	May 6, '64
1326.	Prouty, Wm.	L, 9th Cav.	May 24, '64
2692.	Phenix, A. H.	H, 21st Inf.	June 20, '64
3391.	Pile, Wilson	F, 33d Inf.	July 16, '64
3555.	Pierce, H.	A, 100th Inf.	July 18, '64
4020.	Perkins, W. B.	G, 89th Inf.	July 26, '64
5190.	Piffer, G.	A, 123d Inf.	Aug. 9, '64
5377.	Parker, W.	H, 124th Inf	Aug. 11, '64
5426.	Perrin, N.	A, 72d Inf.	Aug 12, '64
6463.	Parlice, George W.	94th Inf.	Aug. 22, '64
6589.	Potter, H.	E, 72d Inf.	Aug. 23, '64
6690.	Pullen, Samuel	B, 33d Inf.	Aug. 24, '64
6717.	Post, J.	D, 1st Art.	Aug. 24, '64

No. of Grave.	Name.	Co. Regt.	Date of Death.
6984.	Palmer, Samuel	I, 135th Inf.	Aug. 27, '64
7021.	Pease, G. E.	I, 10th Cav.	Aug. 27, '64
7157.	Plunkett, M.	E, 124th Inf.	Aug. 29, '64
7329.	Pelterson, F.	G, 113th Inf.	Aug. 30, '64
7368.	Purcell, John	D, 72d Inf.	Aug. 31, '64
7384.	Pierson, J.	B, 125th Inf.	Aug. 31, '64
7399.	Palmer, F. G.	D, 2d Cav.	Aug. 31, '64
7519.	Patten, W.	D, 21st Inf.	Sept. 1, '64
7644.	Pierce, Wm.	H, 75th Inf.	Sept. 3, '64
7701.	Pruser, H.	B, 1st Inf.	Sept. 3, '64
7724.	Payne, J.	E, 89th Inf.	Sept. 3, '64
8109.	Potts, Jas.	E, 172d Inf.	Sept. 7, '64
8288.	Phillips, H.	I, 33d Inf.	Sept. 9, '64
8534.	Powell, F.	G, 9th Inf.	Sept. 12, '64
8597.	Pror, A. M.	B, 135th Inf.	Sept. 12, '64
8620.	Pinert, F.	C, 21st Inf.	Sept. 13, '64
8753.	Parker, Z.	E, 124th Inf.	Sept. 14, '64
9111.	Parks, J. W.	G, 6th Cav.	Sept. 18, '64
9327.	Parker, J.	H, 49th Inf.	Sept. 20, '64
9470.	Perrin, G.	B, 3d Inf.	Sept. 21, '64
9768.	Pipenbring, George	K, 13th Inf.	Sept. 25, '64
9822.	Preston, Wm.	B, 34th M. I.	Sept. 27, '64
10056.	Parks, E. F.	D, 36th Inf.	Sept. 30, '64
11221.	Piper, E. A.	B, 23d Inf.	Oct. 20, '64
11453.	Patterson, F.	F, 28th Cav.	Oct. 25, '64
11676.	Prouse, P. I.	I, 1st Inf.	Oct. 30, '64
11779.	Preshall, J. A.	C, 113th Inf.	Nov. 3, '64
12038.	Peasley, J.	H, 65th Inf.	Nov. 16, '64
12040.	Porter, W. C.	H, 40th Inf.	Nov. 16, '64
12352.	Powers, J.	K, 21st Inf.	Dec. 28, '64
12651.	Poistan, J.	F, 133d Inf.	Jan. 29, '65
12645.	Piper, I.	F, 64th Inf.	Feb. 13, '65

R

344.	Ricker, Henry	E, 2d Cav.	April 2, '64
908.	Rush, D.	H, 107th Inf.	May 5, '64

Appendix.

No. of Grave.	Name.	Co.	Regt.	Date of Death.
49.	Reed, Harmon	E,	103d Inf.	May 25, '64
1642.	Radabaugh, W. H.	A,	33d Inf.	June 5, '64
1763.	Rei, J.	K,	124th, Inf.	June 6, '64
2030.	Ralston, W. J.	C,	89th Inf.	June 15, '64
2124.	Rawlings, S.	E,	45th Inf.	June 17, '64
2156.	Rancy, A. K.	B,	111th Inf.	June 18, '64
2231.	Rickards, W. V.	B,	33d Inf.	June 20, '64
2410.	Rowe, A.	F,	104th Inf.	June 24, '64
2878.	Rees, Thomas	C,	98th Inf.	July 4, '64
3074.	Rix, Wm.	K,	2d Inf.	July 9, '64
3400.	Rogers, H.	C,	51st Inf.	July 16, '64
3426.	Ralston, J. M.	C,	89th Inf.	July 16, '64
3613	Russell, L. F.	B,	111th Inf.	July 20, '64
3802.	Regman, O.	D,	2d Inf.	July 24, '64
3961.	Robinson, H. H.	H,	110th Inf.	July 25, '64
4061.	Reiggs, H.	F,	21st Inf.	July 27, '64
4335.	Rex, J. W.	K,	3d Cav.	July 30, '64
4777.	Robbins, A.	D,	6th Cav	Aug. 5, '64
5570.	Reichardson, G.	G,	82d Inf.	Aug. 14, '64
5631.	Russell, J. G.	G,	116th Inf.	Aug. 14, '64
5639.	Read, George H.	H,	21st Inf	Aug. 14, '64
5641.	Redder, G.	G,	45th Inf	Aug. 14, '64
6488.	Robbins, D. B.	I,	89th Inf.	Aug. 22, '64
6511.	Rass, J.	A,	59th Inf.	Aug. 22, '64
6835	Ridgeway, John	D,	23d Inf.	Aug. 25, '64
6948.	Redd, C.	H,	172d Inf.	Aug. 26, '64
7174.	Ross, A.	H,	45th Inf.	Aug. 29 '64
7353.	Roberts, Ed	K,	75th Inf.	Aug. 31, '64
7639.	Rutain, E. B.	E,	41st Inf.	Sept. 2, '64
7844.	Russell, James	E,	9th Inf.	Sept. 4, '64
8521.	Rhotin, W.	C,	2d Inf.	Sept. 12, '64
8747.	Riley, W. M.	B,	89th Inf.	Sept. 14, '64
8818.	Robertson, R.	D,	100th Inf.	Sept. 15, '64
9614.	Robinson, J.	D,	65th Inf.	Sept. 23, '64
9617.	Rose, John	H,	72d Inf.	Sept. 23, '64
10165.	Riper, O. H.	G,	110th Inf.	Oct. 1, '64

No. of Grave.	Name.	Co.	Regt.	Date of Death.
10354.	Rogers, C.	H,	13th Inf.	Oct. 5, '64
10378.	Rochelle, John	F,	135th Inf.	Oct. 11, '64
11279.	Romain, J.	H,	59th Inf	Oct. 21, '64
11360.	Reese, A.	C,	80th Inf.	Oct. 23, '64
11413.	Reese, R.	D,	59th Inf.	Oct. 24, '64
11646.	Rapp, N.	A.	19th Inf.	Oct. 30, '64
11657.	Robbins, P.	H,	122d. Inf.	Oct. 30, '64
11672.	Robinson, C.	E,	2d Cav.	Oct. 30, '64
11857.	Rourk, J.	G,	6th Inf.	Nov. 6, '64
12366.	Repan, A.	A	47th Inf.	Dec. 31, '64
12647.	Rapp, D. C.	C,	2d Inf.	Feb. 13, '65
12692.	Ramsbottom, A. F.	D,	99th Inf.	Feb. 22, '65

S

No. of Grave.	Name.	Co.	Regt.	Date of Death.
33.	Smith, J. E.	C,	7th Cav.	March 9, '64
44.	Smith, H. B.	B,	82d Inf.	March 14, '64
58.	Strill, Michael	K,	100th Inf.	March 18, '64
231.	Sears, Samuel	F,	2d Cav.	March 29, '64
260.	Stephen, H.	B.	100th Inf.	March 31, '64
263.	Shields, George	L,	2d Cav.	March 31, '64
284.	Saughessey, John	B,	45th Inf.	April 1, '64
481.	Steele, Abraham	H.	80th Inf.	April 9, '64
594.	Swench, W.	A,	45th Inf.	April 16, '64
653.	Snyder, Lewis	C,	80th Inf.	April 20, '64
726.	Sweeney, Samuel	G,	7th Cav.	April 25, '64
791.	Shannon, Charles	I,	45th Inf.	April 28, '64
804.	Starbuck, F.	E,	62d Inf.	April 29, '64
937.	Storer, John	A,	17th Inf.	May 7, '64
962.	Smith, John	F,	7th Cav.	May 8, '64
994.	Smith, Wm.	E,	103d Inf.	May 10, '64
42.	Sabine, Alonzo	A,	100th Inf.	May 11, '64
1160.	Samse, Wm.	H,	14th Inf.	May 17, '64
1179.	Smith, Conrad	A,	100th Inf.	May 18, '64
1183.	Smith, William	G,	2d Inf.	May 18, '64
1229.	Spangler, A.	E,	45th Inf.	May 20, '64
1231.	Swineheart, J. W.	B,	111th Inf.	May 22, '64

Appendix.

No. of Grave.	Name.	Co.	Regt.	Date of Death.
1404.	Seyman, Aaron	D,	89th Inf.	May 27, '64
1672.	Sprague, W. L.	K,	6th Cav.	June 6, '64
1773.	Simmons, John		Bat. 22.	June 9, '64
2220.	Shannon, E.	A,	35th Inf.	June 20, '64
2230.	Stannett, J.	C,	45th Inf.	June 20, '64
2376.	Stiver, J.	C,	93d Inf.	June 23, '64
2524.	Smith, G. W.	K,	11th Inf.	June 26, '64
2575.	Sampson, C.	D,	89th Inf.	June 27, '64
2638.	Stults, P.	F,	45th Inf.	June 29, '64
2783.	Shiver, L.	B,	31st Inf.	July 2, '64
2792.	Smith, N. H.	H,	1st Inf.	July 2, '64
3116.	Smith, G.	I,	21st Inf.	July 10, '64
3252.	Short, James	A,	4th Cav.	July 13, '64
3288.	Smith, D.	H,	7th Inf.	July 13, '64
3361.	Saffle, J.	E,	2d Inf.	July 15, '64
3536.	Steward, C. S.	K,	33d Inf.	July 18, '64
3602.	Stevenson, D.	B,	111th Inf.	July 19, '64
3298.	Squires, Thomas	C,	49th Inf.	July 20, '64
3744.	Snyder, Thomas	G,	9th Inf.	July 21, '64
3770.	Smith, D.	I.	2d Inf.	July 22, '64
3794.	Sever, H. H.	C,	2d Inf.	July 22, '64
4249.	Shephard, J. H.	E,	2d Inf.	July 29, '64
4275.	Smith, J. B.	B,	1st Inf	July 29, '64
4294.	Steward, J.	K,	2d Inf	July 30, '64
4745.	Steiner, M. J.	F,	72d Inf.	Aug. 5, '64
5018.	Smock. A	D,	93d Inf.	Aug. 8, '64
5054.	Smarz, A.	E,	93d Inf.	Aug 8, '64
5066.	Shipple, John	G,	6th Cav	Aug. 8, '64
5133.	Scott, S. E.	I,	4th Inf.	Aug. 9, '64
5287.	Stevenson, John	B,	111th Inf	Aug. 11, '64
5330.	Spegle, F.	D,	14th Inf	Aug. 11, '64
5373.	Schem, J.	K,	101st Inf.	Aug. 11, '64
5455.	Stevens, G. W.	K,	101st Inf	Aug. 12, '64
5896.	Sullivan, W.	D,	78th Inf	Aug. 16, '64
6010.	Staley, G.	A,	89th Inf	Aug. 17, '64
6632.	Smith, Wm.	G,	9th Cav	Aug. 18, '64

Appendix.

No. of Grave.	Name.	Co.	Regt.	Date of Death.
6178	Simpson, W. J.	F,	32d Inf.	Aug. 19, '64
6199	Sheddy, G.	K,	2d Inf.	Aug. 19, '64
6214	Shaw, George W.	A,	105th Inf.	Aug. 20, '64
6253	Shoulder, E.	F,	24th Inf.	Aug. 20, '64
6779	Soper, P.	G,	72d Inf.	Aug. 25, '64
6870	Scarberry, O.	D,	89th Inf.	Aug. 26, '64
7034	Sutton, J.	A,	4th Inf.	Aug. 27, '64
7065	Shoemaker, J.	E,	47th Inf.	Aug. 28, '64
7436	Stincher, F. E.	A,	101st Inf.	Sept. 1, '64
7475	Shafer, A.	G,	9th Inf.	Sept. 1, '64
7540	Sell, Adam	E,	125th Inf.	Sept. 2, '64
7788	Stewart, John S.	B,	19th Inf.	Sept. 4, '64
7897	Smith, H. H.	A,	2d Cav.	Sept. 5, '64
7986	Selb, Jacob		23d Inf.	Sept. 6, '64
8014	Schriver, George	K,	45th Inf.	Sept. 6, '64
8015	Snider, James	C,	4th Inf.	Sept. 6, '64
8156	Sturtevant, W.	A,	72d Inf.	Sept. 8, '64
8197	Shrouds, J.		6th Bat.	Sept. 8, '64
8200	Stroufe, A.	E,	7th Inf.	Sept. 8, '64
8229	Shaw, W.	I,	15th Inf.	Sept. 9, '64
8300	Smith, N.	H,	121st Inf.	Sept. 9, '64
8319	Sheldon, W.	E,	49th Inf.	Sept. 10, '64
8422	Sullivan, John	F,	135th Inf.	Sept. 11, '64
8728	Sisson, P. B.	H,	18th Inf.	Sept. 14, '64
8752	Sickles, J.	I,	51st Inf.	Sept. 14, '64
8914	Simmonds, S. P.	A,	1st Inf.	Sept. 16, '64
8931	Stull, G.	G,	15th Inf.	Sept. 16, '64
9009	Sharp, S. F.	K,	63d Inf.	Sept 17, '64
9244	Schmall, J. D.	E,	12th Inf.	Sept 19, '64
9386	Smith, L.	H,	153d Inf.	Sept. 20, '64
9645	Scott, J. H.	H,	33d Inf.	Sept. 24, '64
9649	Skiver, J.	H,	114th Inf.	Sept. 24, '64
10250	Sheets, W.	A,	81st Inf.	Oct. 3, '64
10312	Spencer, S. M.	E,	89th Inf.	Oct. 4, '64
10434	Shingle, D.	L,	2d Cav.	Oct. 6, '64
10437	Stanford, P. W.	A,	2d Cav.	Oct. 6, '64

Appendix. XLVII

No. of Grave.	Name.	Co. Regt.	Date of Death.
10576.	Stonechecks, J. D.	F, 51st Inf.	Oct. 9, '64
10618.	Schafer, P.	I, 101st Inf.	Oct. 10, '64
10703.	Stout, Samson	F, 2d Inf.	Oct. 11, '64
10383.	Sheppard, John	D, 34th Inf.	Oct. 13, '64
11139.	Shark, H.	F, 72d Inf.	Oct. 17, '64
11146.	Smith, G. A.	F, 45th Inf.	Oct. 19, '64
11249.	Sullivan, F.	C, 76th Inf.	Oct. 21, '64
11433.	Swaney, E.	A, 124th Inf.	Oct. 24, '64
11579.	Smith, P.	I, 69th Inf.	Oct. 28, '64
11595.	Sapp, W. N.	E, 20th Inf.	Oct. 28, '64
11711.	Spiker, J.	122d Inf.	Nov. 1, '64
11797.	Shaler, F.	E, 72d Inf.	Nov. 4, '64
12105.	Sly, F.	G, 89th Inf.	Nov. 20, '64
12281.	Singer, J.	G, 6th Inf.	Dec. 13, '64
12305.	Sweet, M.	F, 49th Inf.	Dec. 18, '64
12441.	Shoemaker, C.	F, 8th Inf.	Jan. 12, '65
12538.	Stewart, A. F.	D, 2d Inf.	Jan. 27, '65
12562.	Sponcelar, George	B, 71st Inf.	Jan. 31, '65
12668.	Shorter, W.	K, 89th Inf.	Feb. 17, '65
12769.	Sloon, L.	D, 123d Inf.	March 13, '65
12789.	Stroup, S.	B, 50th Inf.	March 17, '65
12793.	Seeley, N.	D, 132 Inf.	March 18, '65
12810.	Scott, R.	G, 75th Inf.	March 24, '65

T

734.	Tweedy, R.	A, 1st Cav.	April 25, '64
743.	Trescott, Samuel	C, 2d Inf.	April 26, '64
999.	Trimmer, Wm.	H, 40th Inf.	May 10, '64
1196.	Turney, U. S.	G, 2d Cav.	May 18, '64
1496.	Thomas, Wm.	M, 10th Cav.	May 30, '64
4784.	Thompson, J.	E, 2d Inf.	Aug. 5, '64
4951.	Toroman, W. R.	F, 13th Inf.	Aug. 7, '64
5356.	Tierney, W.	L, 1st Art.	Aug. 11, '64
5552.	Tinsley, M.	B, 90th Inf.	Aug. 13, '64
5668.	Terrilliger, N.	C, 12th Inf.	Aug. 14, '64
6330.	Tanner, A.	G, 32d Inf.	Aug. 21, '64

No. of Grave.	Name.	Co.	Regt.	Date of Death.
7224.	Thompson, O. B.	C,	26th Inf.	Aug. 29, '64
7246.	Turner, S. B.	B,	45th Inf.	Aug. 30, '64
7340.	Thomas, James	C,	44th Inf.	Sept. 2, '64
8850.	Talbert, R.	F,	135th Inf.	Sept. 15, '64
9774.	Thomas, N.	B,	103d Inf.	Sept. 26, '64
9945.	Townsend, J.	C,	26th Inf.	Sept. 23, '64
10471.	Tattman, B.	C,	123d Inf.	Oct. 7, '64
10800.	Tinway, P.		93d Inf.	Oct. 12, '64
11320.	Townsley, E. M.	B,	89th Inf.	Nov. 5, '64
12577.	Tensdale, T. H.	E,	2d Cav.	Feb. 3, '65

U

12251.	Uebre, S.	E,	12th Inf	Dec. 9, '64

V

2194.	Vining, W. H. H.	G,	45th Inf.	June 19, '64
3902.	Valentine, C.	H,	123d Inf.	July 24, '64
4450.	Vaugh, B.	F,	125th Inf	Aug. 1, '64
4497.	Vangrider, H.	H,	103d Inf.	Aug. 1, '64
5262.	Vatier, J. F.		6th Cav.	Aug. 10, '64
6170.	Vail, John L.	C,	17th Inf.	Aug. 19, '64
6859.	Vanaman, M.	E,	21st Inf.	Aug. 26, '64
6985.	Vanderveer, A.	H,	6th Inf.	Aug. 27, '64
7756.	Victor, H.	D,	1st Art.	Sept. 4, '64
9576.	Volis, J.	H,	34th Inf.	Sept. 23, '64
10252.	Vail, N.	K,	12th Inf.	Oct. 3, '64
10389.	Vail, G. M.	D,	7th Inf.	Oct. 5, '64
10472.	Van Fleet, H.	I,	14th Inf.	Oct. 7, '64
11095.	Van Kirk, G.	B,	135th Inf.	Oct. 18, '64
11097.	Van Malley, J. M.	G,	89th Inf.	Oct. 18, '64
12554.	Vanhorn, S.	C,	9th Cav.	Jan. 30, '65

W

7.	Wiley, Samuel	A,	82d Inf.	March 5, '64
185.	Wickman, Wm.	B,	111th Inf.	March 27, '64
34.	Wright, Wm.	H,	7th Inf.	April 24, '64

Appendix.

No. of Grave.	Name.	Co.	Regt.	Date of Death.
799.	Wooley, John	B,	45th Inf.	April 28, '64
807.	Werts, Lewis	D,	45th Inf.	April 30, '64
1085.	Wood, Wm	A,	89th Inf.	May 14, '64
1449.	Wenthing, Joseph	K,	130th Inf	May 29, '64
1604.	Wood, Joseph	B,	15th Inf.	June 4, '64
1836.	Wilkinson, W.	D,	89th Inf.	June 11, '64
1913.	Wilson, James	I,	93d Inf.	June 13, '64
2020.	Way, Jno.	I,	44th Inf.	June 15, '64
2041.	Windgrove, S. R.		15th Inf	June 15, '64
2172.	Webb, E.	A,	45th Inf	June 19, '64
2358.	Walters, F.	E,	9th Inf.	June 23, '64
2536.	Wing.	M,	2d Cav.	June 26, '64
2815.	Willis, A.	A,	89th Inf	July 3, '64
2840.	Wroten, L.	H,	89th Inf	July 3, '64
3188.	Williams, D.	A,	90th Inf	July 12, '64
3310.	White, H	A,	15th Inf.	July 15, '64
3325.	Whitten, G.	K,	75th Inf.	July 14, '64
4214.	West, J. B.	B,	89th Inf.	July 29, '64
4681.	Witt, Jno. T.	G,	93d Inf.	Aug. 4, '64
4688.	Won, J	B,	111th Inf.	Aug. 4, '64
4695.	Wile, A.	D,	33d Inf.	Aug. 4, '64
4833.	Webricks, Josh H.	G,	9th Inf.	Aug. 6, '64
5121.	Winder, I.	D,	70th Inf	Aug. 9, '64
5211.	Wood, N. L.	L,	4th Cav.	Aug. 10, '64
5726.	Winters, George	K,	145th Inf.	Aug. 15, '64
6314.	Wainwright, S. G.	G,	89th Inf	Aug. 20, '64
6318.	Wisser, F. J.	A,	35th Inf.	Aug. 20, '64
6362.	Wistman, N.	G,	9th Cav.	Aug 21, '64
6397.	Wilson, E.	A,	4th Inf.	Aug. 21, '64
6700.	Watson, G.	A,	21st Inf.	Aug. 24, '64
6761.	Wood, S.	A,	123d Inf.	Aug. 25, '64
7056.	Wood, W. H.	E,	59th Inf.	Aug. 28, '64
7373.	Wyatt, J.	B,	90th Inf	Aug. 31, '64
7582.	Wentworth, L.	A,	72d Inf.	Sept. 1, '64
8298.	Wright, J. S.	E,	49th Inf.	Sept. 9, '64
8696.	Warner, T.	C,	14th Inf.	Sept. 10, '64

No. of Grave.	Name.	Co.	Regt.	Date of Death.
8907.	Wyckman, D.	G,	73d Inf.	Sept. 16, '64
9384.	Worte, J.		116th Inf.	Sept. 20, '64
9527.	Woodruff, J. M.	F,	135th Inf.	Sept. 22, '64
9691.	Wagner, J.	F,	93d Inf.	Sept. 24, '64
10007.	Whitney, E.	K,	21st Inf.	Sept. 29, '64
10230.	Williams, Orland	K,	7th Cav.	Oct. 2, '64
10309.	Weaver, M.	H,	72d Inf.	Oct. 4, '64
10402.	Ward, Francis	H,	21st Inf.	Oct. 6, '64
10464.	Whitehead, A. B.	E,	33d Inf.	Oct. 7, '64
10528.	Wiley, A.	I,	26th Inf.	Oct. 8, '64
10733.	White, I.	E,	73d Inf.	Oct. 11, '64
10844.	Westbrook, R. L.	F,	135th Inf.	Oct. 13, '64
11013.	Walker, C.	I,	65th Inf.	Oct. 16, '64
11034.	Waldron, H.	A,	14th Inf.	Oct. 16, '64
11418.	Williams, S. M.	F,	60th Inf.	Oct. 24, '64
11770.	Worthen, D.	B,	122d Inf.	Nov. 3, '64
11874.	Weason, J.	F,	36th Inf.	Nov. 6, '64
12042.	Wickham, J.	H,	14th Inf.	Nov. 16, '64
12073.	White, R. M.	D,	15th Inf.	Nov. 18, '64
12158.	Warner, B. F.	E,	35th Inf.	Nov. 25, '64
12584.	Whitaker, E.	A,	72d Inf.	Feb. 4, '65
12722.	Wells, E.	A,	57th Inf.	March 3, '65
12759.	Winklet, T.		McL's. Sqn.	March 12, '65
12786.	Warner, M.	G,	132d Inf.	March 16, '65

Y

638.	Yulerler, W. A.	E,	45th Inf.	April 20, '64
5477.	Younker, S.	F,	80th Inf.	Aug. 13, '64
6068.	Young, John	E,	7th Inf.	Aug. 18, '64
7816.	Yeager, John	B,	7th Cav.	Sept. 4, '64
7876.	Young, J.	F,	9th Inf.	Sept. 5, '64
10583.	Young, W.	G,	6th Inf.	Oct. 10, '64
12659.	Young, W.	A,	15th Inf.	Feb. 16, '65

Z

3225.	Zubers, J. M.	B,	100th Inf.	July 12, '64
11253.	Zink, A. J.	E,	72d Inf.	Oct. 21, '64

www.ingramcontent.com/pod-product-compliance
Lightning Source LLC
Chambersburg PA
CBHW020759230426
43666CB00007B/762